SHARING RESPONSIBILITY

Human Rights and Crimes against Humanity
Eric D. Weitz, Series Editor

For a full list of titles in the series, go to https://press.princeton.edu/catalogs/series/title/human-rights-and-crimes-against-humanity.html.

Sharing Responsibility: The History and Future of Protection from Atrocities, Luke Glanville

A World Divided: The Global Struggle for Human Rights in the Age of Nation-States, Eric D. Weitz

The Crime of Aggression: The Quest for Justice in an Age of Drones, Cyberattacks, Insurgents, and Autocrats, Noah Weisbord

The Killing Season: A History of the Indonesian Massacres, 1965–66, Geoffrey B. Robinson

Evidence for Hope: Making Human Rights Work in the 21st Century, Kathryn Sikkink

"They Can Live in the Desert but Nowhere Else": A History of the Armenian Genocide, Ronald Grigor Suny

Child Migration and Human Rights in a Global Age, Jacqueline Bhabha

The Young Turks' Crime against Humanity: The Armenian Genocide and Ethnic Cleansing in the Ottoman Empire, Taner Akçam

The International Human Rights Movement: A History, Aryeh Neier

All the Missing Souls: A Personal History of the War Crimes Tribunals, David Scheffer

Against Massacre: Humanitarian Interventions in the Ottoman Empire, 1815–1914, Davide Rodogno

Stalin's Genocides, Norman M. Naimark

"If You Leave Us Here, We Will Die": How Genocide Was Stopped in East Timor, Geoffrey B. Robinson

Terror in Chechnya: Russia and the Tragedy of Civilians in War, Emma Gilligan

Torture and the Twilight of Empire: From Algiers to Baghdad, Marnia Lazreg

Sharing Responsibility

The History and Future of Protection from Atrocities

Luke Glanville

PRINCETON UNIVERSITY PRESS

PRINCETON AND OXFORD

Published by Princeton University Press
41 William Street, Princeton, New Jersey 08540
6 Oxford Street, Woodstock, Oxfordshire OX20 1TR

press.princeton.edu

All Rights Reserved
ISBN 978-0-691-20502-1
ISBN (e-book) 978-0-691-20501-4

British Library Cataloging-in-Publication Data is available

Editorial: Eric Crahan, Priya Nelson and Thalia Leaf
Production Editorial: Jenny Wolkowicki
Jacket design: Layla Mac Rory
Production: Danielle Amatucci
Publicity: Kate Hensley and Amy Stewart
Copyeditor: Joseph Dahm

This book has been composed in Adobe Text and Gotham

Printed on acid-free paper. ∞

Printed in the United States of America

10 9 8 7 6 5 4 3 2 1

For Clare

CONTENTS

Introduction

"I stand before you to awaken the conscience of the world, and to arouse the voice of the international community," declared Minister of Justice Abubacarr Tambadou, opening The Gambia's case against Myanmar at the International Court of Justice (ICJ) in 2019. "Another genocide is unfolding right before our eyes, even as I make this statement to you today. Yet we do nothing to stop it. This is a stain on our collective conscience and it will be irresponsible for any of us to simply look the other way and pretend that it is not our business because it *is* our business."[1] Fourteen years earlier, at the 2005 United Nations (UN) World Summit, states unanimously agreed that they share a responsibility to protect people the world over from genocide and other atrocities. The UN Security Council reaffirmed this agreement repeatedly over subsequent years.[2] And yet, when Myanmar government forces and local militias launched "clearance operations" in Rakhine State in 2017, killing at least ten thousand Rohingya Muslims and forcing more than seven hundred thousand to flee to Bangladesh, the international community failed to act.[3] The Security Council did not adopt a single resolution condemning the atrocities, much less authorize measures to bring them to an end and to ensure the protection of civilians. It was left to The Gambia, a small West African state that had itself only recently emerged from the twenty-two-year presidency of Yahyah Jammeh that was marked by violations of rights and threats of atrocities, to bring a case to the ICJ accusing Myanmar of genocide and seeking an order for provisional measures to protect the Rohingya.

This book examines the idea that states share responsibilities for the protection of people beyond their borders from atrocities. We are often told that this is a new idea, conceptualized as the responsibility to protect (R2P) at the beginning of this century. While histories of humanitarian intervention and human protection proliferate, we are nevertheless told that states until recently conceived and claimed—or denied—merely a *right* to protect distant vulnerable people. States were not thought to be burdened by any obligation to care for strangers when they did not want to.[4] But this is false. When justifying action taken to protect people beyond borders, or when exhorting others to act, states have almost always deployed the language of responsibility, of duty, of obligation, of an imperative to love their neighbor, to uphold justice, and to defend the interests of humanity.

Political leaders, moreover, have long engaged with this idea of a responsibility to protect in ways that are familiar to us today. We will see that they have at times put it into practice with a measure of integrity and at other times knowingly manipulated and abused it. Compare for example Britain's costly nineteenth-century efforts to abolish the slave trade with Leopold II's brutal administration of the Congo at the end of that century, both of which were justified in terms of the duties of humanity. Some have sought to dilute expectations for action by claiming that duties toward outsiders are outweighed by national interests, while others have sought to bolster popular support for action by asserting a convergence of duties and interests. This was a feature of the famous dispute between Benjamin Disraeli and W. E. Gladstone, current and former prime minister, concerning how Britain should respond to atrocities against Bulgarian Christians in the 1870s. Leaders have also often highlighted how protection obligations ought to be shared among states, sometimes seeking to persuade other states to contribute to protection efforts, as Frederick William I of Brandenburg-Prussia did on behalf of vulnerable Protestants in Nassau-Siegen in 1710, and sometimes hoping to shift blame for a failure to protect onto those who impede effective action, as British prime minister Lord Salisbury did in the context of atrocities against Armenians in the 1890s. In some instances, responsibilities for the protection of the vulnerable beyond borders have even been written into the mandates of international institutions and codified in international law. We find this as early as the Peace of Westphalia in 1648, which, far from establishing a right of states to freedom from external interference, as myth would have it, actually bound contracting parties to peacefully and, if necessary, forcefully protect the religious liberty of individuals in the princely states of the Holy Roman Empire. We hear echoes of each of these efforts to perform, abuse, negotiate, evade, and codify responsibilities beyond borders in the global politics of human protection today.

This is not to say that there have not been real and significant changes over time. There have been. For starters, in previous centuries, responsibilities for extraterritorial protection were commonly constructed and claimed by an exclusive club of European powers and imposed upon particular communities and peoples outside the club. For all the inequities and hypocrisies that continue to mark the politics of human protection today, it is noteworthy that *all* states have agreed that they share a responsibility to protect, described at the 2005 World Summit as a responsibility to encourage and help each other prevent atrocities and to take timely and decisive action—peaceful if possible, coercive if necessary—to put an end to atrocities when they break out.[5]

But whatever the successes of international efforts this century to act on these commitments and to more consistently and effectively protect people from atrocities—and I argue that there have been such successes—the project of human protection is in crisis today as multiple forces push against the commitment of states to protect the vulnerable beyond borders. Rising populist nationalism in many Western states, not least the United States, sees them turning their backs on global responsibilities that they have long championed at least in word, if not always in deed. Increasing weariness of Western hypocrisy emboldens other states, not least Russia, to resist whatever efforts the West continues to muster to shame them into facilitating the protection of strangers. And rising confidence of non-Western powers, not least China, leads them to more brazenly challenge prevailing notions of global rights and responsibilities, the application of which by Western powers in recent years has so often revived traumatic and humiliating memories of imperialist interventionism beyond the West. Rohingya civilians suffer as a result. So too do Yemeni, Syrian, and Congolese civilians, and many others besides.

How might we think through this crisis of abandoned responsibilities? Should we even conceive it as a crisis given how often such responsibilities have been mishandled? It will prove useful to begin with a historical question: how have theorists and practitioners derived and discharged, contested and evaded, and manipulated and abused responsibilities for the protection of the vulnerable beyond borders in the past? Armed with answers to that question, we can derive richer and more robust answers to crucial questions about the responsibility to protect today than we can when we overstate the novelty of this responsibility and occlude its history. Questions to be asked include these: How should the responsibility to protect be shared among states to ensure that populations are consistently and effectively protected without placing unfair burdens on particular states and without opening the door to abuse? To what extent might these shared responsibilities be made legally binding? To what extent have states actually embraced their shared responsibilities? And what, if anything, might lead them to take up their shared responsibilities more responsibly, more consistently, and more effectively? Confronted as we are today with atrocity crises that are killing hundreds of thousands of civilians and wounding, displacing, and traumatizing many millions more, these questions are as urgent as they have ever been. Answering them is the task of this book.

Five Lenses for Viewing the Responsibility to Protect

The book looks at the shared responsibility to protect through five different lenses in order to answer these questions. The lenses are (1) the history of international thought, (2) the history of international practice, (3) international ethics, (4) international law, and (5) international politics. I devote a chapter to each. All of these lenses represent fields of research that have in different ways been undergoing something of a turn (or more precisely a return) from a focus on rights to a focus on responsibilities in recent years, or at least a reinvigorated engagement with how the fulfilment of rights requires the identification and assignation of responsibilities, and the book makes a contribution to each of these "turns" in the process of contributing to our understanding of R2P.[6]

However, as becomes clear as we move through the book, these five perspectives on responsibilities are closely related and in some respects inseparable. We are more likely to produce poor answers to ethical questions about whether and when military intervention is required and who in particular should undertake the intervention, for example, if we neglect to grapple with the history of powerful states justifying the forcible subjugation of weaker others in languages of a duty to protect and civilize the tyrannized and the barbaric. A deeper understanding of each field of research helps enrich our understanding of each of the others, leading to a fuller understanding of the possibilities, limits, and hazards of shared responsibilities for human protection.

I was prompted to write the book in part by frustration with existing treatments and prevailing assumptions about each of these five perspectives. I deal more fully with these faulty treatments and assumptions in the chapters that follow. For now, let us consider just one example: Rajan Menon's recent, prominent, and relentlessly skeptical book *The Conceit of Humanitarian Intervention*.[7] This thoughtful and engaging work, which focuses on the military interventionist aspect of R2P, utilizes each of the five lenses at different points, but in each instance reproduces pervasive myths and misunderstandings that scholars and commentators have embraced for too long.

In Menon's hands, the *history of international thought* regarding the moral obligation to intervene is reduced to Hugo Grotius's famous seventeenth-century defense of a mere *right* of intervention, failing to recognize that the Dutchman actually prioritized considerations of reason of state over the care of vulnerable foreigners, whereas numerous other theorists both before and after him argued in favor of weighty *duties* to intervene to assist and rescue people beyond borders.[8] Menon's treatment of the *history of international practice* is grounded in the long-demolished myth that the Peace of West-phalia established a principle of nonintervention, hampering his ability to draw appropriate lessons from practices of intervention across the centuries that followed.[9] And his discussion of *international ethics* is marred by the fact that he argues both that intervention to protect the vulnerable does not work and also that states do not intervene enough, unintentionally imitating the opening joke of Woody Allen's *Annie Hall* about two elderly women complaining both that the food at their resort is terrible and also that the portions are so small.[10]

Menon's treatment of *international law* focuses on the tired question of whether there is a *right* of military intervention in the absence of UN Security Council authorization.[11] This is understandable given that some Western governments have an uncanny knack for finding lawyers willing to make the case for such a right when needed. But the vast weight of legal scholarship has long been against this right, and in rehearsing this scholarship, Menon neglects to grapple with the live and pressing issue of whether efforts to protect populations beyond borders, where legally permissible, are also legally *obligatory*. Finally, his discussion of *international politics* proceeds from the blunt claim that states will always act in their own interests, ignoring a wealth of research demonstrating that these interests themselves are socially constructed and subject to change and that they both can and often do include an interest in caring for vulnerable outsiders.[12]

I correct each of these myths and misunderstandings over the course of the book. But correcting the claims of others is only a minor aim. More importantly, I "think with history" in order to help us understand the present-day shared responsibilities of states to protect the vulnerable beyond their borders.[13] I engage with past ideas and practices for three purposes: first, to clarify precisely what, if anything, is novel about present ideas and practices regarding responsibilities for human protection; second, to retrieve forgotten or neglected ways of thinking about responsibilities that can help us understand the possibilities, limits, and hazards of protection (including three senses of "imperfection" that I outline in a moment); and third, to appreciate the implications of past uses and abuses of protection responsibilities, such as the ethical obligations produced by historical abuse and the traumas and temptations of abuse that continue to mark the politics of protection.

I am conscious that the book wrestles with a number of questions and concepts that were unfamiliar to past theorists and practitioners. In order to control for *some* anachronism and to limit the distortion of the past, I seek first, in chapters 1 and 2, to carefully depict historical arguments and actions as they were understood by the people involved. Only then, with these con-textualized historical materials in hand, do I turn to think about present-day ethics, law, and politics in chapters 3, 4, and 5. Other than a few moments when it seems useful to help orient the reader, I refrain in the first two chapters from noting how the historical material relates to the discussions of the present-day that follow. That said, while I strive to not impose present understandings on past ideas and practices, I am aware that, in zeroing in on past constructions and performances of protection responsibilities in the first two chapters, my selection and presentation of historical material is shaped by presentist concerns. My hope is that such moderate anachronism proves useful for helping us think about the debates and dilemmas about human protection that confront us today.[14]

I outline the findings and arguments of each chapter shortly. Let me first detail one broad contribution of the book that cuts across all chapters and that helps us better understand not only R2P but international responsibilities more generally, which is an explication of the many implications of the fact that the responsibility to protect is rightly understood as an "imperfect" responsibility.

An Imperfect Responsibility

Since the end of the Cold War, there has emerged a large body of research examining the development and impact of a range of human-rights-based international norms. Most of these norms entail "negative" duties. That is, they require states to refrain from certain behaviors. Examples include duties to *not* engage in practices of slavery,[15] colonialism,[16] or apartheid,[17] and duties to *not* use chemical weapons,[18] nuclear weapons,[19] or land mines.[20] Violation of each of these duties involves doing something that is almost universally condemned. States tend to be fully capable of complying with these duties in all instances. Violation, therefore, is always inexcusable and commonly subject to social sanction and even material punishment. As such, these negative duties are also known as "perfect" duties.

In contrast, R2P entails a "positive" duty. That is, rather than a duty to refrain from doing something abhorrent, it is a duty to do something good. It requires that states take action on behalf of the international community to protect vulnerable people beyond their borders. When we think carefully about what is required of any individual state, we find that this positive duty is "imperfect" in three different senses. Recognition of these imperfections helps us to more rightly grasp the nuances of the ethics, law, and politics of R2P, and to better calibrate our expectations.

We can understand the three senses of imperfection through the works of three historical thinkers whom we get to know in chapter 1: Samuel Pufendorf, Emer de Vattel, and Immanuel Kant. We find in chapters 2 and 5 that each sense of imperfection has marked the politics of human protection for centuries and continues to do so today.

The first sense of imperfection was first articulated by Pufendorf in the late seventeenth century: the duty to care for those beyond borders is imperfect because it is rightly subject to the judgment of each state, which needs to weigh the costs and risks of protecting outsiders against the duty to care for the well-being and interests of its own population.[21] Political leaders often appeal to this idea even if they do not speak in terms of imperfect duties. Disraeli, for example, justified his refusal to intervene on behalf of persecuted Bulgarians in the Ottoman Empire on the grounds that the duties Britain owed to vulnerable foreigners were at that moment trumped by the duty "to maintain the Empire of England."[22] Likewise, more recently, US president Barack Obama responded to pressure to do more to protect vulnerable Syrians by insisting that his job as president was to measure efforts in Syria "against my bottom line, which is what's in the best interest of America's security."[23]

The second sense of imperfection was alluded to by Vattel in the mid-eighteenth century: while every person may have a right to be protected from atrocities, the duty to ensure such protection when a host government is unable or unwilling to provide it falls on no particular state.[24] We see that

several British leaders deployed this idea in the nineteenth century, rejecting calls for greater efforts to protect vulnerable Christians in the Ottoman
Empire on the grounds that Britain did not have a "special" or "peculiar"
responsibility that fell more heavily on them than any of the other European
powers. More recently, both Obama and US president Donald Trump have
lamented the unwillingness of other states "to put any skin in the game" and
to share with the United States the burden of responsibility for responding
to crises of human protection.[25]

The third sense of imperfection is extrapolated from Kant's late
eighteenth-century discussion of duties of virtue: given that the international community will usually be confronted with multiple situations involving the threat or perpetration of atrocities, each state that seeks to discharge
its duties has a "playroom for free choice," meaning they have freedom to
choose whom in particular they should protect and what measures they
should use to protect them.[26] This idea has long been echoed by leaders
seeking to dilute pressure for a stronger response to a particular crisis. Queen
Victoria, for example, queried why the Bulgarians were supposed to be more
deserving of England's assistance than any other vulnerable people, "as if
they were more God's creatures and our fellow-creatures than every other
nation abroad."[27] More recently, Obama asked, "How do I weigh tens of
thousands who've been killed in Syria versus the tens of thousands who are
currently being killed in the Congo?"[28]

While the Pufendorfian dilemma of how to weigh duties to others against
duties to oneself and the Vattelian dilemma of who among many should do
the protecting in a given situation have received a reasonable amount of
attention from moral philosophers in recent years, the Kantian dilemma
of who among many should be protected by a given state has been almost
entirely neglected. Theorists have tended to proceed on the assumption that
the world is confronted with only a single atrocity crisis at a time and that our
task is to identify which state or states bear responsibility for responding on
behalf of the international community. This has severely hampered the development of ideas about how to work toward optimal coverage in the protection of civilians the world over from atrocities. When we place the Vattelian
(who should protect?) and Kantian (who should be protected?) senses of
imperfection alongside each other, it becomes clear that the answers to each
need to be woven together. The responsibility to protect needs to be shared.
I pursue this idea in chapter 3 and explain how the imperfections identified
by Vattel and Kant might be overcome. This involves the identification of
guiding principles for the fair and efficient distribution of responsibilities

among states, so that the plurality of threatened and actual crises confronted at a given time can be adequately addressed insofar as is possible.

When first developing the idea of imperfect duties, Pufendorf explained that a fundamental implication of the fact that a duty is imperfect is that states cannot be compelled to perform it.[29] States are at liberty to judge for themselves what they can contribute to the protection of vulnerable strangers and should be considered answerable to no one else. We find politicians, from British Leader of the House Arthur Balfour in the nineteenth century through to US ambassador to the UN John Bolton in the twenty-first century, making use of such an idea, seeking to dilute expectations for humanitarian intervention by emphasizing that the imperative to protect beyond borders is a moral rather than legal responsibility. In chapter 4, I examine how the ICJ and the International Law Commission (ILC) have tried to "perfect" this responsibility in recent years in the sense of making it legally enforceable, by codifying extraterritorial obligations for the prevention of atrocity crimes. I argue, however, that such codification can never be fully coherent until the international community "perfects" its answers to the Vattelian question of who among many should act and the Kantian question of who among many should be protected. This requires much more substantial institutionalization of the distribution of global obligations than presently exists.

Some skeptical observers point to the absence of more comprehensive legal codification as evidence that the R2P norm cannot have a meaningful impact on the behavior of states.[30] However, we see in chapters 2 and 5 that, even in the absence of legal enforceability, the felt imperative to protect beyond borders does at times move states to make meaningful efforts, individually and collectively, to care for strangers. The imperfect and shared nature of the responsibility generates opportunities for problematic buck passing and opportunistic (even if often justifiable) blame shifting, but also creative burden sharing and courageous action for the sake of the distant vulnerable.

Overview of the Book

The book begins with two chapters that examine the intellectual and diplomatic histories of duties of protection beyond borders.[31] As noted above, I largely refrain in these chapters from looking ahead to note how past ideas and practices are similar to or different from those of the present day. To do so would risk compromising our understanding of these histories. Instead,

I seek to convey historical debates and events as they were understood by the people involved. I encourage readers to simply soak up these histories safe in the knowledge that the three chapters that follow will make good use of them to illuminate how we might best understand the ethics, law, and politics of the shared responsibility to protect today.

Chapter 1 sketches a history of thinking about the duties of states to care for vulnerable people beyond their borders. While histories of human rights have proliferated in recent years, past thinking about duties to vindicate these rights remains relatively underexplored. This is particularly the case for extraterritorial duties. I focus on one strand of theorizing—Western natural law—which has given sustained attention to such duties, producing a range of arguments and frameworks for thinking that remain influential as well as others that are largely forgotten and can reward renewed attention. I sketch multiple and disparate theories of duties beyond borders, from Francisco de Vitoria deliberating the justice of the conquest of the Americas in the early sixteenth century through to the supposed eclipse of natural law theorizing by Kant at the end of the eighteenth century. I retrieve debates waged across these three centuries about how to conceive tensions between duties to strangers and duties to one's own people. I examine how theorists comprehended not only duties of military intervention in nonconsenting states, but also duties of consensual aid and assistance. And I explore contrasting claims about the nature of these various duties and the implications of violation. This sketch provides us with important tools for probing in later chapters how states commonly perceive, and how they might more fruitfully comprehend, their shared responsibility to protect today.

Chapter 2 considers the historical practices of (mostly Western) states, focusing on how they have constructed and performed responsibilities in realms related to R2P, including humanitarian intervention, minority protection, and the colonial subjection of "backward" peoples to the supposedly beneficial rule of "civilized" powers. Covering the period from the Peace of Westphalia to the end of the Cold War, I give particular attention to key developments in the nineteenth and early twentieth centuries—an especially innovative period in the international construction of shared responsibilities due initially to the advent of great power management by European powers and subsequently the transfer of some of their managerial roles to the League of Nations. Of particular interest is how states grappled with questions about how they should share their acknowledged protection responsibilities.

The historical record is at best mixed. Constructions of responsibilities, even when aimed at assisting and protecting people beyond borders, have typically been shaped by the interests of the most powerful states. Too often, they have been cynically manipulated to justify abuse and exploitation. Performances of these responsibilities, even when seemingly motivated by concern for vulnerable people, have commonly been marked by selectivity, hypocrisy, paternalism, and racism. Too often, they have done more harm than good. Understanding this history helps us think through the contemporary ethics, law, and politics of international human protection, enabling us, for example, to appreciate how responsibilities can be variously evaded or perverted by the powerful and to grasp both the historical traumas and the enduring temptations that continue to shape protection debates and practices.

Turning to the present, chapter 3 examines the ethics of the shared responsibility to protect. As I noted earlier, existing accounts commonly proceed on the assumption that the world is confronted with only a single atrocity crisis at a time and that our task is to identify which state or states bear the responsibility to respond on behalf of the international community. I take as my task to develop an account of the ethics of R2P fit for a world in which there are typically multiple situations involving the threat or perpetration of atrocities requiring international attention. Noting both the history of imperial abuse and the more recent failure of the 2011 intervention in Libya, the chapter begins by considering whether responsible international protection is even possible. Wrestling with postcolonial critiques of R2P, I cautiously argue that, as disastrous as the Libyan intervention turned out to be, the broader contemporary record suggests that the possibilities and opportunities for responsible international protection—both coercive and noncoercive—remain much more substantial than critics suggest. I then examine the "imperfections" inherent to the shared responsibility to protect, derived from Pufendorf (how should competing responsibilities be weighed?), Vattel (who should do the protecting?), and Kant (who should be protected?), and theorize how this imperfect responsibility might be made more "perfect" by clarifying what we should ask of states confronted with the threat or perpetration of atrocities beyond their borders. Specifically, I propose a set of principles that might fruitfully guide the fair and effective distribution of responsibilities among multiple states in response to multiple situations of concern.

Chapter 4 clarifies the legal status of the shared responsibility to protect, offering a twofold argument: extraterritorial obligations for the prevention of atrocities have become more firmly established in law in recent decades than many people realize, but these legal developments are troublingly incoherent. The ICJ and the ILC have offered bold statements indicating that states have a legal obligation to do whatever they can to protect populations beyond their borders from atrocity crimes. The ICJ has gone so far as to say that states are obliged "to employ all means reasonably available to them, so as to prevent genocide so far as possible," regardless of where the genocide occurs.[32] These are monumental legal developments. But they are limited in three crucial respects, which stem from a failure to reckon adequately with the obligation's Pufendorfian, Vattelian, and Kantian "imperfections": there is a lack of clarity around questions of enforcement and reparation, and it is unclear how these questions could be given coherent answers; the ICJ's claim that the scope of protection obligations should be grounded in the capacities of states places an unfair burden on those that have diligently culti-vated such capacities; and there is ambiguity about how a state can be legally obligated to respond to a particular atrocity crisis in a given instance since it will usually be confronted with multiple crises to which it could justifiably direct its resources. I suggest that, while recent and ongoing legal develop-ments are certainly significant, the way forward in encouraging states to respond to the threat or perpetration of atrocities beyond their borders lies less in the further development of law than in the diffusion and internaliza-tion of social norms that lead states to accept risks and costs in protecting vulnerable outsiders. This political dimension of the shared responsibility to protect is the focus of chapter 5.

Chapter 5 tells the story of the politics of human protection in the era of R2P, explaining how the felt imperative to protect strangers from atrocities has had a real impact on the behavior of many states in recent years, while avoiding the temptation to exaggerate the historical novelty or contemporary success of the R2P norm. Reflecting on the long history of international protection explored in chapter 2, I argue that what is particularly new in the R2P era is that international engagement with atrocities has become almost a matter of routine. The international community, and especially the members of the Security Council, recognize a need to attend to not only the most prominent crises, but also those many other situations of concern that neither attract substantial media attention nor engage the strategic or economic interests of powerful bystander states. However, I also recognize that states continue to fail to adequately discharge their responsibilities in many ways. Not only do they too often fail to respond quickly enough or commit the necessary resources to protect vulnerable civilians, but they too often shield those committing atrocities and too often themselves contribute to the perpetration of these crimes. And things have been getting worse in recent years as several states that have long provided the impetus and accepted much of the burden of responsibility for international protection efforts embrace norms of populist nationalism and abandon global responsibilities and as the growth of post-truth politics and the global exposure of great-power hypocrisies combine to weaken the potential for proponents of R2P to push other states to care better for vulnerable strangers. A brief conclusion, making further use of the idea of "imperfection" to reflect on some of the limits and possibilities of encouraging states to embrace and discharge their shared responsibility to protect, brings the book to a close.

PART I

Historical Responsibilities

1

International Thought

For all the attention paid to the international community's responsibility to protect today, the long history of thinking about such responsibilities is commonly overlooked. Histories of human rights have proliferated.[1] But little attention has been given to the history of responsibilities to protect these rights beyond the confines of the sovereign state.[2] Certainly, we have a good understanding of the history of arguments for and against military intervention to protect tyrannized and persecuted populations.[3] I make use of this research in what follows. But such scholarship has largely focused on arguments about the *permissibility* of such actions, rather than whether, and in what circumstances, the care of strangers might be considered *obligatory*.[4] To tell the story of the development of the idea that states have not merely a right but a responsibility to protect vulnerable people beyond their borders, we need to explore not only tensions between sovereignty and intervention, as many have, but also tensions between responsibilities to strangers and responsibilities to one's own people. We need to examine not only responsibilities of military intervention in nonconsenting states, but also responsibilities of consensual aid and assistance. And we need to analyze a variety of contrasting and competing claims about the nature and scope of these responsibilities and the implications, if any, of violation.

In this chapter, I merely sketch this story. While I stake out a position on several ongoing historiographical debates, I do not purport to overhaul existing interpretations of any particular past thinkers. Rather, I take as my task to bring to the surface their engagement with questions about responsibilities for strangers and foreigners and, in so doing, lay foundations for a richer and more informed discussion of contemporary ethics, law, and politics in the second part of the book. It is worth emphasizing that I do not seek to discover or derive from intellectual history a foundational argument for the responsibility to protect. I explain in chapter 3 that I take this responsibility as given on the basis that states acknowledge it today in word, if not always in deed. Rather, in examining some of the history of thinking about duties beyond borders, I seek insights into how the responsibility to protect might be fruitfully framed, how its "imperfections" might be conceived and addressed, how its potential perversions and abuses might be recognized and overcome, and how states might be led to discharge it responsibly.

Those who have alluded to the history of thinking about duties to assist and protect the vulnerable beyond borders have often misrepresented it. They have tended, in particular, to truncate it such that ideas of duties to strangers and foreigners are said to have emerged only in recent centuries. "It was the Enlightenment," Anthony Pagden claims, "which made it possible for us . . . to think beyond the narrow worlds into which we are born, to think globally. It was the Enlightenment which made it possible for anyone to imagine that any nation had any kind of responsibility for the welfare of any other."[5] This is a curious claim particularly given that Pagden's earlier scholarship did so much to bring to our attention the writings of the sixteenth-century Spanish Thomists, who, as we will see, wrote so clearly of the responsibilities of Spaniards for the welfare of the native peoples that they encountered in the Americas.[6] Similarly, Seyla Benhabib has argued that it was specifically Immanuel Kant, in his 1795 essay "Toward Perpetual Peace," who paved the way for a transition from "Westphalian sovereignty" to "liberal international sovereignty," in which states who were once concerned exclusively with the welfare of their own people were now bound to also give heed to the needs of vulnerable outsiders.[7] Yet, as we will see, many of those who had written before Kant had suggested much more demanding duties to vulnerable strangers and foreigners than those articulated in "Toward Perpetual Peace." Indeed, Kant's insistence on a strict right of noninterference rendered his understanding of sovereignty not only more "Westphalian" than many who preceded him but also more "Westphalian" than the provisions of the Peace of Westphalia itself, negotiated a century and a half before Kant penned his essay.[8]

The idea of an international responsibility to protect is one that has resonance within a diverse range of intellectual, religious, and cultural traditions predating Kant.[9] This chapter focuses on one strand of theorizing—Western natural law—that has pursued and probed this idea in particular detail and has bequeathed a range of concepts and claims that remain particularly influential. It focuses on the development of Western natural law thinking about duties to vulnerable people beyond borders, from its deployment by Spaniards thinking about the legitimacy of the conquest of the New World in the early sixteenth century through to its supposed eclipse by Kant at the end of the eighteenth century. Even within the confines of Western natural law we find multiple and disparate languages of thinking—including Thomists, Humanists, Moderns, Perfectionists, and Kant himself.[10] Debates have been waged both within and across these languages about the nature and scope of duties to strangers and foreigners, and the applicability of such duties to relations between states. I can only sketch some key aspects of these debates. I focus on the contributions of natural lawyers whose arguments proved particularly pivotal and whose claims subsequent natural lawyers wrestled with and responded to when developing their own ideas. Insofar as is possible in a single chapter, I take account of the different intellectual and political contexts in which they wrote, offering a compressed genealogical study of the kind that some contextualist historians have produced in recent years.[11] Among other things, we will see that ideas about extraterritorial duties were frequently constructed in response to, and often in the service of, European imperialism. While it is merely a sketch, the narrative that follows tells us important things about the histories of ideas that we commonly reason with and invoke today—ideas such as the unity of humankind, the love of neighbor, and the morality of "enlightened" self-interest—as well as retrieving alternative arguments or ways of thinking that have been too quickly forgotten and that can reward renewed attention.

Thomists

Western philosophers, jurists, and theologians have long contemplated duties owed to strangers and foreigners.[12] Through the course of the sixteenth century, however, theorists felt an urgent need to interpret and apply the ideas of earlier theorists anew given, on the one hand, the European encounter with the peoples of the New World and, on the other hand, the emergence of the concept of sovereignty and the increasing division of Europe into independent, territorially bounded commonwealths. A number of Spanish Thomist theologians at the Universities of Salamanca and Alcalá, the most influential of whom was Francisco de Vitoria, were unpersuaded by several prevailing justifications for the Spanish conquest and subjugation of Native Americans and troubled by reports of the loathsome treatment of indigenous peoples at the hands of colonists. These Catholic scholastics firmly rejected papal and imperial claims to dominion over the whole world as well as assertions of a universal right of the church to punish sins or unbelief. Instead, they envisaged a world of independent polities, each with jurisdiction over their own affairs. Nevertheless, drawing on Scripture, the writings of the church fathers, and the rediscovered writings of Aristotle, read through the lens of Thomas Aquinas, they insisted that all people were united by the principle of human fellowship, the duty to love one's neighbor, and the sacred demands of justice and charity. In turn, they acknowledged that while Native Americans did rightly possess dominion, the Spaniards had solemn duties to preach to them the Christian faith, to protect converts to the faith, and to rescue innocents from tyrannical indigenous rulers and their injurious rites.[13]

The theologians' understanding of duties relied heavily on the formulation articulated by Aquinas in the thirteenth century. While Aquinas sometimes treated duties to care for the vulnerable as matters of justice, he more commonly framed them as matters of charity.[14] However, in contrast to its common usage today, he did not consider matters of charity less binding or compulsory than those of justice. Rather, the distinction he drew between justice and charity was primarily that they directed actions toward different goods. The proper object of justice was the common good, whereas the proper object of charity was the divine good. Failure to take appropriate action to succor those in need, therefore, might constitute an injustice against the common good, but more dangerously, it could constitute a mortal sin against God.[15] Given the impossibility of any one individual caring for all who are in need, how should one determine whom to assist? Aquinas proposed that individuals should be guided by the "order of charity," such that they should love most those who are closely united to them. However, he also insisted that the demands of beneficence vary according to circumstance such that in certain cases individuals should succor a stranger rather than even their own father because of the degree and urgency of need. Moreover, he indicated that individuals ought to care particularly for vulnerable people who would not otherwise be assisted by anyone.[16]

It was with this understanding of duties that the Spanish theologians approached the "affair of the Indies." While they often relied on the language of charity and love of neighbor rather than justice, they insisted that the Spaniards had a sacred obligation to care for vulnerable Native Americans with whom they came into contact. Not only did they posit duties to preach the Christian faith and to protect converts from persecution, both of which were commonplace at the time, but they also suggested a duty to protect unbelievers from unjust harm. It was not the business of Christians to punish the Native Americans, who were outside the church, merely for violating the natural law, Vitoria insisted in a 1539 lecture.[17] But the Spaniards ought to restrain the Native Americans from violations that harmed innocents, specifically sins of human sacrifice and cannibalism, and to defend the victims of these crimes. "The proof," Vitoria claimed, "is that God gave commandment to each man concerning his neighbor. . . . The barbarians are all our neighbors, and therefore anyone, and especially princes, may defend them from such tyranny and oppression." Further proof was said to be given by the scriptural command to "deliver them that are drawn unto death, and forbear not to deliver those that are ready to be slain."[18] A close associate of the theologians at Salamanca and Alcalá, the missionary and defender of indigenous rights Bartolomé de Las Casas similarly claimed that while it was not the business of the church to pass judgment on the Native Americans, "it is the concern of the Church and the Pope, to whom the pastoral care of the whole world has been entrusted by Christ, to prevent the slaughter of such innocent persons lest their souls should perish forever." This duty to liberate innocents, he said, was a work of "piety or charity" analogous to the obligation to give alms to the poor.[19]

The Thomists cautioned, however, that the duty to care for the Native Americans did not necessarily provide just grounds for the Spaniards to wage war. They were conscious of the grave ills that tended to result from the use of force and the danger that Christian princes would unjustly seek to advance their own interests under the pretext of loving their vulnerable indigenous neighbors. Vitoria, for example, cautioned that Christian princes should act "only as far as is necessary to ward off injustices and secure safety for the future."[20] Some of his colleagues at Salamanca and Alcalá went further, expressing clear reservations about the justice of using force in protecting the Native Americans.[21] In this, they were likely influenced by Las Casas, who cautioned that the Spaniards must consider the decision to resort to arms carefully, lest, in trying to prevent the death of a few innocents, a multitude of people, including innocents, are killed, and those who survive are led to hate the Christian faith. Rather than resorting to war, he suggested, the Spaniards should encourage the Native Americans to refrain from inhumanity through "warnings, entreaties, or exhortations."[22]

Before proceeding further, it is important to note that in addition to the duties of Spaniards to care for the Native Americans, Vitoria also spoke of

the duties of the indigenous peoples to grant the Spaniards hospitality and
freedom to dwell, travel, and trade in their lands. Appealing to scriptural
injunctions to love one's neighbor, he declared that "to refuse to welcome
strangers and foreigners is inherently evil" and could, under certain conditions, justify the resort to force.[23] Some of Vitoria's colleagues firmly rejected
his suggestion that this duty of hospitality was enforceable,[24] and indeed Vitoria himself was reluctant to conclude that the Native Americans had violated
their duties of hospitality toward the Spaniards in a manner that gave just
cause for war. Nevertheless, this construction of duties would be confidently
reasserted and expanded by later theorists, such as Alberico Gentili and Hugo
Grotius, and by Spanish, English, and Dutch colonizers through the sixteenth
and seventeenth centuries, before giving way to alternative justifications for
the conquest and subjection of non-European peoples.[25]

Humanists

Through the course of the fifteenth and sixteenth centuries, a language of
humanism emerged in opposition to the scholasticism of the Thomist theologians. Disillusioned with the supposedly obscurantist philosophizing of the
scholastics and critical of their perceived enslavement to Aristotle and theological authorities, the Humanists turned to the combination of eloquence
and wisdom that they found in the Roman oratorical tradition, and most completely in the works of first-century BCE statesman and philosopher Cicero.
They embraced a skepticism that emphasized the contingency of political
knowledge, the virtue of prudence, and the art of practical judgment as essential qualities for successful political action. Princes were advised to cultivate
such qualities if they wished to maintain their state in a dangerous world.[26]

A key innovation of Gentili, Regius Professor of Civil Law at Oxford
University, writing toward the end of the sixteenth century, was to translate humanist categories of necessity (*necessitas*) and expedience (*utile*) into
the language of natural jurisprudence. Most crucially, whereas Renaissance
Humanists such as Niccolò Machiavelli and more recent *raison d'état* theorists such as Justus Lipsius had framed self-preservation as a principle that
sometimes required considerations of justice to be set to one side, Gentili
sanctified self-preservation, framing it as a fundamental aspect of justice
and a primary precept of natural law.[27] Self-defense is "the most generally
accepted of all rights," Gentili declared in *De jure belli* (*On the Law of War*,
1588–89/99), and it justifies actions that might otherwise be considered
unjust: "There is one rule which endures for ever, to maintain one's safety

by any and every means."[28] The Spanish theologians had accepted the right of princes to resort to force in defense of the commonwealth.[29] But Gentili put the principle of self-preservation to much more expansive ends, suggesting that it could justify wars not only of necessity but also of expedience, including preventive wars, wars of acquisition, and even wars fought for the reputation of the sovereign.[30]

Writing in the context of the upheaval and violence that accompanied the end of ecclesial unity brought about by the Reformation and the efforts of princes to consolidate sovereign authority in their respective polities, Gentili contemplated not only the duty of princes to maintain their own state but also their duty to assist persecuted and oppressed peoples in other European states. Again, he put the language of humanism to work. He insisted that, in addition to principles of necessity and expedience, wars could, indeed should, be justly fought for the humanist ideal of honor (*honesta*). Such wars were said to be fought for the sake of others and without concern for one's own interests. In support of such wars, he offered a Stoic-Ciceronian account of the unity of humankind and the bonds of fellowship between all people: "It remains to speak of defence for honour's sake, which is undertaken without any fear of danger to ourselves, through no need of our own, with no eye to our advantage, but merely for the sake of others. And it rests upon the fundamental principle, that nature has established among men kinship, love, kindliness, and a bond of fellowship."[31] Gentili applied this idea of universal human fellowship to relations between sovereigns. Sovereigns were particularly bound to come to the defense of allies, neighbors, those of common blood, and those united by common religion, he claimed.[32] In addition, they were bound to defend the subjects of other sovereigns from cruel and unjust treatment. While sovereigns should have some freedom in exercising authority over their own subjects, he claimed, "the subjects of others do not seem to me to be outside of that kinship of nature and the society formed by the whole world," and thus sovereigns ought to be accountable to that society for the treatment of their subjects.[33]

This claim was directed toward answering what Gentili described as "a burning question, namely, whether the English did right in aiding the Belgians against the Spaniards." In justifying Elizabeth I's decision in 1585 to intervene in the Low Countries, Gentili drew some lessons for the relationship between honor, necessity, and expedience. The Spanish theologians had insisted that wars fought to defend innocents should be waged only for the benefit of innocents, rather than for the benefit of Spain.[34] Gentili himself had begun his discussion by claiming that wars of honor should be fought "with no eye to our advantage."[35] He now noted, however, that the defense of others would tend to coincide with reasons of necessity and expedience and insisted that this was entirely appropriate. England's resort to arms to aid the Low Countries was justified by the need to vindicate the "bonds of kinship" between the English and the Belgians and to secure their liberty, he claimed, but it was also justified on the necessary and expedient grounds of protecting England's allies against a threatening enemy, maintaining "that bulwark of Europe" that the Spaniards wished to break down, and securing a favorable peace with Spain.[36]

But what was to be done if the demands of honor were at variance with the requirements of necessity and expedience? What was to be done if the duty to vindicate the bonds that unite the universal society of humankind failed to complement the duty to seek the security and advantage of one's own state? Gentili conceded that no one was obliged to attempt to rescue others if it would put their own safety at risk, "for no one is bound to place himself in danger; no one is bound to rush into a fire for the sake of another."[37] However, he otherwise said little about how to resolve the tension between the need to assist vulnerable outsiders and the virtue of maintaining and strengthening the state. This was a tension with which natural law theorists would begin to grapple the following century.

Moderns

It was Grotius who "broke the Ice" by explicating "the true fundamental Principles of the Law of Nature, and the right Method of explaining that Science," supplanting the perverse dominance of Aristotelianism and the barbarous methods of the Scholastics, Jean Barbeyrac declared in 1709.[38] The task of further illuminating the "true" law of nature, Barbeyrac claimed, was subsequently taken up by others such as the Englishmen Thomas Hobbes and Richard Cumberland, and most successfully by Samuel Pufendorf, German professor of the law of nature and nations.[39] This suggestion that Grotius broke from the past is challenged by some who insist that the Dutchman drew heavily on the natural law reasoning of the Thomist theologians and also the ideas of Humanists such as Gentili.[40] But Benjamin Straumann rightly adjudicates that while Grotius certainly borrowed ideas from the theologians, he departed from them by developing a system of natural law that was grounded not in an Aristotelian, eudaemonist account of the ultimate purpose of human activity, but in fundamental principles of human nature that right reason obliges us to acknowledge. The formulations of virtues that the Thomists had produced were supposed to guide action toward goods of happiness and perfection. Grotius's system, in contrast, produced strict rules that were to be obeyed simply because they were dictated by reason.[41] In the hands of Grotius and those "Moderns" who followed him, duties of charity and neighborly love that proceeded from considerations of virtue were marginalized and what remained was a much thinner account of the law of nature that emphasized duties to preserve oneself and to refrain from injuring others.

As Richard Tuck highlights, a characteristic feature of the reasoning of the modern natural law theorists was their use of the concept of a "state of nature"—an ungoverned realm in which humans could be conceived to exist and interact prior to their entry into civil society—and their transposition of that concept to the realm of relations between sovereigns.[42] While the "state of nature" would be most famously developed by Hobbes, Grotius had already made use of the concept when developing his system of natural law.[43] In his influential work, *De jure belli ac pacis* (*The Law of War and Peace*), first published in 1625, Grotius built a system of law upon the Stoic-Ciceronian notion of a natural human inclination to sociability (*appetitus societatis*).[44] The desire for society, when combined with the human capacity for reason and speech, was said to provide the source of the law of nature. However, the duties to others that supposedly followed from this sociability were quite circumscribed. Indeed, they were almost identical to those that Grotius had derived from the principle of self-preservation in an earlier unpublished work, *De jure praedae* (*Commentary on the Law of Prize and Booty*).[45] He declared, "To this sphere of the law belong the abstaining from that which is another's, the restoration to another of anything of his which we may have, together with any gain which we may have received from it; the obligation to fulfil promises, the making good of a loss incurred through our fault, and the inflicting of penalties upon men according to their desserts."[46] These negative duties to refrain from injuring others were said to be matters of "law properly so called." Their observance was compulsory. Violation involved breaching the "rights" of others and was appropriately subject to punishment. In contrast, Grotius claimed that the observance of principles of charity and the provision of kindness and liberality, while praiseworthy, was not obligatory because no one could properly be said to have a "right" to these things. Thus, departing from the Thomists, he drew a stark distinction between charity and justice, insisting that liberality toward others was not rightly understood as a duty of natural law to which the word "ought" could be applied.[47] Positive duties to care for the interests of others and offer relief in time of distress, he claimed, arose only when individuals united to form a commonwealth or state. Only once a group of individuals transitioned from natural to civil society, covenanting with each other for the sake of the common good, could they perceive a benefit and an obligation to provide for each other's protection and contribute to each other's necessities.[48]

Grotius made clear that it was those negative duties that obtained within natural society rather than the more demanding positive duties of civil society that were applicable to relations between states. One implication of this was that while he famously justified a *right* of war to rescue people beyond borders from tyranny and oppression, he made clear in his published work at least that there was no *duty* to engage in such acts of rescue. In his unpublished *De jure praedae*, which he was commissioned to write by the Dutch East India Company in 1604, Grotius did briefly argue in favor of a positive duty to rescue victims of tyranny and oppression. In this work, a study of the law of nature, which was essentially an exhaustive defense of Dutch privateering in the East Indies, Grotius momentarily ignored the strict system of rights and duties that he was developing in order to argue that the Dutch had rightly acted upon a positive duty in taking up arms in defense of the peoples of the East Indies, particularly the Sultan of Johore, who had been harassed and injured by the Portuguese. He marshaled all the usual authorities to which earlier theorists had appealed—Scripture, the church fathers, philosophers, and jurists—in order to make the case that the Dutch had performed a sacred and universal duty to protect the vulnerable. Indeed, he asserted, should the Dutch have failed to protect the East Indians from harm they would have been no less culpable than the Portuguese who inflicted the harm.[49]

In *De jure belli ac pacis*, however, written twenty years later, at a time when Grotius no longer had political or commercial incentives to construct demanding duties of rescue, he adhered to his strict system of rights and duties and insisted that while one was *permitted* to take up arms for the sake of others, the maintenance and advantage of one's own state should always take priority. The protection of the subjects of others from oppression was lawful and even praiseworthy, he observed, but it should not be undertaken at trouble or inconvenience to oneself.[50] Grotius thus made clear what had been only hinted at in the writings of Gentili: war to rescue the vulnerable beyond borders was rightly waged where possible and prudent, but it should not properly be called a duty. A sovereign prince in an international state of nature was bound to protect his own state and to refrain from unjustly injuring others, but he bore no duty to accept risks or costs for the protection of those outside his care.

In contrast to Grotius, Hobbes bluntly declared that even if humans were naturally desirous of society, they were not capable of it. The notion that man was "an animal born fit for Society," he claimed, was an error that "proceeds from a superficial view of human nature."[51] If Grotius had derived from the inclination to sociability an account of the law of nature that demanded little in terms of positive duties to succor those in need, Hobbes now stripped the law back even further. In *Leviathan* (1651), the Englishman painted a notoriously bleak picture of the state of nature as a condition of war "of every man, against every man," and suggested that this natural condition of war could be recognized in the posture of sovereigns to one another.[52] In such a condition, he claimed, natural individuals and, by extension, sovereign states were at liberty to do whatever was conducive to their preservation.[53]

In recent years, scholars have helpfully shown that the laws of nature that Hobbes derived from this principle of self-preservation provided more substantial grounds for restraint and cooperation in relations between sovereign states than has often been recognized.[54] Nevertheless, it remains that such laws followed solely from considerations of utility. Properly speaking, Hobbes insisted, there could be no justice or injustice in a realm that lacks a common power to promulgate and enforce laws; there could only be the liberty to preserve oneself.[55] He acknowledged that there might be occasions in which a state should extend benevolence to those in need beyond its borders. But this would be generated only by consideration of the benefits to be derived to oneself from such action, rather than consideration of what was just or unjust.[56]

When Pufendorf came to formulate his own system of the law of nature in *De jure naturae et gentium* (*The Law of Nature and Nations*), first published in 1672, he sought to combine Grotius's emphasis on sociability with Hobbes's emphasis on utility. Wary of the charges of anti-Aristotelianism and impiety that had been leveled at Hobbes, Pufendorf made sure to endorse man's capacity for sociability. But, in contrast to Grotius, he grounded his system not in a natural desire for such sociability, but in the utility to be derived from sociable behavior.[57] Pufendorf shared Hobbes's belief that life in the state of nature is unstable and dangerous, but he insisted that actors in this natural condition can recognize that they cannot secure their preservation without the assistance of others. This in turn gives them reason to extend assistance to others in time of need so as to gain their trust and favor and be free from harm.[58] Rather than being a natural characteristic of individuals, therefore, sociability is an imperative produced by the principle of self-preservation. For this reason, it is a precept of nature: "And so it will be a fundamental law of nature, that 'Every man, so far as in him lies, should cultivate and preserve towards others a sociable attitude, which is peaceful and agreeable at all times to the nature and end of the human race.' . . . By a sociable attitude we mean an attitude of each man towards every other man, by which each is understood to be bound to the other by kindness, peace, and love, and therefore by a mutual obligation."[59] In a response to critics, published in 1686, Pufendorf insisted that his was a Stoic conception of the law of nature and that it was directly opposed to the Epicurean theories of Hobbes.[60] Some scholars accept this claim, submitting that Pufendorf's system generated demanding duties of mutual assistance that are not found in Hobbes (or, for that matter, in Grotius). Pagden, for example, suggests that Pufendorf's law of nations "involves an obligation on the part of one social group not merely not to harm, but actively to promote the welfare of all others."[61] But such claims are too strong. Pufendorf's theory, proceeding from a basic concern for self-preservation and grounded in considerations of utility, was fundamentally much closer to Hobbes's than he was willing to admit.[62]

Certainly, in contrast to Hobbes, Pufendorf acknowledged the possibility of justice and injustice in the state of nature and further developed Grotius's account of the rights and duties of natural individuals and, by extension, sovereign states. Crucially, he developed a notion of "imperfect" duties, which reaccorded the language of "duty" to the performance of those principles of beneficence and liberality that Grotius had marginalized. While the performance of "perfect" duties, which require refraining from injuring others, was necessary for the ongoing existence of (international) society, he explained, the performance of "imperfect" duties contributed merely to the improvement of (international) society. States, moreover, needed to weigh the duties that they owed imperfectly to outsiders against the duties that they owed to themselves and their citizens. As such, while it is a good thing to discharge these "imperfect" duties, their performance should remain subject to the discretion of the duty bearer and never enforced.[63]

In contrast to earlier theorists, who had suggested that the provision of hospitality, free passage, and trade could be compelled, Pufendorf indicated that the duty to provide such things was imperfect since violation entailed withholding a benefit rather than doing an injury, and thus violation was not rightly subject to enforcement.[64] Thus he disposed of a perverse set of arguments that Europeans had developed to justify the conquest and colonization of the Americas. But while Pufendorf thereby refused to facilitate the subjugation of vulnerable peoples, he gave little indication that his system entailed positive duties requiring the assistance and protection of those in need. On the question of the resort to arms to rescue oppressed peoples, he simply referred his readers to the opinion of Grotius.[65] And crucially, having grounded sociability in considerations of utility, he even recommended that states be prepared to act unsociably if utility demanded it, suggesting, for example, that states could expel foreigners in time of famine for the sake of their own citizens.[66] Such exceptions suggested a serious shortcoming in Pufendorf's utility-based argument for sociability, which G. W. Leibniz would soon expose.

Perfectionists

Hobbes and Pufendorf were driven by a circumscribed vision of the aims and possibilities of law and politics. Responding to decades of violence and instability, both within and between states, they posited systems of the law of nature and nations that sought merely to facilitate the maintenance of peace and order. The purpose of law, for them, was to restrain and pacify a violent humanity. Other natural law theorists of the early Enlightenment, however, most prominently Leibniz and Christian Wolff, embraced the Aristotelian-Thomist claim that law and politics should aim higher and seek to facilitate the natural human inclination to "perfection." They offered an expansive vision of the ends of social life that required individuals to pursue the well-being and happiness not only of themselves but also of others.[67]

Asked for his opinion on Pufendorf's political theory, Leibniz offered a fierce critique. In a letter penned in 1706, the German philosopher declared that Pufendorf's decision to ground his system in considerations of material utility and to exclude consideration of the ultimate ends of human life had forced him "to be content with an inferior degree of natural law."[68] Across numerous works, Leibniz developed a theory of the law of nature that grounded moral action not in material utility but in the lasting pleasure and perfection that individuals derive from benevolently promoting the perfection and well-being of others.[69] Over subsequent decades, Wolff elaborated and systematized Leibniz's ideas and, in *Jus gentium methodo scientifica pertractatum* (*The Law of Nations According to the Scientific Method*), published in 1749, he applied them to relations between states. Rejecting "the perverse idea . . . that the mainspring of the law of nations is personal advantage," Wolff insisted that every nation ought to instead "have the fixed and lasting desire to promote the happiness of other nations." Just as "every man ought to love and cherish every other man as himself," he claimed, "every nation too ought to love and care for every other nation as for itself." He acknowledged that each nation was bound to preserve and perfect itself, perfection entailing "a sufficiency for life, tranquility and security." But he also maintained that "every nation owes to every other nation that which it owes to itself," insofar as it can perform it without neglecting its duty to itself.[70]

The following decade, the Swiss diplomat and jurist Emer de Vattel developed these ideas further. Vattel is often read as a disciple of the modern natural law theorists, particularly Grotius and Pufendorf.[71] Kant likely bears some responsibility for this, having artfully grouped the three writers together in order to dismiss them in a single stroke as "sorry comforters."[72] Certainly, Vattel knew the works of the Moderns well and made use of many of their claims. However, he was at least as positively disposed to the perfectionist theories of Leibniz and Wolff. His most famous work, *Le Droit des Gens* (*The Law of Nations*), published in 1758, echoed Wolff in grounding the law of nations in a Leibnizian concept of perfection, recommending that nations contribute to each other's perfection insofar as they can without neglecting their duties to preserve and perfect themselves.[73]

Vattel's primary purpose in writing *Le Droit des Gens* was to advance the security and well-being of the small Swiss principalities and republics in which he lived amid the large and often predatory militarist and commercial powers of Europe. While other Swiss theorists, such as Jean-Jacques Rousseau, recommended isolationism as the means of protecting Swiss liberty, Vattel argued that the freedom and welfare of vulnerable states would be better advanced by binding Europe more tightly together through the cultivation of mutual commitment to the common good.[74] Nature has established society among individuals, he declared, and the "general law" of that society is that "each individual should do for the others every thing which their necessities require, and which he can perform without neglecting the duty that he owes to himself." While groups of individuals were free to unite with each other to form states, they could not thereby liberate themselves from their duties to the rest of humankind. Rather, in so uniting, "it thenceforth belongs to that body, that state, and its rulers, to fulfil the duties of humanity towards strangers." These "duties of humanity" were imperfect duties whose performance could not be compelled by other states. External compulsion would violate the liberty and independence of the state, Vattel explained. But this did not mean that states were morally free to act as they chose. Rather, duties of humanity were internally binding on the conscience of each state and a state that refused to perform them, when in a position to do so, was "guilty of a breach of duty"—something Grotius and Pufendorf had refused to say.[75] The rejection of international enforcement of these duties was not a concession to the exigencies of national self-interest or an endorsement of reason of state, as some scholars charge.[76] Rather, it was a concession to the need to maintain international peace and security. Permission to enforce duties of humanity, Vattel explained, would mean "opening the door to endless discussions and quarrels."[77] It remained, then, for each state to weigh their duties to others against their duties to themselves on a case-by-case basis, according to the dictates of their conscience.[78] But rather than leaving it there, he proceeded to provide principles and guidelines for how such duties should be so weighed.

States, Vattel claimed, should always exercise prudence when weighing their obligations, but this in no way justified unreasonably neglecting the needs of others. By way of example, he suggested that Russia had recently carried out a "prudent performance" of its duties in that it had "generously assisted Sweden when threatened with a famine," but had refused to allow other nations to purchase corn that it needed for its own people.[79] Moreover, in direct contrast to Grotius, he insisted that while a state should give heed to its own security and material interests, it should nevertheless be willing to bear costs and inconveniences for the sake of the vulnerable beyond its borders. While a state was under no obligation to aid another if this would require doing "an essential injury to herself," it ought not to refuse to assist others out of fear of "a slight loss, or any little inconvenience: humanity forbids this; and the mutual love which men owe to each other requires greater sacrifices."[80]

Several other of Vattel's suggestions are worth noting. First, in a significant break from earlier theorists, who had tended to focus on the question of military force to put down tyranny when contemplating extraterritorial duties, Vattel also gave attention to duties of nonforcible assistance to those afflicted with "famine or any other calamities." He declared that "if a nation is afflicted with famine, all those who have provisions to spare ought to relieve her distress, without however exposing themselves to want. . . . Whatever be the calamity with which a nation is afflicted, the like assistance is due to it." By way of example, he endorsed the "noble generosity" of Protestant Britain, which had responded to the Lisbon earthquake of 1755 by providing a hundred thousand pounds worth of assistance to the Catholic Portuguese. The obligations to perform these duties of humanity, he explained, were "solely founded on the nature of man." No nation can refuse them to another on the grounds of difference of religion. Rather, "to be entitled to them, it is sufficient that the claimant is our fellow creature."[81] Second, Vattel added that a nation is bound not only to contribute to the perfection of other nations by providing for their necessities and helping them secure peace and justice within their territories but also to contribute, "occasionally, and according to its power," to the capacities of these nations so that they are better able to procure such things for themselves.[82] Duties of humanity, thus, are owed not only in time of crisis. Rather, they are to be discharged whenever possible, so that nations may be made more capable of preventing or responding to such crises themselves. Third, Vattel insisted that a nation is bound not only to seek to benefit others insofar as it is presently capable. Rather, for a nation to truly perfect itself, it should endeavor to cultivate ever greater capacity to promote the perfection and happiness of others.[83]

Finally, in a discussion of the plight of strangers exiled from their homeland, Vattel alluded to a feature of imperfect duties that we will explore throughout this book: the problem of how to determine which among many states should discharge an imperfect duty. An exile, he argued, has a perfect right to live somewhere. But the duty to accept the exile is imperfect and therefore unenforceable with respect to any particular state.[84] We will see that this question of identifying who among many should take up the duty to assist and protect the vulnerable in a particular instance has long plagued the international politics of protection.

Immanuel Kant

In "Groundwork of the Metaphysics of Morals," published in 1785, Kant questioned the attempts of natural law theorists to derive morality from consideration of human nature: "One need only look at attempts at morality in that popular taste. One will find now the special determination of human nature (but occasionally the idea of a rational nature as such along with it), now perfection, now happiness, here moral feeling, there fear of God, a bit of this and also a bit of that in a marvellous mixture; without its occurring to them to ask whether the principles of morality are to be sought at all in acquaintance with human nature."[85] The principles of morality should not be drawn from experience of human nature, Kant insisted. Rather, they are to be found "altogether a priori, free from anything empirical, solely in pure rational concepts and nowhere else."[86] He proceeded to produce a "metaphysics of morals" that was purportedly derived from reason alone.[87] He then put these principles to work to explicate the laws that should apply in relations between states. He did so most famously in his 1795 essay, "Toward Perpetual Peace," and most completely in his 1797 study, "The Metaphysics of Morals."

Kant offered a Hobbesian vision of a state of nature in which "each has its own right to do *what seems right and good to it*," and he echoed the Englishman's suggestion that individuals have a duty to escape this natural condition by uniting with others to enter into "a civil condition."[88] However, in contrast to Hobbes, who was content to stop at the level of the sovereign state, Kant insisted that states also had a duty to leave the (international) state of nature by contracting with each other to establish a condition of peace. He rebuked Grotius, Pufendorf, and Vattel, describing them as "sorry comforters," whose "code . . . has not the slightest *lawful* force and cannot even have such force (since states as such are not subject to a common external constraint)."[89] What was needed, he claimed, was ideally "a universal *association of states*," in which "rights come to hold *conclusively* and a true *condition of peace* come about."[90] He conceded that this ideal was ultimately unachievable, but insisted that states nevertheless had a duty to continually seek to approximate it so as to "bring the human race ever closer to a cosmopolitan constitution."[91]

However, in contrast to some present-day "Kantian" scholars who purport to draw demanding international duties of assistance and protection from the philosopher's principles, Kant himself indicated that the obligations borne by states in their relations with each other in his ideal "cosmopolitan constitution" were rather minimal. Morality required not the establishment of a "friendly" community of nations, but merely a "peaceful" one, he claimed.[92] Therefore, despite observing that the community of nations had developed to the point where "a violation of right on *one* place of the earth is felt in *all*," he insisted that "cosmopolitan right shall be limited to conditions of universal *hospitality*," and this entailed merely "the right of a foreigner not to be treated with hostility because he has arrived on the land of another."[93] Rather than offering a "Kantian" system of positive duties of assistance and protection beyond borders, as some of his present-day disciples are wont to do, Kant prioritized negative duties to refrain from interfering in the affairs of other states, to refrain from undermining trust among states, and to eventually abolish standing armies so as to secure international peace.[94]

Those searching for positive duties to assist and protect in Kant's "Metaphysics of Morals" will find them not in his "Doctrine of Right," which is where we find his consideration of relations between states outlined above, but in his "Doctrine of Virtue," the focus of which is restricted to relations between individuals. This "Doctrine of Virtue" entails a rich discussion of positive duties to perfect oneself and to advance the happiness of others. Duties of virtue (or "ethical duties"), in contrast to "duties of right," Kant explained, are imperfect and unenforceable. But, in contrast to Pufendorf's treatment of duties, the "imperfection" of Kant's duties of virtue stems not from the idea that the duty bearer can choose whether or not to perform them. And in contrast to Vattel, the "imperfection" stems not from the fact that there are multiple potential duty bearers. Rather, these positive duties are imperfect because each duty bearer has a "wide" range of options—"a playroom for free choice"—regarding how and for whom they are performed.[95] This is the third sense of imperfection that we will explore throughout the book.

Contemplating such imperfect positive duties, whereas Vattel suggested that actors ought to seek to cultivate greater material capacity to contribute to the happiness of others, Kant posited a need to cultivate sympathetic feeling so that they will be inclined to so contribute. Since beneficence is a "universal duty" owed to all "rational beings with needs," he claimed, individuals ought to actively cultivate compassion for vulnerable people, so that they are more positively disposed to discharge their duties to them. Indeed, Kant explicitly framed such cultivation as a moral duty:

> But while it is not in itself a duty to share the sufferings (as well as the joys) of others, it is a duty to sympathize actively in their fate, and to this end it is therefore an indirect duty to cultivate the compassionate natural (aesthetic) feeling in us. . . . It is therefore a duty not to avoid the places where the poor who lack the most basic necessities are to be found but rather to seek them out, and not to shun sickrooms or debtors' prisons and so forth in order to avoid sharing painful feelings one may not be able to resist. For this is still one of the impulses that nature has implanted in us to do what the representation of duty alone might not accomplish.[96]

Nevertheless, we should remember that while individuals were obliged to cultivate compassion for and seek to contribute to the happiness of all humankind, Kant gave no indication that states should also be so concerned. He offered no principle of "cosmopolitan virtue" to complement his principle of "cosmopolitan right." His ideal international legal order did not include any obligation to care for the vulnerable beyond borders. And we ought not to attribute this absence of positive duties of mutual assistance among states to the idea that such concepts were not known to Kant. After all, as we have seen, such duties had been examined in detail in previous centuries by theorists whose works he knew well. Rather, it would seem that, given his overriding concern with establishing the conditions for "peace" rather than "friendship" among states, he consciously chose not to impute to states extraterritorial duties of assistance and protection. We are of course free to draw on Kant's ideas as we develop our own accounts of duties beyond borders, as I do in chapter 3, but we should hesitate before calling such a system "Kantian," and we should be careful not to neglect the prudent concern for international peace that appears to have driven Kant's wariness of interventionism in relations between states.

———

Today, so much theorizing about the ethics of the international protection of vulnerable populations operates in a "Kantian" mode that is grounded in a dehistoricized and idealized caricature of Kant's ideas. Much of this theorizing is valuable. But in addition to doing an injustice to Kant's actual arguments, it fails to make use of the rich resources for theorizing about duties offered by those who preceded him. This chapter has examined some key arguments offered by Western natural law theorists, revealing a range of ideas about the nature and scope of the duty to assist and protect vulnerable people beyond sovereign borders and the material and ideational interests that might motivate compliance with these duties, as well as making clear how constructions of duties have so often been driven, at least in part, by political and commercial opportunities and fears. We will return to many of these ideas as the book proceeds.

The chapter has also detailed the emergence of three different senses in which duties can be imperfect, each of which applies to international protection duties. Pufendorf, who first articulated the idea of imperfect duties, helps us perceive that the shared responsibility to protect is imperfect in the sense that it is rightly subject to the judgment of states that need to weigh the costs and risks of protecting vulnerable foreigners against the responsibility to care for the interests and well-being of their own populations. Vattel helps us see that the responsibility is imperfect in the sense that it is often unclear which among many states are obliged to protect a given group of foreigners at risk of atrocities. And Kant alerts us to the reality that it is often unclear which among many vulnerable groups of foreigners a given state is obliged to protect. We will see in chapters 3, 4, and 5 that it is vital that we grapple with each of these senses of imperfection if we are to understand the contemporary dynamics of the ethics, law, and politics of R2P. Recognition of these senses of imperfection will also help us understand the historical construction and performance of shared international responsibilities for the protection of vulnerable people—historical practices to which I now turn.

2

International Practice

Recent years have seen a proliferation of impressive studies that have begun to piece together the history of the international community's engagement with the plight of vulnerable people. We are increasingly well served with histories of humanitarian intervention,[1] humanitarianism,[2] minority protection,[3] refugee protection,[4] and the subjection of "backward" peoples to the supposedly beneficial rule of "civilized" powers.[5] These histories have exposed examples of international actors displaying integrity and hypocrisy, wisdom and foolishness, selflessness and selfishness, and often combinations of each, generating policies and actions that have variously done substantial good and terrible harm. In this chapter, I draw on and contribute to this literature by zeroing in, as per chapter 1, on the idea of *responsibility*—focusing here on the question of how imperial powers, sovereign states, and international institutions have constructed and performed responsibilities for the protection of the vulnerable since the seventeenth century. I examine how responsibilities have been claimed by particular actors or attributed to them by others, and I explore how these responsibilities have been at times embraced and discharged and at other times contested and evaded or manipulated and abused.

Most of the chapter focuses on the construction and performance of responsibilities by Western actors. There are certainly important stories to be told about historical non-Western practices of extraterritorial assistance and protection.[6] But so many of the practices and institutions of shared responsibilities for human protection that we work with today were produced within the West and subsequently globalized in ways that largely reflected Western interests.[7] Indeed, as we will see in chapters 3 and 5, the Western-centric nature of this history has implications for the ethics of R2P and informs much of its politics. While R2P is framed in universal terms, its clear parallels with earlier Western constructions of responsibilities, which so often legitimated the paternalistic, racist, hypocritical, and violent subjugation of non-Western peoples, leads many non-Western states to be skeptical of the interventionist aspects of R2P and emboldens them to resist or reshape the norm today.[8]

This chapter sketches numerous aspects of the international construction and performance of protection responsibilities from the Peace of Westphalia in 1648 through to the end of the Cold War. There are of course many strands to this history that I do not explore. I have chosen those that seem most useful for giving us a sense of the historical politics of shared responsibilities and also the legacies that continue to mark the international discussion of R2P today.[9] I pay particular attention to key developments in the nineteenth and early twentieth centuries. This was an especially innovative period in the international construction of responsibilities due to, initially, the advent of great power management of the international system and, subsequently, the transfer of some managerial functions to the League of Nations. A large portion of the chapter focuses on responsibilities for the protection of minorities—from Protestant and Catholic minorities in the German princely states of the Holy Roman Empire, through Christian minorities in the Ottoman Empire, to national minorities in eastern European and Balkan states whose protection was supposedly guaranteed by the league. Particular attention is given to the construction and performance of responsibilities for minorities since these activities were commonly attended with illuminating politicking about how responsibilities should be shared. I then examine responsibilities for the liberation, protection, and "civilization" of non-Europeans borne by imperial powers and league-mandated authorities. While there is less of a sense of shared responsibility here, since responsibility for each colonial and mandated territory was typically held by an individual power, it is vital that we consider these imperial projects since they have left legacies of temptation and trauma that color discussion of the ethics and politics of R2P today.[10] Finally, I briefly trace the marginalization of international responsibilities in the negotiation of the UN Charter and the gradual reassertion of such responsibilities by states, particularly with respect to the international promotion of human rights, through the 1970s and 1980s.

We will see that some responsibilities were inscribed in positive international law, in bilateral and multilateral treaties, covenants, and conventions. But we will also see that those deliberating the construction of these responsibilities and debating their performance frequently appealed to natural law arguments encountered in chapter 1. They invoked, for example, notions of love of neighbor and duties of humanity. They appealed also to considerations of self-interest to justify helping others, citing the benefits of advancing one's reputation, securing the regional balance of power, and preserving the broader international order.

Many political leaders contemplated the need to weigh duties to vulnerable strangers against duties to one's own people—a feature of such imperfect duties highlighted by Samuel Pufendorf. Some insisted that the interests of one's polity always trumped the needs of outsiders. Others rejected such claims as problematically selfish. Occasionally, a leader would echo Immanuel Kant's notion of a "playroom for free choice," insisting that the imperfect nature of duties beyond borders meant that their state was not bound to help any one group of vulnerable strangers more than any other. In contrast to Kant, who encouraged actors to therefore determine for themselves whom to assist, this idea was usually deployed to justify assisting no one. Frequently, political leaders addressed a question arising from the sense of imperfection to which Emer de Vattel had alluded: which state, collectivity of states, or multilateral institution bears the duty to succor those in need in a given instance? In certain cases, states determinedly claimed responsibility, and thus authority, to act to protect a group of people. In other instances, they acknowledged responsibility reluctantly and only under sustained domestic or international pressure, and sought to portray themselves as no more bound by a burden of responsibility than any other state. In other situations, states worked to shift the burden of responsibility onto other states or international institutions.

The historical record is at best mixed. Responsibilities have been repeatedly constructed for the assistance and protection of distant vulnerable people, but the nature and scope of these responsibilities have commonly reflected the interests of the most powerful states, ranging from broad interests in securing some common good to narrow interests in pursuing their own material advantage. Efforts to discharge these responsibilities have, at times, saved the lives of substantial numbers of people, but such efforts have often also been marked by troubling selectivity, manifest hypocrisy, appalling racism, and sheer brutality. While some of the international community's historical practices may prove worthy of renewed consideration and replication, others are worth our engagement today for the very different reason of helping us recognize how shared responsibilities can be rejected or evaded or, worse, manipulated or abused, all of which can help us as we grapple with the responsibility to protect today.

Protecting Liberty of Conscience at Westphalia

Scholars debating the merits of R2P often build their arguments upon a story about the Peace of Westphalia. The story goes that the peace brought into being an international system of equal and sovereign states, each with an indefeasible right to govern itself as it wished. Critics of R2P express concern that this Westphalian system, which for so long enabled peoples to pursue their respective conceptions of the good life free from external interference, is being undone by a new and specious principle of intervention. Supporters of R2P celebrate that the Westphalian system, which for too long provided a shield for tyranny, is being undone by a new and welcome principle of human protection. This Westphalian story, however, is false. For more than two decades now, scholars have been demonstrating that the Peace of Westphalia did not inaugurate a noninterventionist system of equal and sovereign states. Rather, the negotiators of the peace embraced and codified heteronomous forms of political community, hierarchical relationships between communities, and provisions for legitimate intervention.[11] Indeed, a close look at the provisions of the Westphalian treaties and their subsequent use by actors reveals that 1648 represents a crucial early instance of the construction of international responsibilities for the protection of the vulnerable. In my previous book, I explained that the peace imposed duties on the rulers of the German princely states for the care of their subjects, and a *right* of other contracting parties to intervene in response to violation of these duties.[12] I now go a step further and observe that the peace imposed a *responsibility* on contracting parties to ensure the German rulers discharged their duties.

The Peace of Westphalia brought to an end the Thirty Years' War (1618–48) that had engulfed and ravaged much of Europe. It was composed of the Treaty of Osnabrück, struck between the Holy Roman Empire and the Protestant queen of Sweden, and the Treaty of Münster, struck between the empire and the Catholic king of France. After decades of conflict between Catholics and Protestants in Europe, it had become clear that one of the keys to preventing religious conflict *between* political communities would be to secure agreement on the protection of religious minorities *within* political communities. Consequently, in the process of granting certain measures of autonomy to the German princely states within the empire, negotiators of the peace also made sure to impose upon the rulers of those states clear obligations for the exercise of religious tolerance within their territories. The Treaty of Osnabrück, for example, declared that subjects that chose to embrace a confession different from their prince, so long as it was Catholicism, Lutheranism, or Calvinism, were to "be patiently suffer'd and tolerated, without any Hindrance or Impediment to attend their Devotions in their Houses and in Private, with all Liberty of Conscience, and without any Inquisition or Trouble."[13] The contracting parties, moreover, indicated that they each bore an obligation to ensure that the German princes adhered to these provisions. "All Partys in this Transaction," they declared, "shall be oblig'd to defend and protect all and every Article of this Peace against any one, without distinction of Religion." If the violations of the conditions of the peace could not be peacefully resolved within three years, "all and every one of those concern'd in this Transaction shall be oblig'd to join the injur'd Party, and assist him with Counsel and Force to repel the injury."[14] Authorities within the empire and the guarantors of the peace beyond the empire were understood to be bound by these provisions to take peaceful and, if necessary, coercive measures to uphold religious liberty in the princely states.

Within the empire there was contestation over who could rightfully claim responsibility to ensure that the princes respected the liberties of their subjects. This dispute has been recently examined by Patrick Milton.[15] Milton explains that it was generally accepted that the Reichshofrat (Imperial Aulic Council), which was largely controlled by the emperor, had the authority to intervene in the affairs of the princely states. The council did so on numerous occasions, suspending or deposing princes found to have abused their authority. However, a group of Protestant princely states, called the Corpus Evangelicorum (CE), also claimed authority to intervene to protect coreligionists in situations where the Reichshofrat refused to act. They argued that this authority was derived from the provisions of the Westphalian treaties and the law of nature. In 1707, for example, the CE received an appeal for assistance from Protestant subjects of William Hyacinth, the Catholic ruler of Nassau-Siegen. They claimed to be victims of physical and financial persecution that "run contrary to law and justice, the Peace of Westphalia, Christian love itself." The CE responded not only by appealing to the emperor for redress but also by instructing "all neighboring Protestant Estates . . . to lend a helping hand" to restore the liberties established at Westphalia to all subjects. In

1710, as persecutions in Nassau-Siegen continued, the CE requested that the Protestant rulers of Brandenburg, Hanover, and Hessen-Kassel intervene. King Frederick William I of Brandenburg-Prussia responded by dispatching a contingent of troops to protect Protestants in Nassau-Siegen. A Prussian memorandum distributed at the Reichstag defended Frederick William's actions, claiming that Protestant princes could not be blamed for "assisting their suppressed and innocently persecuted coreligionists against all acts of violence contrary" to Westphalia. Indeed, failure to intervene would be "unjustifiable before God and the world." In an early example of the kind of tensions that can accompany shared responsibilities, however, Frederick William informed his Hanoverian counterpart, via an envoy, that he "hoped he would not be expected to settle this business alone. He had done his part and would have to lower his fists if he were not seconded."[16]

The other contracting parties to the Westphalian treaties, Sweden and France, were also understood to have a role to play as guarantors of religious liberty within the empire. Despite the language of obligation found in the treaties, it does not seem that the guarantor powers felt they were bound to intervene in instances where they did not wish to. Nevertheless, it is clear that when they perceived a particular moral duty or political interest in interceding, the treaties provided them with a clear mandate to do so. Certainly, states had often claimed that a duty to forcibly protect coreligionists could be derived from natural law alone. Elizabeth I, for example, justified her intervention on behalf of the Dutch revolt against Spain in terms of a need to restore ancient liberties and Christian government to an oppressed people.[17] However, it was perceived that such justifications were stronger when tied to legal agreements.[18] This is particularly evident in Britain's response to the persecution of Protestants of the Palatinate in 1719. At the time, one of the Westphalian guarantors, Protestant Sweden, was busy fighting for survival against Russia, and the other, Catholic France, had little interest in intervening on behalf of Protestants. George I, king of Britain and elector of Hanover, considered the protection of Protestants in the Palatinate important for the defense of the "Protestant interest," a concept that comprised an inseparable mixture of confessional sentiment and strategic self-interest.[19] He declared, "We cannot abandon our religious relatives in the face of such hard persecution and oppression" and expressed a desire to intercede, not only in his capacity as elector of Hanover, but also as king of Britain. His British secretary of state, James Stanhope, worried about the legality of British involvement and suggested that Britain should explore the possibility of becoming a guarantor to the Westphalian settlement. This, he explained, would enable George to "intervene with more justification and weight for the cause of the Protestants of the Empire."[20] It was understood that, while natural law arguments were potentially powerful, treaty law was a particularly authoritative way to establish and allocate international obligations for the protection of the persecuted.

Guarantees for the protection of Christian minorities would be a routine feature of treaties contracted among European polities after Westphalia, including Oliva (1660), Nijmegen (1678–79), Ryswick (1697), Dresden (1745), Paris (1763), and Hubertusburg (1763).[21] They would also be a feature of treaties contracted between European powers and the Ottoman Empire through the eighteenth and nineteenth centuries. These treaties would play a central role in a range of new debates about the scope and distribution of international responsibilities and the conditions for their performance.

Protecting Christians in the Ottoman Empire

At the Congress of Vienna (1814–15), convened to reconstruct the European order in the wake of the Napoleonic Wars (1799–1815), a small group of materially powerful states formally claimed for themselves the status of great powers. Britain, Russia, Austria, Prussia, and a restored France authorized themselves to direct the congress and accepted guardianship of the new order that they established. As British foreign secretary Lord Castlereagh explained to Cabinet, "The Great Powers feel that they have not only a common interest, but a common duty to attend to."[22] They assumed responsibility for the implementation of the mandates of the Congress of Vienna and the ongoing management of the balance of power.[23]

The great powers were soon confronted with what would become known as the "Eastern Question"—a complex set of issues concerning Europe's engagement with the supposedly decaying Ottoman Empire.[24] Among these issues was the matter of how to protect Christian minorities within the empire who, often due to their own provocations or rebellions, were frequently targets of atrocities by Muslim authorities. Over the next one hundred years, the great powers repeatedly coordinated to intervene in the Ottoman Empire, most notably in Greece (1827), Lebanon and Syria (1860–61), Crete (1866–68 and 1896–1900), and Macedonia (1903–8), to protect Christians from persecution and misrule.

The reasons why they undertook these interventions are complex. Some scholars emphasize power of moral sentiment, bolstered by the emergence of mass media, which stirred citizens, particularly in Britain and France, to pressure their leaders to alleviate the suffering of fellow Christians. These leaders, in turn, were moved to act, if not due to their own moral sensibilities then at least because they were concerned for their reputations both domestically and internationally.[25] This is certainly part of the story. An expanding body of scholarship has traced the emergence of a "humanitarian sensibility" among peoples and their rulers in Europe in the eighteenth and nineteenth centuries, which generated a new culture of compassion in response to distant suffering.[26] Feelings of empathy and pity for distant strangers helped to prompt numerous diplomatic and coercive interventions to protect the persecuted, as well as other activities that I touch on later in this chapter such as humanitarian relief for those in crisis, abolition of the slave trade, and efforts to promote more humane governance of colonized peoples.

It is important to note, however, that with the exception of Britain's forcible efforts to abolish the slave trade, the European powers intervened militarily to protect the vulnerable only in the Ottoman Empire, and only for the purpose of protecting fellow Christians. To the extent that moral sentiment generated a felt obligation to intervene, it did so only with respect to those with whom the European powers felt a particular affinity.[27] While they occasionally interceded diplomatically on behalf of persecuted Jews in European states, they never did so with force.[28] The interventions in Ottoman territories, moreover, were marked not only by this troubling selectivity but also by appalling hypocrisy. While the European powers cast the Turks as a people of "elaborate and refined cruelty," they themselves committed pogroms at home (Russia against Jews in 1881–84 and 1903–6) and genocides in their colonies (Britain against Aboriginal Tasmanians across the nineteenth century and Germany against the Herero and the Nama in 1904–7).[29]

Furthermore, even with respect to the protection of Christians in the Ottoman Empire, moral sentiment explains only so much. After all, while the great powers repeatedly intervened to protect Christians, they refrained from doing so on behalf of Christians in Armenia (1894–96 and 1909), despite clear evidence of atrocities and significant public pressure for them to respond. As Davide Rodogno rightly insists, ongoing competition among the great powers and the imperative of managing the balance of power are central to the story of when and where intervention took place as well as who intervened and how they conducted their intervention.[30] One further factor worth highlighting is that the great powers felt they had acquired rights and incurred obligations for the protection of Christians through treaties contracted with the empire. While none of these treaties explicitly provided for a right, much less a duty, to intervene militarily to protect Christians, they commonly contributed to the generation of felt sociopolitical obligations to do so—much like the Convention on the Prevention and Punishment of the Crime of Genocide (1948) in more recent times. Let us briefly explore the construction, distribution, and performance of this obligation to aid persecuted Christians in the Ottoman Empire via two examples of intervention and two of nonintervention.

GREECE 1821–27

In the Treaty of Küçük Kaynarca (1774), which concluded the Russo-Turkish war of 1768–74, Russia claimed authority for the protection of Orthodox Christianity in the Ottoman Empire, cutting into the right and responsibility for *all* Christians within the empire that France had claimed since the establishment of the Franco-Ottoman alliance in 1536.[31] When Ottoman authorities responded to a Greek revolt in 1821 by massacring Christians, pillaging churches, and hanging the patriarch of the Orthodox Church, Russia invoked its role of guarantor, protested, and threatened to intervene.[32] In a letter to the Duke of Wellington penned the following year, British foreign secretary George Canning admitted that Russia's quarrel with the Turks "was founded upon treaties, which gave the Emperor a right of interference, to a certain extent, in the internal affairs of the Turkish government; a right to which we had no pretension."[33] But Britain and the other great powers feared that war between Russia and the Turks could draw in all of Europe and destroy the balance they had carefully constructed at Vienna.

Britain and also Austria thus worked to frame the Greek crisis as a common European, rather than solely Russian, concern. Rather than endorsing Russia's special guardianship of Orthodox Christianity, they emphasized the bonds of Christianity and humanity that all the great powers shared with Greek Christians. At the same time, they warned against intervening on behalf of Greek rebels, noting the dangers that popular revolutions posed to European stability.[34] Castlereagh wrote to Czar Alexander I in 1821, encouraging him to "suffer the tempest to exhaust itself." He admitted that "humanity shudders at the scenes," but insisted "it is in vain hope that we can materially alter [the Greeks'] lot, or deliver them from their sufferings, and preserve the system of Europe as it now stands."[35] In a second letter, he acknowledged the pull of the moral duty to rescue the Greeks, but encouraged the czar to resist it, cautioning that one should not "be tempted, nor even called upon in moral duty under loose notions of humanity and amendment, to forget the obligations of existing Treaties, to endanger the frame of long established relations, and to aid the insurrectionary efforts now in progress in Greece."[36] For a time, war was avoided.

Over the next few years, however, the pressures on great power unity generated by the Greek crisis grew. The Greek rebels increased in strength, as did the civil society movement in Britain that championed the Greek cause. Canning responded by recognizing the Greeks as belligerents and allowing activists such as Lord Byron to travel to Greece to support their cause. Russia felt its role as guarantor was under threat. Rising tensions between Britain and Russia were resolved by an agreement to cooperate to address the crisis. The two parties convened in 1826 to produce a protocol. This formed the basis for the Treaty of London, adopted by the two powers and also France the following year.

These three powers acknowledged in the treaty that they were motivated to end the crisis in part because it had impeded European commerce and created opportunities for piracy that were costly to suppress. But they also insisted that they were "animated with the desire of putting a stop to the effusion of blood, and of preventing the evils of every kind which the continuance of such a state of things may produce." Their actions were called for, they claimed, "no less by sentiments of humanity, than by interests for the tranquility of Europe." They demanded an armistice, offered to mediate negotiations between the Ottomans and the Greeks, and suggested the outcome of negotiations should include Greek self-government, under the sovereignty of the empire. The powers added a "self-denying clause," stating they would not seek "any augmentation of territory, any exclusive influence, or any commercial advantage for their subjects" through these arrangements.[37] Ottoman rejection of the treaty led to the imposition of a blockade and subsequently a confrontation in the Bay of Navarino, in October 1827, in which the three powers easily defeated the Turkish forces. Three years later, the great powers granted independence to Greece.

Through the 1820s, accounts of Ottoman atrocities had generated public outrage, particularly in Britain, that helped keep the Greek crisis on the political agenda. Political leaders were led to acknowledge a moral duty to do what they could to relieve the Greeks, even if they were reluctant to resort to force.[38] While humanitarian sentiment had remained an important motivator as the pressure to intervene mounted, great power competition and a desire to preserve the European order were more important in determining the timing and conduct of the intervention. Nevertheless, regardless of the actual reasons for the intervention, a belief emerged among the great powers that they had successfully coordinated to stop atrocities against Christians by Ottoman authorities.[39] This would contribute to the generation of a felt obligation to do so again and again across the nineteenth century and early twentieth.

SYRIA 1860–61

Upon allying with France, Britain, and Sardinia to defeat Russia in the Crimean War (1853–56), the Ottoman Empire was rewarded with admission into the European system of states. The contracting parties to the Treaty of Paris (1856) declared the empire "admitted to participate in the advantages of the public law and system (concert) of Europe," and they undertook to respect its independence and territorial integrity. The treaty noted with approval the Hatt-i Hümayun, issued by the sultan earlier that year, that guaranteed the protection of Christians under his rule. It also noted that acknowledgment of this decree did not give the great powers "the right to interfere, either collectively or separately, in the relations of His Majesty the Sultan with his subjects, nor in the internal administration of his Empire."[40] But Britain and France interpreted this provision as putting an end to Russia's unilateral claims to guardianship of Orthodox Christianity rather than as a general disavowal of European involvement in Ottoman affairs. Umut Özsu rightly notes, "Having gained the right to partake in the European state system's 'advantages,' [the empire] now had to comport itself accordingly."[41] And crucially, responsibility for supervision of Ottoman behavior was now understood to be formally accorded to and shared among the great powers.

When conflict between Druze and Maronite populations in Syria devolved in 1860 into the massacre of thousands of Maronites, first by Druze and then also by Ottoman troops, France in particular was outraged. For centuries, the French had guaranteed the protection of Maronite Christians under Ottoman rule. The French people pressured their leaders to act to relieve the suffering, and these leaders appear to have genuinely felt a moral obligation to do so. But there were other factors also pushing them to intervene. "French prestige and influence in the Middle East, the completion of the Suez Canal, defending the Syrian silk trade, and diversion of the French public's attention from home affairs (the dismemberment of the Papal State had . . . alienated the sympathies of the Catholics in France) were all issues of great concern at this time," Rodogno explains.[42] French officials realized, however, that they would have no right to intervene militarily without the agreement of the other great powers.

Foreign minister Edouard-Antoine de Thouvenel impressed upon the other powers that "European public sentiment" demanded a response to the crisis, and he claimed they had a shared obligation to work together to develop a solution. "In the face of these massacres, reproducing from city to city and everywhere Christians live," he declared, "it is impossible not to recognize that humanity commands the Powers to interpose their actions." France was not motivated by self-interest, he claimed. Rather, its sole object was "to co-operate with the Powers, by an equality of right, in the interest of peace in the East, to re-establish tranquility and order."[43] Britain was suspicious of the intentions of the French. But public pressure to act within Britain combined with a desire not to let France act alone, much less to act in alliance with Russia in a way that would leave Britain isolated, led foreign minister John Russell to agree to a concerted European intervention.

The great powers convened in July and August 1860 and adopted two protocols authorizing intervention. The first grounded the legitimacy of the intervention in the provisions of the Treaty of Paris that required Ottoman protection of Christians. The second authorized the dispatch of twelve thousand troops to Syria, half of which would be provided by France (in the end, those six thousand French troops were the only soldiers deployed), as well as European naval forces to monitor Syrian coastal towns. The troops were to act in the name of all the powers and in conjunction with the Ottoman authorities. They would stay in Syria for no more than six months—long enough, it was thought, to pacify the region. Echoing the Treaty of London, the great powers declared that neither of them would seek any territorial advantages, exclusive influence, or commercial concessions from intervention. The protocol noted the sultan's consent to the intervention due to his desire "to stop, by prompt and efficacious measures, the effusion of blood in Syria."[44] American jurist Ellery Stowell would later note that the sultan provided consent only "through constraint and a desire to avoid worse."[45]

The French troops who were deployed worked with Ottoman authorities to protect Christians who had survived the atrocities, nourishing them and rebuilding their schools and churches. They also sought to hold to account those responsible for the atrocities and to implement reforms that would establish conditions for peace. Rodogno helpfully summarizes, "They conceived humanitarian intervention not as a 'hit-and-run' operation but as a complex operation encompassing a perhaps rudimentary peace-enforcement process."[46] As the six-month intervention was drawing to an end, France requested that the great powers approve an extension for another six months to ensure the prevention of further atrocities. The

British were again resistant. While admitting there was no guarantee atrocities would not recur, they feared a prolonged occupation would eventually lead to the annexation of Syria, which could become a precedent for the gradual partition of the empire.[47] The French again insisted their motives were pure and invited the other powers to contribute troops. Moreover, they warned, if French forces were required to leave Syria and fresh massacres were to occur, it would be on the head of those who opposed the extension. Emperor Napoléon III wrote to Russell, "If your Government urge this evacuation, remember that they make themselves responsible if massacres and outrages against the Christians are renewed."[48] The European powers eventually agreed to an extension of three months, after which the French troops returned home.

France's initial motivations in pushing for agreement on the intervention may not have been exclusively humanitarian. But they proceeded with the intervention even with the limited mandate granted by the other great powers, and they adhered to that mandate. Having repudiated the acquisition of material advantages, it was largely the felt moral duty of French leaders, as well as their desire for domestic and international esteem, that led them to go ahead with it. Napoléon may have been speaking hyperbolically when he condemned the "pitiful jealousies and unfounded distrust of those who suggested that any interests except those of humanity had induced him to send troops to Syria."[49] But those "interests . . . of humanity" do seem to have played a pivotal role in the decision to intervene. The process of securing agreement among the great powers to either share or delegate the burden of responsibility to protect Ottoman Christians, however, would not always be so straightforward, as the powers would discover when confronted with atrocities in Bulgaria the following decade.

BULGARIA 1876-78

A peasant revolt that began in Herzegovina in 1875 soon spread to Bosnia, Serbia, Montenegro, and Bulgaria, provoking numerous atrocities from Ottoman troops and culminating in the massacre of an estimated twelve thousand Bulgarian Christians in May 1876. While Russia pushed for a forceful response by the great powers, the British government resisted. Reports of horrific atrocities in British newspapers inflamed public opinion and moved numerous public figures, including former prime minister W. E. Gladstone, to argue forcefully for intervention. But Prime Minister Benjamin Disraeli and his supporters feared Russia's designs on Ottoman territories. They also feared how Indian Muslims might react if Britain went to war against the Muslim Turks. Edward Bulwer-Lytton, the British viceroy in India, cautioned Queen Victoria that a war against the Ottomans would "cause a Mohammedan rising in India," which could be put down only by "blood and iron."[50] Disraeli sent a fleet of British warships to Besika Bay, just outside the Dardanelles, assuring the queen that he had done so "not . . . to protect Christians or Turks, but to uphold your Majesty's Empire."[51]

The debate that emerged within Britain about how to respond to the atrocities in Bulgaria is worth examining in some detail since it is often cases of resistance to and violation of normative expectations, rather than compliance, that reveal most clearly the substance and weight of these expectations.[52] Particularly revealing is a House of Commons debate of August 11, 1876, in which Disraeli was pushed to defend Britain's response to the atrocities. Liberal Party member William Harcourt claimed that Disraeli's government had a "duty . . . to remonstrate [with Ottoman authorities] and to see that their remonstrance was attended to."[53] This was particularly so because Britain had diplomatic influence with the Ottomans and its ability to exert pressure was enhanced by the presence of the fleet in Besika Bay. But the government had failed to discharge its responsibility, Harcourt declared. The government had tacitly admitted that it had "a responsibility in this matter towards this country and Europe" by tardily sending a vice consul to Philippopolis and a military attaché to Serbia. But their protests were delivered too late.[54] Harcourt invoked the rescue of the Greeks a half century earlier, and the scriptural command to "do justice and to work mercy," and declared, "It was time that the great interests of civilization and humanity should cease to be the base counters in a game of diplomatic chicane." Each of the great powers was urging England to cooperate, he observed. The moment was "never more favorable" for a concerted European response.[55]

Disraeli responded, "Certainly the slaughter of 12,000 individuals, whether Turks or Bulgarians, whether they were innocent peasants or even brigands, is a horrible event which no one can think of without emotion."[56] But Britain did not possess any "peculiar responsibility" to respond that distinguished it from any of the other great powers: "The hon. and learned Gentleman said also that Her Majesty's Government had incurred a responsibility which is not possessed by any other country as regards our influence with the Turks. I say we have incurred no responsibility which is not shared with us by all the other contracting Powers to the Treaty of Paris. I utterly disclaim any peculiar responsibility."[57] The recent dispatch of a vice consul and a military attaché did not amount to a concession of "peculiar responsibility," he insisted. This was merely the queen exercising her regular rights and duties.[58]

Turning to the question of military intervention, Disraeli invoked the independence of the Ottoman Empire, which was confirmed in treaties with the great powers that should not be treated "as idle wind and chaff." He accepted that, should the Ottoman government be found "incompetent for its purpose," there would be an obligation to act, and "neither England nor any of the Great Powers will shrink from fulfilling the high political and moral duty which will then devolve upon them." But such a moment had not yet been reached.[59]

In the meantime, Disraeli declared, England's duties toward itself trumped whatever obligations it had toward the Bulgarians: "Those who suppose that England ever would uphold, or at this moment particularly is upholding, Turkey from blind superstition and from a want of sympathy with the highest aspirations of humanity are deceived. What our duty is at this critical moment is to maintain the Empire of England. Nor will we ever agree to any step, though it may obtain for a moment comparative quiet and a false prosperity, that hazards the existence of that Empire."[60]

Agitation within Britain reached a climax the following month when Gladstone published a pamphlet titled *Bulgarian Horrors and the Question of the East*. It sold two hundred thousand copies in its first month.[61] The former prime minister castigated the Disraeli government for its "moral and material support" for "the one great anti-human specimen of humanity," the Turks.[62] Britain's leaders, he claimed, had failed to understand their duties to the Christian subjects of the Ottoman Empire incurred in the Treaty of Paris and failed to appreciate "the broad and deep interests of humanity." They had instead been content "to consult and flatter the public opinion of the day in its ordinary, that is to say, its narrow, selfish, epicurean humor."[63]

Gladstone charged that the government had deflected questions about why they were not doing more to protect the vulnerable, first by denying knowledge of the atrocities and then by downplaying the extent of the violence, casting it as a civil war, insisting that both sides were equally guilty of wanton cruelty, framing it as a momentary outbreak of fanaticism, and suggesting that it was the kind of thing that should be expected among savage races from time to time.[64] Such excuses have long since been staples of those seeking to reduce pressure to respond to atrocities beyond their borders.

Gladstone then rebuked Disraeli for insisting that the interests of Britain needed to take priority over the needs of vulnerable Bulgarians: "I object to this constant system of appeal to our selfish leanings. It sets up false lights; it hides the true; it disturbs the world." The fleet at Besika Bay should be used not to protect British interests, he declared, but "for purposes of humanity . . . in concert with other Powers, for the defense of innocent lives, and to prevent the repetition of those recent scenes, at which hell itself might almost blush."[65] Indeed, he claimed, such action would serve British interests. Thus far, Russia had "played the part which we think specially our own, in resistance to tyranny, in befriending the oppressed, in laboring for the happiness of mankind." By refusing to cooperate with Russia out of fear of its intentions, the Disraeli government risked leading Slavic Christians to conclude that "Russia is their stay, and England their enemy," which would only further advance Russia's interests in eastern Europe.[66]

The arguments of those pushing for a stronger British response to the atrocities had an impact. By September 11, Disraeli was claiming that the fleet in Besika Bay had actually been sent "to defend H.M. subjects and their property, and to prevent Xtian massacres."[67] He then instructed Britain's ambassador in Constantinople, Sir Henry Elliot, to read a British report on the atrocities directly to the sultan and demand that the Ottomans punish the killers, assist the victims, and provide guarantees against further oppression.[68] Nevertheless, Disraeli continued to resist calls for military intervention.

Over the next few months, the great powers sought to resolve the crisis by negotiating with and issuing ultimatums to the Ottomans. As the campaign for action within Britain lost steam, Disraeli informed Parliament of his belief that, while the people of Britain were rightly interested in "humanitarian and philanthropic questions," there was "a yet deeper sentiment on the part of the people of this country . . . and that is—the determination to maintain the Empire of England."[69] But Russian ambassador Nikolay Ignatyev encouraged the European powers to "not lose sight of the grave responsibility which devolve[d] upon them before history and before humanity."[70] Russian chancellor Alexander Gorchakov claimed that since the Ottomans had violated their obligations under the Treaty of Paris, "Europe had the right and duty to dictate [the] sole conditions on which it will maintain the political status quo," and, if necessary, to "substitute its own action for the Porte's incapacity."[71]

Queen Victoria, however, responded to Russian efforts to unite Europe against the Ottomans by questioning why the Bulgarians were supposed to be more deserving of England's assistance than any other people. "This mawkish sentimentality for people who hardly deserve the name of real Christians, as if they were more God's creatures and our fellow-creatures than every other nation abroad, and forgetting the great interests of this great country—is really incomprehensible," she wrote to Disraeli.[72] For Victoria, as for many others over the centuries, the question—"why should we help this group in particular?"—was posed to justify helping no group at all.

Eventually, in April 1877, after negotiations fell apart, Russia declared war against the Ottoman Empire. Russia, it seems, was driven in part by a desire to acquire new territory and control of the straits and in part by a genuinely felt obligation to protect fellow Christians.[73] In March the following year, Russia and the Ottomans signed the Treaty of San Stefano. This treaty was challenged by the other European powers, who believed that it altered the balance of power in favor of Russia. This led to the adoption of the Treaty of Berlin in July 1878.

The Treaty of Berlin, signed by the original five great powers plus Italy and the Ottoman Empire, authorized the occupation of Bosnia and Herze-govina by Austria and granted independence to Serbia, Montenegro, Roma-nia, and part of Bulgaria. Recognition of the sovereignty of these four new states was conditioned on their conformity to guarantees for the protection of the rights of minorities, including not only Christians but also Muslims and Jews. Additionally, the Ottomans undertook to protect religious liberty across their territories and, in particular, to carry out improvements and reforms in provinces inhabited by the Armenians and to guarantee the security of the Armenians against the Circassians and Kurds.[74] Eric Weitz rightly concludes that these provisions made the protection of certain religious and national minorities "a constituent element of the international system, not the cause of an individual state, but in fact it entangled them in the vicissitudes of Great Power politics."[75] The European powers were motivated to impose these provisions to ease domestic pressures to end the abuses of minorities in the East and also to prevent the mass movement of abused and displaced minorities into the West. But they had little interest in assuming obligations themselves for the protection of these minorities. Thus, they refrained from including in the treaty any mechanisms for enforcement.[76] In 1880, Britain, France, and Germany washed their hands of the persecution of Romania's Jews by formally bestowing unconditional recognition on the Romanian state, accompanied by a note acknowledging that the new state failed to fully comply with the treaty.[77] The following decade, the European powers stood by as eighty to one hundred thousand Armenians were massacred.

ARMENIA 1894-96

The growth of nationalist sentiment and revolutionary activism among Armenians from the 1880s onward provoked a chain of state-sanctioned massacres of Armenian civilians between 1894 and 1896. The response of Britain and Russia was the reverse of that seen in Bulgaria. Britain's strategic interests in the Ottoman Empire were now much diminished, and British statesmen were free to act upon popular sentiment and their own felt obligation to intercede on behalf of the vulnerable. Russia, in contrast, along with Germany, now had an interest in defending the territorial integrity of the empire and resisting British proposals for intervention.[78]

Lord Salisbury, who represented Britain as foreign secretary at the Congress of Berlin in 1878, came into office as prime minister for a third time in June 1895 and immediately began to explore the possibility of military action. He hoped Russia's desire to uphold its reputation as defender of Ottoman Christians, and also its reluctance to antagonize its own Armenian subjects, would mean its opposition to intervention would be tempered. The European powers managed to agree to send a few gunboats up the Dardanelles. But the massacres continued. Austria-Hungary proposed the dispatch of a joint fleet that was prepared to use force. Salisbury agreed to the proposal, but Russia opposed it and readied a fleet of its own to respond if any other fleet entered the Dardanelles. When Salisbury sounded out Austria-Hungary about the possibility of nevertheless joining Britain in an armed intervention, Austria-Hungary insisted it would not risk setting the European powers against each other. Salisbury gave up.[79]

In a speech delivered to the Nonconformist Union Association on January 31, 1896, and in a subsequent defense of that speech given in the House of Lords on February 11, Salisbury sought cover for inaction in the idea that responsibility for the protection of the Armenians was shared. He made clear his horror at the massacres, but insisted that Britain was not obligated to do more to protect the Armenians than any of the other European powers under the Treaty of Berlin. Britain and the other European powers were rightly discharging their obligations incurred at Berlin by seeking to pressure and persuade the sultan to implement reforms that would protect the Armenians, he claimed. Given the other powers refused to contemplate the additional step of applying military force, and given it would not be possible for a naval power like Britain to relieve the Armenians on its own, Britain was under no obligation to intervene. Indeed, given Russia's expressed opposition, such an intervention would risk plunging the great powers into war.[80]

In the House of Commons, also on February 11, several Liberal Party members, including longtime advocate for the Armenians James Bryce, pushed back.[81] Bryce insisted that Britain did have a "special duty" to succor the Armenians that was not shared by the other powers. He explained that Russia had originally guaranteed the protection of the Armenians in the Treaty of San Stefano and it was Britain that insisted that an article be included in the Treaty of Berlin transferring this obligation to the six European powers. Britain therefore bore responsibility for ensuring that the protection that had been guaranteed by one power was now provided by the six. Moreover, he continued, Britain had quickly recognized the protection guaranteed by the Treaty of Berlin might prove inadequate and had thus taken upon itself "sole responsibility" for protecting the Armenians by contracting a separate Anglo-Turkish Convention later that year. "Every English Government that had been in office since 1878," he claimed, "had felt it to be their special duty, beyond other Powers, to endeavor to fulfil their obligations in the matter and to protect the Armenians."[82]

The Leader of the House, Arthur Balfour, and the First Lord of the Admiralty, George Goschen, defended the prime minister. While the obligations of the sultan to implement reforms and to guarantee Armenian protection were clear, they noted, neither the Treaty of Berlin nor the Anglo-Turkish Convention ascribed to either the collective European powers or Britain alone a legal obligation to go to war with the Ottoman Empire to ensure this protection was provided.[83] Bryce responded that there could of course be no "legal obligation" for one sovereign (Britain) to protect the subjects of another sovereign (Turkey). But Britain had incurred a "moral obligation."[84] Goschen replied that Britain had "done the utmost that any Power could do" to discharge that moral obligation. It had continually pressured the sultan to succor the Armenians. And it had done so, he insisted, "not because we were bound to do so by any clause in a convention or in a treaty, but because we felt bound to do it as a civilized Power." Responsibility for the failure to protect the Armenians, therefore, lay not with Britain but with the other powers:

> We only wish we had been able to convince other Powers of the absolute necessity of putting a stop to these massacres which have lasted so long. It is not the fault of the Government; it is not the fault of the people of this country. . . . It is known throughout Europe that we are horrified at what has taken place. The other Powers do not seem to have shared, I will not say the horror, but the duty, if I may say so, of taking such measures

as might have brought about the cessation of these horrors. . . . We shall not be diverted from the imperative duty which is laid upon us to watch for every opportunity to consult with other Powers to take every possible means short of a European conflagration by which we may bring this Armenian question to an end. . . . Until we are shown a better way we shall believe that we have done our duty under the most difficult circumstances, and that if we have failed and if events have taken place which have shocked our conscience if not the conscience of Europe, it is not on this country at least that the reproach will lie.[85]

In the end, the outbreak of the Greco-Turkish War in 1897 led the Armenian question to be put to one side, only for it to reassert itself with the renewal of massacres in 1909 and then the 1915 genocide in which more than one million Ottoman Armenians were killed. In both cases, the European powers, and also the United States, refrained from intervening militarily, despite popular pressure to do so.[86] The willingness of the great powers to undertake what had by now become known as "humanitarian intervention" declined further in the aftermath of the First World War. The horrific cost of the war made states reluctant to embrace duties to risk blood and treasure for the sake of vulnerable strangers.[87] Indeed, in the process of establishing a globalized system of collective security in the League of Nations, the great powers sought to relinquish some of the obligations for the protection of vulnerable strangers that they had arrogated to themselves the previous century, placing these unwanted burdens upon the new international organization.[88] In the absence of any appetite among member states for forcible intervention, this necessitated the construction and institutionalization of a range of international responsibilities for the noncoercive assistance and protection of the vulnerable.

Institutionalizing Shared Responsibilities for Minority Protection

The practice of forcible intervention for the protection of Ottoman Christians had emerged in the nineteenth century alongside other practices of caring for vulnerable strangers within and on the fringes of Europe (as well as imperialist practices further afield, which I address in the next section). This included demands for governance reforms and security guarantees for minorities, as we have already noted, as well as the provision of relief and refuge in the aftermath of atrocities.[89] Such nonforcible responses to the threat or perpetration of atrocities would be internationalized and institutionalized to varying degrees in the aftermath of the First World War. This was a rich and complex period of negotiation, construction, and variable implementation of a range of responsibilities toward the vulnerable.[90] A particularly instructive example is the establishment of an international regime for the protection of minorities.

Seeking to reconstruct the (European) international order on a principle of national self-determination, but recognizing that the creation of nation-states inevitably entailed the creation of national minorities, the great powers agreed to impose provisions for minority protection on new and reorganized states across eastern Europe and the Balkans. Czechoslovakia, Greece, Poland, Romania, and Yugoslavia were required to sign minority treaties. Austria, Bulgaria, Hungary, and Turkey were required to accept the inclusion of minority protection obligations in their peace treaties. Albania, Estonia, Finland, Latvia, and Lithuania, and then later Iraq, were required to issue public declarations on minority protection as a condition of admission to the league.[91]

The treaty that the Allies and Associated Powers signed with Poland on June 28, 1919, served as the model for subsequent agreements. In Article 2, Poland undertook "to assure full and complete protection of life and liberty to all inhabitants . . . without distinction of birth, nationality, language, race or religion." Articles 3 to 11 delineated what protection should entail, and Article 12 declared that these stipulations "constitute obligations of international concern and shall be placed under the guarantee of the League of Nations." Any difference of opinion between Poland and a member of the Council of the League was to be referred to the Permanent Court of International Justice, whose decision would be final.[92]

Georges Clemenceau, French prime minister and president of the Paris Peace Conference, attached a cover note to the treaty justifying the imposition of these provisions by the great powers. "This treaty does not constitute any fresh departure," he insisted. Citing the precedent of the Treaty of Berlin, he claimed it had long been established procedure that recognition by the great powers of a new or reorganized state should be accompanied by a binding requirement for the protection of minorities. "There rests, therefore, upon these Powers an obligation, which they cannot evade, to secure in the most permanent and solemn form guarantees for certain essential rights which will afford to the inhabitants the necessary protection whatever changes may take place in the internal constitution of the Polish state."[93]

But while the great powers had an obligation to insist on provisions for minority rights, Clemenceau continued, the obligation to guarantee execution of the provisions was best entrusted to the league. The earlier practice of vesting guarantees for protection in the great powers had proven "ineffective." And it had been open to the criticism that it gave the great powers "a right to interfere . . . which could be used for political purposes." By entrusting the guarantee to the league, it was made clear that Poland would not be "under the tutelage" or in "danger of political interference" by the great powers.[94]

While Clemenceau was right to note fears of great power interference, it seems that the decision to entrust the guarantee to the league was largely the result of the unwillingness of the great powers to continue to themselves bear the burden of responsibility for minority protection. The great powers no longer had any appetite for enforcement—and understandably so, given the enormous human and material costs of the war. In her authoritative study, Carole Fink observes, "despite the widespread anguish over the Armenian tragedy during the war and over the postwar violence against the Jews throughout Eastern Europe, the peacemakers . . . deliberately omitted any specific means of punishing governments that transgressed against the new treaties." They viewed the new regime as "more of a deterrent than a vital element of the peace settlement." The treaties were "essentially transitional measures, to reassure minorities, restrain their governments, and help settle things down."[95] In his letter, Clemenceau expressed a hope that knowledge of the league's guarantees for protection would mean minorities "will be more easily reconciled to their new position," thereby reducing hostility between minorities and majorities and obviating the need for enforcement.[96]

Whatever the humanitarian concerns driving the great powers in seeking minority protection within Europe, the protection regime was also marked by selectivity and instrumentality. In instances where a minority was deemed too vulnerable to protect or too volatile to appease with a minority rights treaty, they could simply be deported. The Treaty of Lausanne (1923), for example, included provision for the compulsory transfer of over one million Orthodox Christians from Anatolia to Greece and around 350,000 Muslims from Greece to Turkey.[97] The great powers, moreover, insisted that provisions for minority protection should be imposed upon new and reorganized states only, and not on all states, and certainly not on themselves. One British official recalled that negotiators considered in 1919 the possibility of including a general clause in the covenant, giving the league "the right to protect minorities in all countries which were members of the League," but he strongly opposed it since it was better to allow potential "injustice and oppression" than to allow "anything which would mean the negation of the sovereignty of every state in the world."[98]

The Covenant of the League provided for the establishment of ad hoc Minorities Committees to address complaints lodged by minorities or states. These committees considered hundreds of petitions, issued hundreds of reports, and in some cases helped alleviate the persecution of minorities. But by the mid-1930s the regime had broken down. The unwillingness of the great powers to contribute to enforcing the treaties or to subject themselves to international scrutiny for their own treatment of minorities were but two reasons. Most problematically, the regime was effectively hijacked by revisionist powers, particularly Weimar and then Nazi Germany, who deployed the principle of minority protection for irredentist purposes. While persecuting minorities at home, Germany presented itself as the champion of minority rights abroad, issuing vexatious petitions and overt threats against vulnerable neighbors with respect to their treatment of German nationals. In September 1934, Polish foreign minister Józef Beck stood before the league and disavowed the Polish peace treaty. Twelve months later, Adolf Hitler's Reich issued the Nuremberg laws.[99]

Liberating, Protecting, and Civilizing Non-Europeans

Before we move any further into the twentieth century, we should briefly backtrack and document some of the ways in which European powers constructed and institutionalized responsibilities for the care of non-Europeans, and also how they performed or evaded these responsibilities, through the nineteenth and early twentieth centuries. Let us begin with the gradual acceptance of a duty to prevent and punish the slave trade before turning to the related construction of a duty of imperial powers to subject backward peoples to civilized rule for their protection and advancement.

ABOLISHING THE SLAVE TRADE

The centrality of evangelical-humanitarian sentiments in Britain's decision to abolish the slave trade within its empire in 1807 is well established.[100] Britain's subsequent effort to extend abolition across the globe was also driven in part by such sentiments. But there were additional motivations in play. As John Stuart Mill acknowledged in 1859, even if Britain's decision to give up the lucrative trade was not prompted by self-interest, she did have an interest in encouraging others to do the same: "The fox who had lost his tail had an intelligible interest in persuading his neighbors to rid themselves of theirs."[101] Furthermore, as Lauren Benton and Lisa Ford have shown, Britain's international efforts to abolish the trade served to consolidate its imperial-legal control of the Atlantic Ocean.[102]

At the Congress of Vienna, eight years after Britain's Parliament had passed the Act for the Abolition of the Slave Trade, Castlereagh successfully persuaded the other great powers to declare the slave trade "repugnant to the principles of humanity and universal morality" and to acknowledge "at length the public voice, in all civilized countries, calls aloud for its prompt suppression." The powers proclaimed "their wish of putting an end to a scourge, which has so long desolated Africa, degraded Europe, and afflicted humanity" and "the duty and necessity of abolishing it." However, recognizing the need for sovereigns to heed "the interests, the habits, and even the prejudices of their subjects," the signatories insisted that no timeline should be set for each power to definitively abolish the trade.[103]

While the agreement at Vienna made no mention of enforcement, at least some British abolitionists argued that it provided a mandate for international action. James Stephen, the principal lawyer of the abolitionist movement, produced a pamphlet in 1816 that interpreted the Vienna declaration as asserting "the duty of all civilized Powers to suppress the trade as soon as possible, not only by prohibiting it to their own subjects, but by employing all the means they possess to procure its universal abolition." The restraint and punishment of violations of the law of nature and nations and the rescue of those oppressed by such violations, he declared, "are duties, and therefore rights, not peculiar to Great Britain . . . but belong to all the branches of the human family, and pre-eminently to every civilized nation." He noted that Vattel wisely claimed that states retain the right to judge themselves absolved from such duties of humanity if they lack capacity to perform them or have reason to fear for their own preservation. But he insisted, at least in the case of the Spanish slave trade with which the pamphlet was concerned, Britain faced no such obstacles. He added, moreover, that Britain's past sins against Africans did not undermine its duty to deliver them from slavery. Rather, "the duty is enhanced in a high degree by that very consideration."[104]

Over the next few years, Britain negotiated numerous bilateral treaties that not only banned the trade, but provided for enforcement through international "courts of mixed commission." Britain deployed the Royal Navy to enforce these treaties, in what has been described as the "most expensive international moral effort in modern world history."[105] All told, the effort to suppress the trade cost about five thousand British lives (mostly due to disease) and an average of 1.8 percent of British national income annually from 1808 to 1867. And the effort was remarkably successful. Whereas in the first decade of the nineteenth century an estimated 609,000 slaves had been transported to the New World, by the late 1860s the trade had been reduced to a few hundred per year.[106]

In the final decades of the nineteenth century, the major powers finally confirmed not only that the trade was illegal but also that they each had a responsibility to prevent and punish its occurrence. Article 9 of the General Act of the Conference of Berlin (1885), signed by the major European powers, including Turkey, and the United States, declared that "trading in slaves is forbidden" and each signatory state bound itself "to employ all the means at its disposal for putting an end to this trade and for punishing those who engage in it."[107] Five years later, in the preamble to the General Act of Brussels (1890), the powers declared their "firm intention of putting an end to the crimes and devastations engendered by the traffic in African slaves" and bound themselves to take practical action to repress the trade, punish offenders, and liberate and protect captured slaves.[108] In both treaties, however, the noble obligation to abolish the trade was tied to a duty to civilize Africans by subjecting them to European rule.[109]

PROTECTING AND CIVILIZING THE UNCIVILIZED

The responsibility to liberate slaves was commonly perceived to go hand in hand with a responsibility to contribute to their moral and material improvement. This notion of responsibility for the care and advancement of vulnerable and "backward" strangers was central to justifications offered by European powers first for colonial rule and then, in the aftermath of the First World War, for a system of internationally supervised governance of nonsovereign peoples. We should not too quickly write off these justifications as the self-serving rhetoric of predatory powers. Certainly, the deployment of "protection" and "civilization" language was often self-serving, as is evidenced by the systems of forced labor and wealth extraction so often introduced and the cruelties and atrocities so often perpetrated by colonial powers. But in many instances, heads of state and colonial officials appear to have genuinely felt and genuinely sought to perform solemn responsibilities for the care of the bodies and souls of those under their authority.[110] Any history of international protection needs to find a place for the European colonial project, and anyone seeking to advance international protection today needs to wrestle with both the horrific legacies and enduring temptations of this project. I attempt such wrestling in chapter 3. For now, let us get a handle on the construction and performance of responsibilities of colonial rule.

Guided by a hierarchical view of humanity and a liberal narrative of progress, many nineteenth-century Europeans believed that they had an obligation to use their supposed cultural, economic, political, and even biological superiority to impose progress on backward peoples beyond Europe and to guide them toward civilization.[111] This civilizing mission was said to justify the annexation of non-European territories by European empires and the subjection of non-European peoples to European rule. Annexation and subjection were commonly framed in terms of a need to educate, improve, Christianize, and civilize the uncivilized. They were also frequently cast in the language of a duty to protect. Protection was an obligation of empire, and its invocation legitimated empire. The duty to protect people from native tyranny and oppression justified the incorporation of new territories, as in the case of the British invasion of the Kingdom of Kandy in 1816. And, once incorporated, the duty required—and justified—the imposition of imperial provisions for indigenous protection.[112]

The tensions in this imperial protectionist project were widely recognized, particularly in the case of settler colonialism. In the eighteenth of a series of lectures on colonization that he delivered between 1839 and 1841, Oxford political economist Herman Merivale, who would go on to become permanent undersecretary at the Colonial Office, contemplated the duty of colonial governments to protect and civilize indigenous people. He began by lamenting "the ferocity and treachery which have marked the conduct of civilized men, too often of civilized governments, in their relations with savages," across South Africa, Australia, Newfoundland, New Zealand, and the US interior. "Desolation goes before us," he declared, "and civilization lags slowly and lamely behind." He conceded that laws and regulations could not prevent this (and he pinned the blame not on colonial authorities but on "the perverse wickedness of those outcasts of society whom the first waves of our colonization are sure to bring along with them"). And yet, refusing to give up on the settler-colonial project, he insisted that "our errors are not of conception so much as of execution" and proceeded to outline a range of new laws and measures that might better ensure the protection of indigenous peoples.[113] This pattern would be repeated again and again. Focusing on Australia, Ann Curthoys and Jessie Mitchell summarize that Britain's settler-colonial project involved "an inherent contradiction concerning Indigenous people that was never resolved." Some British governments "did attempt to enact a policy of Aboriginal protection and 'civilization.'" But even when colonial authorities knew the spread of settlement would harm Indigenous people, Britain continued to colonize, with the effect of producing "the widespread destruction of Indigenous societies."[114]

The notion of a duty to protect and civilize uncivilized peoples was collectively confirmed by the European powers and the United States with respect to Africa in the 1885 General Act of Berlin. Delegates to the Berlin Conference acknowledged that their efforts to carve up Africa among the European powers served the purpose of furthering the development of trade, but they insisted it also facilitated the improvement of the natives, declaring in Article 6, "All the Powers exercising sovereign rights or influence in the aforesaid territories bind themselves to watch over the preservation of the native tribes, and to care for the improvement of the conditions of their moral and material well-being, and to help in suppressing slavery, and especially the slave trade. They shall, without distinction of creed or nation, protect and favour all religious, scientific or charitable institutions and undertakings created and organized for the above ends, or which aim at instructing the natives and bringing home to them the blessings of civilization."[115]

In contrast to most international agreements examined in this chapter, responsibility for the care of the well-being of a particular colonized people was not understood to be shared among multiple states. Rather, each imperial power was attributed responsibility for the people in the territories over which they exercised authority. Most notoriously, the General Act recognized King Leopold II of Belgium's International Association of the Congo as the authority responsible for the administration and care of the Congolese Free State. Conference delegates endorsed Leopold's professed mission of bringing civilization to the Congo. The Italian delegate, Count de Launay, celebrated, "The whole world cannot fail to exhibit its sympathy and encouragement on behalf of this civilizing and humane work which does honor to the nineteenth century."[116] After the conference, however, Leopold set about establishing a brutal system of wealth extraction marked by forced labor and atrocities that resulted in the deaths of ten million Congolese.[117] After twenty years of barbarity, Belgium was eventually compelled by other European powers and the United States to implement reforms, though of course those powers were themselves guilty of atrocities, even if on a smaller scale, against those they claimed a responsibility to civilize: the British against the Boers, the Germans against the Herero and the Nama, and the Americans against civilians in the Philippines.[118]

The idea of an obligation to care for the well-being and development of peoples who were supposedly not yet capable of self-government was institutionalized after the First World War. Delegates to the Paris Peace Conference were initially divided on what should be done about African, Pacific, and Middle Eastern territories that Allied powers had seized from Germany and the Ottomans. Most of the Allies believed they should be allowed to annex seized territories as compensation for the blood and treasure expended in winning the war. Only after much negotiation did they consent to administer these territories as mandated powers on behalf of, and subject to the supervision of, the League of Nations. "Only reluctantly did they bend to American pressure and the wave of internationalist and anti-imperialist sentiment sweeping the globe," Susan Pedersen reports, "and even so they kept their obligations, and the League's powers, limited and vague."[119]

The broad contours of the system were laid out in Article 22 of the Covenant of the League. The care of the "well-being and development" of peoples once governed by the German and Ottoman empires and "not yet able to stand by themselves under the strenuous conditions of the modern world" was said to constitute "a sacred trust of civilization," and the best method of securing its performance was that "the tutelage of such peoples should be entrusted to advanced nations who by reason of their resources, their experience or their geographical position can best undertake this responsibility, and who are willing to accept it, and that this tutelage should be exercised by them as Mandatories on behalf of the League."[120] The article added that a permanent commission should be constituted to examine annual reports from mandatory powers and to advise the Council of the League on the observance of mandatory responsibilities. In an early study of the peace conference, Harold Temperley celebrated, "What sharply distinguishes the Mandatory System from all such international arrangements of the past, is the unqualified right of intervention possessed by the League of Nations."[121] But this was an exaggeration. As Pedersen notes, the covenant said nothing about what the league could or should do if a mandatory power violated the "sacred trust of civilization," and the mandatory powers proved "reluctant to negotiate the terms of their rule and quite uninterested in establishing the oversight apparatus at all."[122]

The Permanent Mandates Commission was eventually convened in 1921. Its task was to oversee the administration of fourteen territories in Africa, the Pacific, and the Middle East by seven mandatory powers. Despite the intransigence of some mandatory powers, the commission managed to develop significant independence and expertise and to establish various procedures—examining reports and petitions, convening hearings, and issuing its own reports—which brought a degree of international publicity to the mandate system and compelled the mandatory powers to justify at the international level their treatment of those under their "tutelage." Mandated territories were in general not better governed than colonial territories, and in some instances they were governed much worse. But the system of international supervision did at least render the mandatory powers answerable for failures to discharge their responsibilities.[123]

In some instances, mandated powers successfully resisted or bypassed the commission's restraints. As Priya Satia summarizes, "France violated the Syria mandate by giving Alexandretta to Turkey without allowing the commission to weigh in, Japan incorporated the South Sea mandated islands, and all powers imperialized their Africa holdings."[124] But in other instances, the commission's oversight made mandatory administration more burdensome and less attractive to imperial powers. Indeed, it contributed to Britain's decision in 1932 to relinquish its institutionalized responsibilities by giving up its mandatory authority in Iraq. Britain thereby released itself from administrative burdens while retaining the benefits of favorable treaty arrangements with a newly independent state. Upon receiving assurances that Britain would accept moral responsibility should Iraq prove itself unworthy of independence, the Permanent Mandates Commission agreed that Iraq could be granted membership in the League of Nations, on the condition that Iraq subject itself to the league's minority rights regime. Iraq agreed, thus entering into a protection regime that was quickly crumbling. Soon after independence, the Iraqi Army set upon dozens of minority Assyrian villages, massacring between several hundred and several thousand Assyrians. Little was done by either Britain or the league to prevent or punish the atrocities.[125] Instead, they set about looking to forcibly resettle the Assyrians elsewhere, perpetuating an international program of forced population transfer that was tied so troublingly to programs of minority protection and mandated protection in the interwar years.[126]

It might be noted that the duties of colonial and mandated authorities have less direct parallels with the duties of the international community under R2P than do the duties of great powers for protection of minorities in the Holy Roman Empire, the Ottoman Empire, and the new and reorganized states of early twentieth-century eastern Europe and the Balkans discussed earlier. Most obviously, responsibility for each colonial and mandated territory was borne by an individual power (even if that power was to some degree internationally accountable) rather than shared among many, and these individual powers bore a measure of sovereign authority over the non-self-governing people for whom they were responsible.[127] Nevertheless, this imperial project was increasingly woven into the fabric of international institutions in the first half of the twentieth century such that comparisons with present-day efforts to institutionalize international responsibilities for human protection are not out of place. The humiliation, oppression, and often genocidal violence suffered by those supposed to be the beneficiaries of Western civilizational responsibilities under this project, moreover, produced an enduring legacy that rightly colors so much of the discussion of R2P today. I wrestle with its ethical implications and consider its political ramifications in chapters 3 and 5.

The Fall and Rise of Protection Responsibilities after the Second World War

In the aftermath of the First World War, the great powers had sought to pass some of the burdens of international protection onto the league. In the wake of the Second World War, they did away with such responsibilities almost completely. There were some exceptions. The responsibilities of administrative powers to protect the interests and well-being of non-self-governing peoples over whom they exercised a trust were reaffirmed in the UN's international trusteeship system that replaced the mandates system. This system, however, was soon rendered obsolete by decolonization.[128] A more enduring construction of international responsibilities was found in the 1951 Convention Relating to the Status of Refugees and its 1967 Protocol, which replaced the weakly institutionalized refugee regime of the interwar period. The new refugee regime, including a binding responsibility of *non-refoulement*, retained a reasonable degree of support through the Cold War, not least because western European powers understood that the provision of refuge to people fleeing communism could serve as a useful propaganda tool.[129] But, when it came to the care of vulnerable people beyond sovereign borders, the great powers chose to replace the broken minority rights regime, for which the league had acted as guarantor, with a new principle of international human rights that was guaranteed by no one.

The memory of German abuse of the ideas and instruments of minority rights protection had left European states with no enthusiasm for reviving that failed protection regime. The great powers sought to resolve some pressing minority rights issues in the aftermath of the war by permitting a new wave of forced population transfers, including the expulsion of more than ten million Germans from central and southern Europe. More generally, in place of international guarantees for minority protection, they offered in the UN Charter mere affirmations of human rights.[130] Human rights had been given a central place in the wartime declarations of the United States, the United Kingdom, and other allied powers, and this encouraged numerous South American states, India, New Zealand, Australia, and others to insist that the charter include substantial references to rights. But the great powers were reluctant to bind themselves to protecting these rights. Serving as advisor to the British foreign office, historian Charles Webster reported that "our policy is to avoid '*guarantee* of human rights' though we might not object to a declaration."[131] The great powers had their way. Article 1(3) of the UN Charter, for example, noted that "promoting and encouraging respect for human rights and for fundamental freedoms" was one of the purposes for which the organization was created. A suggestion by the Panamanian delegation at San Francisco in 1945 that the draft article refer also to the "protection" of human rights was quickly rejected by the United States and Britain on the grounds that it would raise undue expectations and risk improperly implying that the organization "should actively impose human rights and freedoms within individual countries."[132]

The end of the Second World War is conventionally cast as a pivotal moment in which the centuries-old "Westphalian" principle of unconditional sovereignty began to be revised as states became increasingly accountable to the international community for the treatment of their populations. In fact, as I have argued elsewhere, the reverse is true.[133] Westphalia did not establish the sovereign right to nonintervention. Such a right emerged gradually in Europe in the nineteenth and early twentieth centuries and was unambiguously established in international law only for the first time in the UN Charter. This right, anachronistically labeled "Westphalian sovereignty" since the end of the Cold War, was instituted not in 1648, but in 1945.[134] While human rights may have been recognized as a legitimate matter of international concern by the charter and by numerous international conventions negotiated through the Cold War, it was generally accepted that states no longer possessed any right, much less a responsibility, to enforce the protection of the vulnerable beyond sovereign borders.

Any lingering appetite among Western states for humanitarian intervention had vanished in the wake of its exploitation in the 1930s, first by fascist Italy, which justified the invasion of Ethiopia on the grounds of a need to suppress slavery, and then by Nazi Germany, which justified the annexation of Austria, occupation of Czechoslovakia, and invasion of Poland on the grounds of an obligation to protect oppressed and mistreated German minorities.[135] Powerful states were eager to outlaw interventions that harmed international peace and security. Weaker states were keen to secure a principle of nonintervention that could protect them from the predations of the powerful. Article 2(4) of the charter satisfied both groups by prohibiting "the threat or use of force against the territorial integrity or political independence of any state, or in any other manner inconsistent with the Purposes of the United Nations." This article was complemented by Article 2(7), which established a generalized principle of domestic jurisdiction: "Nothing contained in the present Charter shall authorize the United Nations to intervene in matters which are essentially within the domestic jurisdiction of any state." The only exception to the prohibition on UN intervention was the application of enforcement measures by the Security Council in response to threats to international peace and security: Article 24(1) accorded the council "primary responsibility for the maintenance of international peace and security," and Chapters VI and VII detailed the enforcement measures available to the council to this end. But the charter gave no indication that the council's responsibility for international peace and security included responsibility for the protection of people tyrannized within their own states.

Over the next few years, due in large part to the tireless efforts of the Polish-Jewish jurist Raphael Lemkin, the international community negotiated and adopted the Convention on the Prevention and Punishment of the Crime of Genocide (1948). The preamble recognized that "international cooperation" was required "to liberate mankind" from the "odious scourge" that is "genocide"—a word Lemkin had invented in 1943—and contracting parties confirmed in Article I that "genocide ... is a crime under international law which they undertake to prevent and to punish." This declared commitment to international cooperation for the protection of *group* rights was somewhat anomalous in this new era of unguaranteed *human* rights.[136] Nevertheless, while subsequent articles outlined the duties of states to prevent and punish the occurrence of genocide within their own territories, the convention was at best ambiguous about whether the international community possessed a duty, or even a right, of enforcement.

Article VIII provided the only clarification about what international prevention of genocide might entail. The first official draft, written by the UN Secretariat, included a strongly worded version of this article, stating that, should genocide be committed anywhere in the world, the contracting parties "may call upon the competent organs of the United Nations to take measures for the suppression or prevention of such crimes. In such case the said Parties shall do everything in their power to give full effect to the intervention of the United Nations."[137] The Soviets took this idea further, positing an "obligation to bring a case of genocide to the attention of the Security Council" since "any act of genocide was always a threat to international peace and security and as such should be dealt with under Chapters VI and VII of the Charter."[138] However, other states, variously wary of binding themselves to unwanted obligations or enlarging the prerogatives of the council, proposed more cautious formulations.[139] In its final form, Article VIII stated merely that contracting parties "may call upon the competent organs of the United Nations to take such action under the Charter of the United Nations as they consider appropriate for the prevention and suppression of acts of genocide." As William Schabas observes, this was something states were already entitled to do.[140]

How did the Security Council engage with international protection issues during the Cold War? On the one hand, it repeatedly condemned and eventually sanctioned the South African government for its policy of apartheid and the illegal regime in Southern Rhodesia for its human rights abuses and denial of self-rule. Such crimes, the council suggested, constituted threats to international peace and security. On the other hand, it refrained from responding to numerous atrocity crises, including those perpetrated against Ibos in Nigeria, Hutus in Burundi, and Tutsis in Rwanda, perpetrated by anticommunist regimes supported by the United States such as Argentina, Chile, El Salvador, Guatemala, and Indonesia, and perpetrated by the governments of the Soviet Union and China against their own people.[141] When India intervened militarily in East Pakistan in 1971, bringing to an end brutal repression by the Pakistani government that had resulted in the deaths of over a million Bengalis, and Vietnam intervened militarily in Cambodia in 1978–79, overthrowing Pol Pot's Khmer Rouge that was responsible for the deaths of between one and two million Cambodians, members of the council responded not with praise, but with condemnation. As regrettable as the atrocities in East Pakistan and Cambodia were, they declared, nothing could justify intervention by one state in the affairs of another.[142]

In Security Council debates about these two interventions, member states contemplated the council's responsibilities. In the debate on East Pakistan, several states concluded that, given the council was charged with maintaining international peace and security, its most urgent obligation was to seek the restoration of peace between India and Pakistan. Britain linked the restoration of peace to the alleviation of suffering: "We cannot evade our responsibilities. . . . Our task, as members of the highest world body charged with the maintenance of world peace and security is to exert our influence to restore peace, to bring the fighting to a stop and to secure the relief of suffering."[143] But no state was willing to acknowledge that the suffering of Bengalis justified India's intervention. On Cambodia, several states concluded that the council's responsibility was to declare its collective disapproval of Vietnam's violation of sovereignty. The United States acknowledged that the invasion of Cambodia presented the council with "difficult political and moral questions." On the one hand, within Cambodia, "some of the worst violations in recorded history have taken place." But on the other hand, Vietnam's invasion had violated the UN Charter. "In these circumstances," the US representative asked, "what is the responsibility of the Council?" He answered, while "the international community long ago should have brought the full weight of international condemnation to bear" on the Khmer Rouge's "brutal violations of human rights," the council was now bound to insist that Vietnam immediately withdraw its armed forces and respect Cambodia's territorial integrity.[144] A draft resolution calling for the withdrawal of "all foreign forces" from Cambodia would have passed had it not been vetoed by Vietnam's supporter, the Soviet Union.[145]

What about the General Assembly? While a state-centric interpretation of "international peace and security," combined with bipolar tensions, prevented the Security Council in most cases from saying much at all about the plight of vulnerable people, the General Assembly gradually came to interpret the charter as imposing upon it a responsibility for promoting human rights. As early as 1946, the assembly concluded that consideration and condemnation of rights violations was not precluded by Article 2(7), and some states soon began to suggest that the assembly had not just a right but a duty to so consider and condemn where appropriate. In 1959, for example, the assembly adopted a resolution condemning China for violating the rights of Tibetans. Several states insisted that the assembly was obliged to do so. Pakistan suggested, "The smaller nations who make up the vast majority of the membership of the United Nations have a moral obligation to rouse the conscience of the world whenever there is a grave violation of human rights and fundamental freedoms."[146] New Zealand declared, "It would be an abdication of responsibility" for the assembly not to denounce the violations of rights.[147] And Malaya claimed the assembly "has a moral duty, in the name of justice and humanity, to record its judgment on the ruthless violation of human rights."[148] From the mid-1970s onward, the assembly routinely affirmed its "responsibility to promote and encourage respect for human rights and fundamental freedoms for all" and its determination "to remain vigilant with regard to violations of human rights wherever they may occur" in annual resolutions expressing concern or condemning rights violations in several states, including Chile (resolutions adopted 1974–89), El Salvador (1980–86), and Afghanistan (1985–94). Certainly, the operative paragraphs of these resolutions tended to merely urge a cessation of rights violations. But this was as much as the assembly was authorized to do.

These General Assembly resolutions, adopted increasingly routinely through the 1980s, pointed to a reemerging willingness among sovereign states—which, in the wake of decolonization, now represented almost all of humanity—to articulate a shared responsibility to work toward protecting people when host states proved unwilling or unable to do so. By the late 1980s, states were routinely declaring this shared responsibility in plain terms. In a 1988 General Assembly debate on humanitarian assistance, Ecuador stated, "All States have a duty to protect [human rights], and their violation anywhere will mobilize the international community to act." Sweden suggested that human rights were a "common responsibility of the international community." And Uruguay declared, "We must share in the responsibility of assisting the millions suffering today because their freedoms are being ignored and their rights violated."[149]

Certainly, most states continued to refrain from suggesting that the performance of this responsibility might include coercive interference in sovereign affairs. But not all. From 1987 onward, French president François Mitterrand and his prime minister, Jacques Chirac, began to speak of a duty to interfere (*devoir d'ingérence*), which required providing humanitarian assistance to vulnerable people even in instances where the host government did not consent. In this, he was following the lead of Médecins Sans Frontières cofounder Bernard Kouchner and other French humanitarians who, having perceived a need to reject humanitarianism's prevailing principles of discretion and respect for sovereignty during Biafra/Nigeria War (1967–70) and the East Pakistan crisis (1970–71), had conceived and championed this *devoir d'ingérence* beyond borders to save vulnerable civilians since the late 1970s.[150] Some commentators have downplayed the importance of the language of duty here, suggesting that French humanitarian actors and political leaders emphasized the right to interfere (*droit d'ingérence*), rather than the duty to do so, and claiming that the language of duty and responsibility was not introduced into international debates about the protection of populations until the development of R2P in 2001. But, in fact, this language was always central to these French claims. A 1987 conference in Paris on humanitarian law and ethics, for example, organized by Kouchner and international legal scholar Mario Bettati and attended by both Mitterrand and Chirac, produced a book titled *Le devoir d'ingérence*.[151] The French invoked the need for a legal right to interfere only because the absence of this right posed a barrier to the performance of the duty to care for those in need in the absence of sovereign consent, which was their fundamental concern (much like James Stephen had argued in 1816 that the existence of a responsibility to abolish the slave trade required that there must also be a right to do so).[152]

————

We will see in chapter 5 that the language of international responsibility would become commonplace through the course of the 1990s, before being famously articulated in terms of R2P the following decade. But, as this chapter has shown, the notion of international responsibilities for the protection of vulnerable people is far from novel. For centuries, states have collectively constructed, distributed, and discharged a wide range of responsibilities for the protection of the vulnerable. Indeed, the denial of such responsibilities during parts of the Cold War was historically exceptional. In some instances, prior to the Cold War, the performance of international responsibilities brought substantial benefit to vulnerable people. In other instances, due variously to naivety and perversity, it made things significantly worse. This history provides much fodder for thinking through the contemporary ethics, law, and politics of international responsibilities for human protection, helping us, for example, to understand the ways in which responsibilities can be challenged and evaded, or manipulated and abused, and to comprehend both the traumatic memories and perilous temptations that continue to color the dynamics and discussions of the shared responsibility to protect.

PART II

Contemporary Responsibilities

3

International Ethics

At the United Nations (UN) World Summit, held in New York in September 2005, leaders of all 191 states declared that they shared a responsibility to protect populations from four crimes: genocide, war crimes, ethnic cleansing, and crimes against humanity. Not only did states acknowledge responsibility for the protection of their own populations (a responsibility that has come to be referred to as pillar 1 of R2P), but they also accepted a collective responsibility to protect vulnerable populations beyond their borders. Specifically, they noted their responsibility to encourage and assist fellow states and to help build their capacity to protect their populations (now referred to as pillar 2), as well as the need to take timely and decisive action, where necessary, to ensure that populations are protected, using appropriate diplomatic, humanitarian, and other peaceful means, and even to take collective action under Chapter VII of the UN Charter should fellow states be manifestly failing to protect (now referred to as pillar 3).[1] We will see in chapter 5 that states have continued to assent to this responsibility to protect in the years since, even if their deeds frequently fail to match their words. Given this international agreement, I make no effort in the present chapter to build an account of the ethics of R2P from the ground up. I proceed instead on the assumption that states share at least a *pro tanto* responsibility to protect.[2] But this still leaves many ethical questions to be addressed.

I aim in this chapter to offer an empirically grounded account of the ethical implications of this acknowledged responsibility to protect—an account that takes seriously historical and contemporary realities and thinks through how these realities inform how the responsibility should be conceived and shared among states. The first question to be addressed, it seems to me, is to consider whether responsible international protection is actually possible. We saw in chapter 2 that the historical record is blotted with examples of myopia, carelessness, and abuse. The instability and suffering that followed the 2011 military intervention in Libya, moreover, confirms for many observers that contemporary constructions of responsibilities for human protection are destined to fare no better. I begin, therefore, by wrestling with postcolonial critiques that charge that R2P reproduces an unjust international order and facilitates replication of imperialism's ills. While I accept much from these critiques, I argue that the contemporary empirical record suggests greater possibilities for careful and successful human protection—both coercive and noncoercive—than critics tend to assume.

The remainder of the chapter then examines the three senses in which the shared responsibility to protect is "imperfect," along the lines identified by Samuel Pufendorf (how should states weigh responsibilities beyond borders against responsibilities to care for the wellbeing of their own people?), Emer de Vattel (who among many should do the protecting?), and Immanuel Kant (who among many should be protected?), noting that the Kantian question in particular has been almost completely and problematically ignored. I theorize how the imperfect responsibility to protect might be made more "perfect," not by making it legally enforceable (the possibility of which is the topic of chapter 4), but by elucidating ethically what we should expect from states confronted with the threat or perpetration of atrocities beyond their borders. After offering a broadly "sufficientist" account of how states should weigh their responsibilities, I propose a set of principles that might fruitfully guide the distribution of responsibilities among multiple states in response to multiple situations of concern. Through such distribution, we can begin to "perfect" the responsibility in the sense of clarifying the tasks that each state might be reasonably expected to perform and for whom.

The Possibility of Responsible Protection

In mid-February 2011, three months into the Arab Spring that had already claimed the leaders of Tunisia and Egypt, large numbers of Libyan civilians rose up against the rule of Muammar Gaddafi. The Libyan leader quickly made clear his willingness to crush dissent and commit atrocities to stay in power. Invoking the Tiananmen Square massacre, he declared his intention to "cleanse Libya house by house" and to execute anyone who threatened the unity of the state. Echoing the language of the Rwandan génocidaires, he urged his supporters to attack the "rats" and "cockroaches" protesting his rule.[3] A series of regional and international responses to ongoing threats and attacks against civilians by Gaddafi's regime culminated on March 17 with the UN Security Council's adoption of Resolution 1973, authorizing the use of "all necessary measures . . . to protect civilians and civilian populated areas under threat of attack."

It seemed clear to many observers that military intervention was both a feasible and necessary means of preventing atrocities. UN Secretary-General Ban Ki-moon commended the council for its action, proclaiming that the resolution "affirms, clearly and unequivocally, the international community's determination to fulfil its responsibility to protect civilians from violence perpetrated upon them by their own government."[4] Over the next seven months, members of NATO and the League of Arab States waged a controversial but successful intervention, removing the immediate threat to civilians in the rebel capital Benghazi and elsewhere and eventually overthrowing Gaddafi's regime. But Libya soon fell into chaos, and that chaos soon impacted neighboring states.

The interim leaders who assumed control of Libya in October 2011 and the publicly elected congress that took power in August 2012 both struggled to contain lawlessness, sectarian violence, and Islamic insurgencies. A flood of mercenaries and arms across Libya's borders fed civil war in Syria and helped trigger civil war in Mali. The renewal of civil war in Libya in 2014 caused the deaths of thousands of civilians and the displacement of four hundred thousand more. This fueled human trafficking networks that have since sent hundreds of thousands of refugees across the Mediterranean, thousands of whom have drowned in transit, and thousands more of whom have been forcibly returned to horrors awaiting them in Libya, from unlawful killings, torture, and arbitrary detention to rape, slavery, and human trafficking.[5] By 2017, the United States was again launching airstrikes in Libya, this time against Islamic State forces that had taken the chaos as an opportunity to set up camp. US president Barack Obama reflected in 2016, "We averted large-scale civilian casualties, we prevented what almost surely would have been a prolonged and bloody civil conflict. And despite all that, Libya is a mess." The intervention, he concluded, "didn't work."[6]

In the years since 2011, political leaders and commentators have offered a range of suggestions as to how the R2P principle might be reformed, or better understood, so as to avoid such negative results in the future—from proposals to clarify the justifications and mandates of military interventions and to make intervening powers answerable for the conduct and progress of their interventions to heightened emphasis on the importance of working *with* states rather than *against* them, wherever possible, to help prevent atrocities and obviate the need to consider resorting to military intervention. Every year since 2009, the UN secretary-general has issued a detailed report on one aspect of R2P or another, seeking to clarify, improve, and promote the execution of international human protection.

This all reminds me of Herman Merivale's mid-nineteenth-century response to the repeated failures of colonial powers to responsibly discharge their claimed duty to protect indigenous people, described in chapter 2. "Our errors are not of conception so much as of execution," he maintained. Rather than questioning the settler colonial project itself, he instead proposed new regulations that he hoped would better ensure indigenous protection, just as others had done before and many would again after him.[7] Are those who, more than a century and a half later, continue to believe in the possibility of responsible and effective international protection despite failure after failure, like Merivale, simply fooling themselves? Perhaps the errors really are of conception after all.

WRESTLING WITH THE POSTCOLONIAL CRITIQUE

Numerous scholars have offered such a critique in recent years, claiming that contemporary claims and performances of a responsibility to protect populations beyond borders contain clear echoes of past imperial practices, and insisting that the flaws of such projects go much deeper than difficulties of execution. Whatever the differences between colonialism and R2P, they charge, both are products of and serve to sustain international hierarchies and inequalities between political communities, which enable the powerful to impose their will on the weak, producing predictably perverse outcomes. Quoting Edward Said, Jessica Whyte asserts that the powerful are "always on top," such that, while they may portray R2P as a novel principle that breaks from the past, the activities they pursue in R2P's name unsurprisingly repeat colonialism's ills.[8] Adom Getachew contends similarly that R2P "generates new forms of international hierarchy," generating tragedies such as Libya that, rather than a misapplication of the principle, should be recognized as one of its "recurring practical entailments."[9]

The critique commonly unfolds into two indictments that are worth distinguishing. The first alleges that R2P obscures how wealthy and powerful states are often implicated or even complicit in the outbreak of atrocities in

poorer and weaker states. Grounded in a notion of "sovereignty as responsibility," R2P attributes primary responsibility for the protection of populations to the host state (pillar 1). The international community is then
accorded supplementary responsibility to assist at-risk states in the prevention of atrocities and to step in to end atrocities when they break out (pillars
2 and 3). Getachew charges that this conceptualization proceeds from "an
impoverished account of international responsibility," which neglects "the
entanglements of domestic and international politics" and "saddles states—
often weak states—with the burden of responsibility for . . . crises that are
not fully of their own making." R2P's proponents are accused of implying
that the international community is an innocent bystander that finds itself
compelled to respond to crises that are solely domestic, whereas in fact those
powerful states that commonly act on the international community's behalf
are already deeply involved, both historically and in ongoing ways, in the
vulnerabilities of weaker states to the threat and outbreak of atrocities.[10] Critics point to how the European colonial project, with its brutal subjugation of
colonized people and extraction of human and natural resources from colonized territories, contributed to the generation of inequalities between, and
vulnerabilities within, political communities. They observe also how these
inequalities and vulnerabilities, far from being repaired by decolonization,
are maintained by unjust global practices and structures, ranging from the
harms of illegal wars and the reckless sales of arms to abusive regimes to the
ills of exploitative economic and trade policies and ongoing environmental
destruction.[11] All of these injustices, past and present, have contributed to
some degree to domestic outbreaks of atrocities in recent years. The international community, Getachew concludes, is "always implicated and should
be understood as already responsible."[12]

This is a vitally important observation. But rather than leading us to
abandon R2P, I suggest that it compels us to conceive the task of preventing
atrocities in the context of a broader project of global justice. R2P is concerned with atrocities. It should not be expected to offer a response to all
global injustices. But neither should it obscure those injustices, and certainly
not injustices that generate or exacerbate the risk of atrocities. Proponents
of R2P, therefore, should be careful not to frame international responsibilities in ways that imply that these responsibilities proceed from a need
to respond to vulnerabilities that are purely domestic. Rather, R2P should
be understood as part of, and compatible with, a broader conception of
international responsibility and accountability. The performance of positive
international duties to prevent atrocities should be attended with efforts to

end and repair the consequences of violations of negative duties, both those that are readily observable and frequently condemned and also those that have been normalized and rendered invisible by global structures.[13] (And the reasons for embracing this more expansive conception of international responsibility are not only ethical, but also political since, as we will see in chapter 5, growing recognition of the hypocrisies of powerful Western states regarding matters of international human protection have weakened the perceived legitimacy and "compliance pull" of R2P in recent years.)

Some critics charge that the fact that international actors are implicated and often complicit in domestic outbreaks of atrocities demonstrates that the international community has no place involving itself in the domestic affairs of states for the purpose of human protection. Others, however, including Getachew, accept that, despite entrenched global injustices, there remains a need to grapple with the question of what should be done to protect populations from atrocities when host states are struggling or refusing to do so.[14] Nevertheless, as noted earlier, Getachew alleges that R2P, grounded as it is in a hierarchical order in which the powerful arrogate to themselves legal authority, via the Security Council, to intervene in the affairs of the weak, produces tragedies such as Libya, not as a misapplication, but as a "practical entailment" of the principle.

As such, R2P is said to mirror European imperial-protectionist projects. This is the second indictment presented against R2P. Critics, such as Lauren Benton and Lisa Ford, acknowledge that there are differences between nineteenth-century imperialism and twenty-first-century human protection, but nevertheless maintain that "the stamp of imperial history is subtly apparent in recent international interventions."[15] But the differences are significant and worth highlighting. In contrast to nineteenth-century norms, R2P does not justify annexation, the extinguishment of sovereignty, and the subjection of peoples to foreign rule. Those who are protected are supposed to remain sovereign and international protection measures are supposed to defend and uphold their sovereign will. Furthermore, in contrast to nineteenth-century agreements such as the General Act of the Conference of Berlin (1885), in which an exclusive club of imperial powers claimed a duty to protect and civilize those outside the club, R2P has been endorsed by all states. And nonconsensual interference in sovereign affairs, according to the 2005 World Summit agreement, requires the assent of the Security Council—a body which, for all its faults, can hardly be accused of authorizing nonconsensual interference too regularly and recklessly. Indeed, while the council has invoked R2P in more than eighty resolutions and presidential statements since 2005, it has only once authorized the resort to force against the wishes of the functioning government of a sovereign state.[16] That was in the case of Libya, and it followed calls for international action from multiple regional organizations: the League of Arab States, the Gulf Cooperation Council, and the Organization of the Islamic Conference.[17] As disastrous as its outcomes have been, the Libyan intervention should not be framed as *yet another* imperialistic R2P intervention gone wrong.

It is telling, I think, that the examples of military intervention that R2P's critics offer as parallels with past imperial practices are often examples that, far from being carried out within R2P's parameters, were and continue to be widely perceived as illegitimate and abusive, not to mention illegal. Whyte highlights the US-led coalition's 2003 invasion of Iraq.[18] Benton and Ford point to Russia's 2014 annexation of Crimea.[19] We do not need to draw parallels with colonialism in order to recognize that these wars were unjust. And while the aggressors did draw on the language of R2P and related protection norms as part of their justifications for resorting to force, there is little reason to think this enabled them to "get away" with their unjust actions any more than they would have had these norms been unavailable to them.[20]

That said, other critics rightly point to Libya, attributing the faults of the 2011 intervention to the same hubris and myopia that marked the European civilizing mission. Siddharth Mallavarapu contends:

> The Libyan invocation has confirmed our worst fears about the R2P. All the checks and balances prior to military resort were not followed through with any diligence, arms were supplied to rebels and regime change was never mandated to begin with. . . . There is nothing in the praxis of R2P that inspires confidence that it is going to be vastly different the next time. If anything, the prior history of interventionism, the hubris of material power and the myopia of a geopolitics that cannot wait do not augur well for serious international redress when warranted, least of all in the garb of "responsibility."[21]

We might quibble with Mallavarapu's analysis of the faults of the Libyan intervention, and we might argue, as Obama has done, that the mistake was not the intervention itself but the failure to "plan for the day after."[22] But this is no less evidence of hubris and myopia corrupting an attempt by the powerful to protect the weak. We might hope to learn from the mistakes of Libya and ensure that future interveners responsibly help establish peace and rebuild the state and its institutions once the intervention is over. But this, again, sounds suspiciously like Merivale's attempt to tinker with issues of execution instead of attending to problems of conception. The lures of civilizational self-confidence and narratives of progress that captured nineteenth-century humanitarians and so often compromised their efforts to protect the vulnerable are still with us. These imperial legacies haunt R2P and should give pause to anyone contemplating the resort to force to protect the vulnerable beyond borders today. At the very least, there is a need to "slow down," as Jeanne Morefield puts it, and to reflect on history before attending to contemporary injustices.[23]

However, the example of Libya provides insufficient grounds for giving up on the possibility of responsibly protecting vulnerable populations. There is much more to the contemporary record of international protection than the failure in Libya. Merivale's problematic response to the repeated failures of colonial protection—focusing on the ills of execution rather than conception—is not so problematic when applied to contemporary efforts to protect vulnerable populations because we actually have a growing body of evidence suggesting that such efforts frequently make a positive contribution to protecting people from atrocities. We certainly ought not to write off Libya as a single problematic data point. It is a tragic example of protection gone wrong and one that political leaders should be wary of replicating. And yet, not only does military intervention not always go wrong, but there are also a range of alternative measures available to the international community that, when carefully and appropriately applied, have a good record of protecting populations from atrocities. Let us briefly consider the current state of knowledge about what works.

WHAT WORKS?

It is worth emphasizing at the outset that nonconsensual military intervention will rarely be the right means of protecting people from atrocities. The sixteenth-century Spanish Thomists were correct to warn against recklessly resorting to arms in defense of tyrannized people since in many instances it leads to more rather than fewer deaths of innocents. It is difficult for international actors to forcibly save lives against the will of a host government without doing more harm than good. Despite the urgings of numerous commentators, intervention in defiance of the Sudanese government to protect victims of atrocities in Darfur between 2003 and 2005 would have risked undermining existing humanitarian relief operations and may have required a protracted counterinsurgency effort against the Janjaweed militia with the likely effect of exacerbating and prolonging civilian suffering.[24] Intervention in defiance of Bashar al-Assad's regime to protect civilians in the civil war waged in Syria from 2011 onward would have risked even greater calamities given the local and regional dynamics of the conflict, not least Russia's willingness to arm and assist Assad and to shield him against Western efforts to restrain or remove him from power.[25]

Indeed, Libya is arguably the only case this century in which the threat or perpetration of atrocities could be credibly read as generating a responsibility to undertake nonconsensual military intervention—and we know how poorly this intervention went. Perhaps the intervention could have worked. The primary reason for failure was that the intervening powers did not do enough to help establish peace and rebuild the state and its institutions after the defeat of Gaddafi. Obama later lamented that his failure to plan for the aftermath of the intervention was his "worst mistake" as president.[26] However, even if the intervening powers and other members of the international community possessed the will to contribute to rebuilding Libya, the task would have been very difficult, not least because the rebels made clear that, once Gaddafi was defeated, they did not want international help in determining Libya's future and would not accept the deployment of a UN peacekeeping mission.[27]

Nevertheless, we should not rule out the resort to arms altogether. Indeed, a case might even be made for forcible regime change in certain circumstances. We can point to Vietnam's defeat of the genocidal Khmer Rouge in 1979 and Tanzania's overthrow of Uganda's tyrannical ruler, Idi Amin, the same year as evidence that successful population protection via regime change is possible.[28] But this will be the right means of responsibly protecting populations only very rarely. That said, we can point to a number of successful examples of military intervention in recent decades that succeeded in averting or ending atrocities *without* regime change. None were perfect, but each saved lives without making things worse than they otherwise likely would have been. Some successful (pre-R2P) interventions were undertaken, as in Libya, without the consent of the host government, such as the US-led intervention to protect Kurds in northern Iraq (1991), in the aftermath of the First Gulf War, and NATO's intervention in Kosovo (1999).[29] Others, such as the Australian-led intervention in Timor-Leste (1999), were undertaken after substantial international pressure led the host state, Indonesia, to grant its consent. Other successful interventions have been undertaken without the consent of the de facto authorities, but with the support of legitimately elected authorities, such as the deployment of UN peacekeepers in Côte d'Ivoire (2011), authorized by the Security Council to "use all necessary means" to protect civilians.[30] And others have been undertaken with host state consent, but in territories controlled by other parties, such as the US intervention to forcibly rescue Yazidis under attack from Islamic State and trapped on Mount Sinjar in Iraq (2014).[31]

Another means of militarized protection, and one that enjoys an even stronger track record of success but which is ignored by many of R2P's critics, is peacekeeping.[32] The potential shortcomings of peacekeeping are well documented, from appalling examples of sexual exploitation and abuse through to concerns about the creation of peacekeeping subcultures and economies that hamper effectiveness.[33] But the overall record of peacekeeping in reducing violence against civilians is strong. Researchers have found that, particularly since the UN began to explicitly mandate peacekeeping operations to protect civilians in 1999, the deployment of peacekeepers has tended to reduce the risk of mass killing of civilians in the context of civil war,[34] shorten the length of conflict episodes and reduce rebel abuses against civilians in the localities where they are deployed,[35] extend the duration of peace once the civil war has ended,[36] and reduce the risk of postconflict victimization of civilians.[37] The larger and better equipped these operations are, moreover, the more effective they tend to be in achieving these goals.[38] And all this despite the fact that peacekeepers have been shown to be often reluctant to discharge fully their protection mandate and intervene with force when civilians are under attack.[39] As Lise Howard explains, peacekeepers instead tend to successfully protect civilians via tactics of verbal persuasion, financial inducement, and coercion in the form of defense, deterrence, surveillance, and arrest—tactics that are sometimes supplemented in moments of crisis by the provision of additional military personnel that *are* willing to use offensive force, such as those provided by Britain in Sierra Leone (2000), the United States in Liberia (2003), and France in Côte d'Ivoire (2011).[40]

In addition to these variously militarized means of responsibly protecting populations, the international community also has at hand numerous nonforcible measures that can likewise be deployed to responsibly protect civilians. It is worth highlighting particularly the potential fruitfulness and cost-effectiveness of efforts to prevent atrocities before they begin. There is a tendency to conceive of duties beyond borders as being generated by crises. Commentators are often found arguing that a particular outbreak of atrocities should "trigger" R2P.[41] But, as the international community acknowledged in the World Summit agreement, states have not only an urgent responsibility to protect in times of crisis (pillar 3) but also an enduring responsibility to encourage fellow states to fulfil their protection responsibilities, to help them build capacity to protect their populations, and to assist those under stress, in order to prevent crises from breaking out (pillar 2). As Ban usefully elaborated in 2014, encouragement involves reminding states to adhere to their protection responsibilities and offering advice on how to mitigate risks of atrocities; capacity building involves assisting states to achieve effective, legitimate, and inclusive governance, establish a security sector and electoral and judicial institutions, and develop early warning and response capabilities; and assistance to those under stress involves providing expertise and resources for human rights monitoring, dispute resolution, law enforcement, and peacekeeping to prevent an emerging crisis from worsening.[42]

The hope is that these pillar 2 prevention efforts will reinforce the endeavors of states to protect their own populations (pillar 1) so that occasions do not arise in which pillar 3 measures to pressure or coerce protection are required. But it should not be assumed that states will consent to being assisted. States commonly resist being labeled vulnerable to atrocities, they are reluctant to acknowledge that they need help in mitigating risks, and they often refuse to accept what they see as impositions by international actors, as was seen in the context of an emerging human protection crisis in Burundi in 2015–16.[43] So long as there is no clear evidence that actors have begun to commit atrocities, states ought not to compel fellow states to accept assistance. But there is strong evidence that, in those instances where states do consent to international assistance, its provision is typically a more effective and less costly way of protecting populations than having to pressure or compel protection once atrocities have begun.[44]

Of course, regrettably, international prevention efforts will sometimes fail to ensure the protection of populations, either because they are insufficient to help the government prevent non-state actors from committing atrocities or because the government itself is intent on committing atrocities against its own people. In such situations, the international community still has in hand a range of nonforcible measures that can, in the right circumstances, be responsibly used to dissuade the perpetration of atrocities or relieve victims. Two prominent means of dissuading perpetrators without resorting to force are diplomacy and sanctions.[45] While there is ongoing debate about the effectiveness of diplomatic criticism in ameliorating human rights violations in general, researchers find that diplomacy can help reduce both the likelihood and the severity of atrocities.[46] In the R2P era, we have seen successful uses of diplomacy to help prevent the escalation of atrocities in cases such as Kenya (2008 and 2013), Guinea (2009–10), and Kyrgyzstan

(2010).[47] The effectiveness of sanctions is more contested. There is some evidence that sanctions can help reduce the duration of atrocities once they have been in place for a few years. But in the short to medium term, they tend to make little contribution to alleviating or reducing the severity of atrocities, regardless of whether they are threatened or implemented, targeted or comprehensively applied, unilaterally or multilaterally imposed.[48] And when they are imposed irresponsibly, they can cause substantial harm to civilians. The application of economic sanctions in Iraq from 1990 to 2003 contributed to a humanitarian crisis that included cholera and typhoid epidemics and widespread malnutrition.[49] The imposition of an arms embargo on Yugoslavia in 1991 hampered Bosnia's efforts to protect its Muslim population against ethnic cleansing during the 1992–95 Bosnian War.[50] While carefully targeted sanctions can succeed in avoiding such unintended harms under certain conditions, more work is needed to improve their effectiveness at alleviating suffering.[51]

Two prominent means of responsibly relieving victims of atrocities are providing humanitarian assistance and granting asylum. Humanitarian assistance is not without its challenges. Some research has found, for example, that the introduction of aid resources in the context of civil war can produce increases in violence against civilians and prolong the fighting.[52] There can also be tensions between the goals of providing relief to vulnerable people and bringing atrocities to an end. The silence of the United Nations in the face of atrocities committed by Sri Lankan government forces against the Tamil population in 2009, due to fear that the government would respond to condemnation by restricting humanitarian access, is a clear example of failure to successfully resolve this tension.[53] But in many contexts humanitarian assistance can be a crucial means of responsible protection. In 2003–4, for example, international and local humanitarian actors protected around two million civilians in Darfur, who had been displaced from their homes by atrocities. The humanitarian effort was so successful that by 2005 the mortality rate in Darfur had returned to prewar levels.[54]

The most straightforward way that states can responsibly provide protection is often to grant temporary asylum or permanent resettlement to those seeking refuge from atrocities, and to assist other states that are willing to do the same. Brian Barbour and Brian Gorlick put the case plainly. Noting that "literally millions of persons" have been saved from atrocities over the last century through the provision of asylum, they conclude that "the grant of asylum is, or would be in many cases, the most practical, realistic, and least controversial response to assisting victims of mass atrocities."[55] By the end of

2019, the UN's refugee agency counted more than six million refugees who had fled the Syrian civil war.[56] The provision of refuge to such vulnerable people constitutes a particularly direct way for states to discharge their shared responsibility to protect with little risk of doing more harm than good.

The possibilities of responsible protection, therefore, across a range of measures, both coercive and noncoercive, consensual and nonconsensual, are extensive. The resort to nonconsensual military intervention is one of the most risky and least cost-effective measures available. Despite the tragedy of Libya, there are enough successful examples of nonconsensual intervention to suggest that this measure need not be abandoned entirely and permanently. But it is one that should be pursued rarely, and with great care. In situations where there are reasonable doubts that military intervention is a responsible means of protection, there will always be alternative means of responsibly protecting, if not in that same situation then in another. (I explore more fully the implications of the fact that the international community is typically confronted with multiple situations of concern later in the chapter.) If powerful states are so intent on benevolently protecting distant strangers, as they inevitably claim to be when seeking to justify doubtful military interventions, they will not lack opportunities to do so by other means, whether it be by consensually helping to build the capacities of fellow states or aiding or resettling vulnerable people fleeing atrocities. When they fail to take up such opportunities, this should surely raise doubts about the sincerity of their professed desire to protect vulnerable people through military intervention.

Finally, we should recognize that not only are there a range of measures available for states who are willing to contribute to the international protection of people at risk of atrocities, but a given situation of concern will often require the efforts of multiple states coordinating with each other, performing a variety of tasks, and accepting a variety of risks and costs at various stages, in order to responsibly discharge their shared responsibility to protect. This brings into relief various senses in which this shared responsibility is "imperfect." In the remainder of this chapter, I think through these imperfections.

Weighing the Responsibility to Protect

The provision of any protection measures, whether coercive or peaceful, can involve substantial costs and risks. Even the application of diplomatic pressure can be costly. One state's criticism of another can result in it losing an ally, or a valuable trade deal, or even much needed foreign aid.[57] In some instances, such as when millions of displaced people flee atrocities and cross borders, recipient states can be confronted with costs and risks that they are not in a position to bear. We need to consider, therefore, what R2P actually demands of individual states. Here we are grappling with the first sense in which the responsibility to protect entails an imperfect duty—the sense articulated by Pufendorf: how should states weigh the responsibility to protect those beyond their borders against the responsibility to care for the well-being and interests of their own people?

To begin, it is worth recognizing that states do not always have to make a choice between protecting distant strangers and securing their own material interests. After all, as Pufendorf observed, it will often be the case that the interests of states are advanced by risking blood and treasure on behalf of vulnerable outsiders, if not in the short term then at least over the long term. Obama repeatedly appealed to such an "enlightened," long-term understanding of the national interest during his presidency. In an address to the UN General Assembly in 2015, for example, he declared that, in a globalized world, the care and protection of vulnerable strangers is in the interests of all: "Of course, in the old ways of thinking, the plight of the powerless, the plight of refugees, the plight of the marginalized did not matter. They were on the periphery of the world's concerns. Today, our concern for them is driven not just by conscience, but should also be driven by self-interest. For helping people who have been pushed to the margins of our world is not mere charity, it is a matter of collective security."[58]

This kind of argument can certainly provide motivation for states to discharge their responsibility to protect. There is value in urging political leaders to perceive their national interests in these expansive terms (and I suggest later that considerations of national interest can sometimes appropriately inform decisions about where to act and who to protect). But we should take care not to reduce R2P to that which is perceived to advance one's own interest. That would be to not actually accept the responsibility after all. And it would likely leave many vulnerable people unprotected. Recall G. W. Leibniz's criticism of Pufendorf's effort to ground duties in utility. Leibniz noted that while considerations of long-term utility may in some circumstances recommend kindness and generosity to strangers, in other circumstances they will recommend neglect. The international community was confronted with this problem in particularly stark terms in the 1990s. NATO member states perceived clear interests in acting to prevent the ethnic cleansing of Kosovar Albanians in 1999, ranging from preventing an influx of refugees and preserving the stability of Europe to maintaining the credibility of the alliance. But five years earlier these same states struggled to conceive what enlightened interests they had in preventing the genocide that engulfed Rwanda. Indeed, it was recognition of this problem that led to the development of R2P, which espouses the responsibilities of states to protect beyond borders even when they perceive they have little to gain materially or strategically from doing so.

That said, states do have responsibilities to care for the interests and needs of their own populations, and so it is appropriate that they weigh their duties to others against their duties to themselves when these duties are not perceived to converge. This is something Obama also repeatedly emphasized as president. Defending the Libyan intervention, he insisted upon its exceptional nature, noted the limitations of US power, and cautioned that, "given the costs and risks of intervention, we must always measure our interests against the need for action."[59] Responding to pressure to do more to alleviate suffering in Syria two years later, he noted that the United States had already "invested" much in terms of humanitarian aid and helping the opposition, highlighted the complexity of the crisis, and explained that his job as president was to measure humanitarian and security concerns in Syria "against my bottom line, which is what's in the best interest of America's security."[60]

So, how should states weigh their duties to others against their duties to themselves? Some might agree with Hugo Grotius that, since the preservation and advantage of the state should always take priority, states are bound to help foreigners only insofar as they can without any risk or cost to themselves. But, again, that would be to not actually accept the responsibility to protect after all. A more justifiable approach, I suggest, is that offered by Vattel.[61] As noted in chapter 1, Vattel argued in *The Law of Nations* that people have every right to unite with others to establish states and to prioritize the care and preservation of each other's well-being and interests, but they cannot thereby liberate themselves from the universal duties that they owe to all humanity. Rather, in so uniting, "it thenceforth belongs to that body, that state, and its rulers, to fulfil the duties of humanity towards strangers."[62] Such an understanding is echoed in the claims of numerous contemporary moral and political philosophers who acknowledge the value of prioritizing duties to fellow citizens for instrumental reasons of efficiency and effectiveness, and even for psychological reasons of communal attachment, but who insist that there remain universal duties to humanity that coexist with and at times override these national duties. Some, such as Robert Goodin, claim that special responsibilities to compatriots derive their moral force from general responsibilities owed among all humanity. The former simply comprises an efficient way of allocating and administering the latter. As such, these special responsibilities "are susceptible to being overridden (at least at the margins, or in exceptional circumstances)" by these enduring general responsibilities. Goodin acknowledges that this mirrors the argument of Christian Wolff, whose ideas were expanded and popularized by Vattel.[63] Others, such as David Miller, insist that special responsibilities owed within national communities have distinct value and force, independent of general responsibilities to humanity, but nevertheless similarly acknowledge that these general responsibilities can at times require states to help foreigners whose basic rights are not adequately protected within their own national communities.[64]

Vattel went on to argue that each state should retain the liberty to exercise practical judgment in weighing their duties to outsiders against their duties to themselves. But he provided guidelines as to how such global and national duties should be so weighed. He accepted that a state should always exercise prudence when considering what it can do for others. No state is obliged to expend blood and treasure for the sake of those beyond its borders to the extent that it does an "essential injury to herself," he declared. And no political leader is permitted "to obey without reserve all the suggestions of a noble and generous heart impelling him to sacrifice his own interests to the advantage of others." The leader's first priority, after all, is to care for "the nation who has committed herself to his care."[65] But, he insisted, a state's prudent concern for its own needs does not justify neglecting the needs of others. Rather, while a state should pay careful attention to the well-being of its people, it should also be willing to accept risks and costs for the sake of vulnerable others. It ought not to refuse to assist others out of fear of "a slight loss, or any little inconvenience; humanity forbids this; and the mutual love which men owe to each other requires greater sacrifices." A state should consider its own needs relative to the needs of others, he explained, and it should not hesitate to sacrifice its interests a little when it can help others a lot: "a nation ought on all occasions to regulate her conduct by reasons proportioned to the advantages and necessities of others, and to reckon as nothing a small expense or a supportable inconvenience, when great good will thence result to another nation."[66]

Vattel's account of responsibilities is similar to the "sufficientist" account of global duties developed by Henry Shue and others in recent decades.[67] This account is commonly directed toward questions of human subsistence, but can be applied also to matters of human protection.[68] It holds that, if there are people beyond a state's borders who lack the basic requirements of protection, the state is bound to contribute to their protection (or to other basic human needs) up to the point at which the provision of basic needs to its own people would be rendered insecure—either because the state would lack the resources to ensure their care or because the state would be made so weak as to leave itself vulnerable to the predations of others. The echoes of Vattel's suggestion that a state should do what it can for others up to the point of doing an "essential injury to herself" can be clearly heard. It may well be, as Samuel Moyn and others argue, that sufficientism does not go far enough and that the historic and ongoing responsibilities of powerful states for global inequalities produce obligations of global egalitarianism that demand equal distribution of resources even above the threshold of basic subsistence and security.[69] However, as suggested earlier, R2P is concerned only with protection against atrocities, rather than pretending to be a comprehensive vision of global justice. Thus, it is enough for its purposes that it demands of states contributions that are sufficient to ensure the protection of vulnerable strangers insofar as is possible. (That said, I suggest in the next section that considerations of historical and ongoing complicity in the vulnerabilities of others should inform how the responsibility to protect is shared among states.) While less demanding than global egalitarianism, a Vattelian-sufficientist conception of global responsibilities still demands much of states. We might not expect states to embrace this conception of global responsibilities anytime soon, and we might instead merely hope that they will be willing to make some substantial sacrifices for the sake of strangers here and there. Nevertheless, it is worth stating it as the ethical mark against which their behavior can be measured.[70]

Vattel was right to suggest that the weighing of duties to outsiders against duties to one's own will appropriately involve the exercise of practical judgment.[71] But a process of weighing that routinely exaggerates the requirements of national security and underestimates the possibilities of generosity—a phenomenon that is unfortunately all too common—will not do. And a decision to seek political advantage by fostering domestic security fears and casting arguments for generosity as naïve and dangerous—a phenomenon likewise all too common—is particularly problematic. German chancellor Angela Merkel's explanation of her decision to open Germany's borders to asylum seekers fleeing the Syrian civil war in 2015 represents a useful model for how a wealthy and capable state should conceive of its responsibilities to vulnerable foreigners. "Germany is a strong country," Merkel observed. "We will manage."[72]

Sharing the Responsibility to Protect

Having considered the first sense of R2P's imperfection, contemplating how much we can reasonably ask of a given state, let us now examine how the collectivity of states ought to coordinate to ensure that those at risk of atrocities are protected. The responsibilities of the collectivity of states can be broadly conceived as "residual" duties, which arise when a host state needs assistance or fails to discharge its own responsibility to protect (notwithstanding that these residual duties may often also be rightly understood as duties of reparation).[73] Goodin helpfully notes that these kinds of duties are appropriately understood as being "shared jointly and severally" by the collective.[74] The collectivity has a responsibility to collectively undertake the various tasks needed to ensure protection of populations, insofar as is possible given the other responsibilities of the collective and the limits of their collective capacity. However, when we try to zero in on what is therefore required of any individual member of the collective, we are confronted with the second and third senses of imperfection.

The second sense of imperfection echoes that suggested by Vattel in his discussion of duties to admit foreign exiles: the duty to protect is imperfect because it falls on no state in particular. While every individual may have a universal right to protection from atrocities, the responsibility to ensure such protection when a host government is struggling or failing to provide it rests with no specific state. Michael Walzer puts it well, focusing on the issue of military intervention: "The general problem is that intervention, even when it is justified, even when it is necessary to prevent terrible crimes, even when it poses no threat to regional or global stability, is an imperfect duty—a duty that doesn't belong to any particular agent. Somebody ought to intervene but no specific state in the society of states is morally bound to do so."[75] This sense of imperfection fuels much political debate. Recall, for example, the British parliamentary debates in 1896 concerning whether or not Britain's obligation to succor oppressed Armenians was greater than that borne by the other great powers. Consider, likewise, controversies among states in recent years about how to fairly distribute the responsibility of providing asylum to those fleeing atrocities in Syria and elsewhere.

The third sense of imperfection is akin to that highlighted by Kant: the duty to protect is imperfect since each state is left with "a playroom for free choice" regarding who in particular beyond their borders they should protect and what measures they should take to protect them. This notion has often been alluded to by political leaders seeking to defend their reluctance to take particular action in a particular situation. Recall, for example, Queen Victoria querying in 1877 why the Bulgarians were supposedly more deserving of England's assistance than any other vulnerable people, "as if they were more God's creatures and our fellow-creatures than every other nation abroad."[76] Consider, similarly, Obama's response to pressure to do more to protect the vulnerable in Syria in 2013: "How do I weigh tens of thousands who've been killed in Syria versus the tens of thousands who are currently being killed in the Congo?"[77]

While the Vattelian dilemma of who among many should do the protecting in a given situation has received much attention by theorists in recent years, the Kantian dilemma of who among many should be protected by a given state has been oddly neglected. Theorists have tended to present a skewed depiction of international life, proceeding on the assumption that the international community is confronted with only one atrocity crisis at a time. This has hampered the development of ideas about how to work toward full coverage—or at least the fullest possible coverage—in the protection of civilians from atrocities. I suggest that, even if the shared responsibility to protect remains largely subject to the judgment of states, it is possible to work toward "perfecting" the responsibility in both the Vattelian and Kantian senses. The identification of principles for the fair and efficient distribution of responsibilities among states is required so that the plurality of threatened and actual crises confronted at a given time can be adequately addressed insofar as is possible. As Shue puts it, we need to identify "waves of duties" and "webs of duty-bearers" so as to generate a "workable allocation" of duties, and we need to work to provide "full coverage" through "a division of labor among duty-bearers."[78] This requires careful cooperation and coordination among the collectivity of states. Indeed, such cooperation and coordination is arguably itself a perfect duty borne by all: while states do not have a perfect duty to act beyond their borders in every instance to ensure every individual's protection, they arguably all have a perfect duty to work together to ensure that their shared responsibilities are distributed effectively and equitably such that protection is provided to the vulnerable as efficiently as possible and without excessive cost to any given state.[79]

WHO SHOULD DO THE PROTECTING?

The first thing to emphasize, when contemplating who should respond to a given situation of concern, is that we do not necessarily need to identify a single responsible agent. While it will sometimes be the case that responsibility to contribute to protection is most appropriately allocated to one state, an effective response to a threatened or actual atrocity crisis will more commonly require contributions from multiple states, collaborating with each other and dividing various tasks among themselves. Nevertheless, we still need to articulate principles for determining who these multiple states ought to be.[80] A useful starting point is to distinguish between backward-looking and forward-looking grounds for allocating responsibility. Looking backward, it can be appropriate to assign responsibility for protection to those that are culpable in some way for the vulnerability of a population or that share special ties with those in need of protection. Looking forward, it can be appropriate to assign responsibility to those that have particular capacity to provide protection due to their material or social power. It turns out there already exists some shared understanding among states about these principles, although there remains frequent contestation about how they should be interpreted in a given instance, a lamentable reluctance to consistently act on them, and examples of states appealing to such principles to justify unjust interference in the sovereign affairs of others.

Those that are culpable in some way for the vulnerability of people beyond their borders have a particular burden of responsibility to ensure their protection. A recent example of the application of this principle is the efforts by members of the coalition that invaded Iraq in 2003 to forcefully protect Iraqi civilians from the threat of atrocities at the hands of Islamic State a decade later.[81] Contemplating intervention to protect the Iraqi state and its people in 2014, British opposition leader Ed Miliband suggested, "While some people would say that our [2003] intervention in Iraq means that we should not intervene in this case, I think that there is a heightened responsibility for us precisely because we did intervene in Iraq, and—with all kinds of implications—the Iraqi state that has emerged is partly our responsibility."[82]

Thinking longer term, former colonial powers will often likewise be understood to bear a special responsibility to protect the vulnerable in their former colonies, due to the historical complicity of the former in the vulnerability of the latter to the outbreak of atrocity crises—though this understanding is only occasionally uttered by those in government.[83] Thinking more broadly, we might also argue that special responsibilities for protection should be borne by those powerful and wealthy states that have benefited from practices of economic exploitation, environmental destruction, and ongoing imperial violence, which have had the effect of perpetuating poverty and instability and heightening the risk of atrocities in poorer states.[84] This source of responsibility tends not to be acknowledged by potential duty bearers. But it is worth highlighting not least because it exposes how the duty to protect borne by powerful and wealthy bystander states often entails not so much a duty of self-sacrificial generosity and beneficence, but a duty to refrain from and make reparations for injustice.

Of course, it may not always be appropriate for culpable states to deploy soldiers, police, observers, or advisors to help protect populations that they have previously harmed. Such involvement may be met with skepticism and resistance and risk exacerbating the trauma of victims. But there will usually be a range of other means of contributing to international protection efforts that culpable states can pursue, such as financing and supporting the efforts of others, contributing to sanctions and embargos, and granting asylum to those who seek it.[85]

Continuing to look backward, we might also allocate protection responsibilities to states that share history, cultural affinity, or kinship with a vulnerable population. In the absence of culpability, this principle of connectedness does not necessarily provide grounds for saying that these states bear a heavier burden of obligation than others. But it does provide a basis for determining which among many potential agents of protection might be particularly expected to act.[86] In 2003, for example, President George W. Bush acknowledged that the United States' "unique history with Liberia" had "created a certain sense of expectations" that it would act to end the violence in the country.[87] However, as with all justifications for extraterritorial interference, we should guard against hypocrisy and abuse. After all, recall that the European great powers repeatedly invoked this principle of connectedness in the nineteenth century to justify intervening on behalf of fellow Christians in the Ottoman Empire, while at the same time committing pogroms in their metropoles and genocides in their colonies. In the twentieth century, the Nazis appealed to ties with German minorities to justify the annexation of Austria, the occupation of Czechoslovakia, and the invasion of Poland. In our own century, Russia has invoked ideas of kinship to justify its invasion of Georgia and annexation of Crimea. While the principle of connectedness can usefully guide expectations about the allocation of duties of protection, it should not be read as providing legitimation for illegitimate action.

Looking forward, we might allocate responsibility on the basis of capability. Indeed, James Pattison insists that the potential effectiveness of the agent of protection should be the primary criterion for assigning responsibility.[88] In situations requiring the resort to force, the United States will often be the most capable agent due to its military superiority. Justifying the intervention against Islamic State and the provision of assistance to civilians harmed and displaced by the terrorist group in 2014, Obama accepted this: "America, our endless blessings bestow an enduring burden. But as Americans we welcome our responsibility to lead."[89] But, given the complexities of atrocity crises, it will often be the case that protection is most capably provided by multiple states coordinating with each other and contributing various measures at various points in time. Furthermore, such multilateral burden sharing is also required by considerations of fairness, as Obama and his successor, President Donald Trump, repeatedly emphasized.[90]

Sometimes a state will have heightened capability to protect due to its social ties to either the perpetrators or victims of atrocities. Considerations of shared history, affinity, and kinship can again be relevant here. In some instances, this will be a particularly clear means of allocating responsibility. We see in chapter 4 that the International Court of Justice found Serbia guilty of failing to discharge a duty to exert its unique influence over Bosnian Serb forces—influence produced by close political, military, and financial ties—to try to prevent the 1995 Srebrenica genocide. Sometimes considerations of geographical proximity will also be relevant. In 2003, Australian prime minister John Howard asserted that Australia had a "special responsibility" to intervene to assist Solomon Islands, which was at risk of state failure, for such a reason—although he expressed it in troublingly paternalistic terms: "The rest of the world expects Australia to shoulder a lot of the burden because this is our part of the world, this is our patch."[91] However, as noted earlier, proximity to atrocities can sometimes lead to a state being confronted with costs and risks in excess of what they can reasonably be expected to bear. The Syrian crisis has produced such an effect as millions of refugees have fled to neighboring states such as Turkey, Lebanon, and Jordan. In such situations, it falls upon other wealthy states to support receiving states so that they can provide adequate shelter and care to asylum seekers in the short term, and these wealthy states are bound also to share the duty of protection themselves, over the medium to longer term, by providing temporary protection or permanent resettlement to refugees.

In a given case, various backward- and forward-looking principles for distribution may point in a range of directions. One state may bear long-term culpability while others bear short-term culpability for the vulnerability of a population. Still others may have particular ties with the population that will create expectations for action. Those states that are best placed to provide protection may be different again, and it may be unclear whether such states are those with the greatest material capability or those with the most relevant local knowledge and influence.[92] Miller usefully recommends that we take a "pluralist" approach when distributing responsibilities: "We should simply look to see which principle or principles apply in a particular case, and if we find that more than one applies, we should weigh their respective strengths."[93] But, as we see in a moment, even this approach is insufficient insofar as it neglects to account for the fact that states will be confronted with multiple threatened or actual atrocity crises beyond their borders at any one time. It risks, for example, unjustly overburdening one powerful state by allocating to it demanding protection responsibilities for multiple crises at once. Rather than clear rules for distribution, therefore, these principles merely provide guidance for the exercise of practical judgment among states with respect to individual cases as they coordinate and cooperate to respond to multiple cases of threatened or actual atrocities.

We should also acknowledge the potential injustice involved in invoking the material capabilities of states as grounds for distributing responsibility. As Miller notes, the capability principle "neglects to ask how variations in capacity have arisen."[94] Distribution on grounds of material capability imposes unfair burdens on those who have diligently developed capacities for human protection and creates disincentives for others to do the same. Vattel usefully suggests that, if states have responsibilities for the care of outsiders, then they are bound not merely to make use of their existing capacities, but also to build their capacities so that they may benefit the vulnerable beyond their borders to an even greater extent.[95] As such, refraining from developing capacity to contribute to international protection efforts and choosing instead to free-ride on the efforts of others is not just selfish. It is a violation of duty. But, in the absence of institutionalized and enforceable targets for capacity building, unequal distribution of the duties of protection is likely to continue. Some states will refuse to make use of their resources to enhance their capacity to protect. Others will have significant capacity, but refuse to draw on it. This leads to questions about whether states that are already doing their fair share have a responsibility to also take up the slack produced by the inaction of others. I will briefly address this question later. But first, let us address the Kantian dilemma of who among many potential recipients of protection should a given state seek to protect at a given time.

WHO SHOULD BE PROTECTED?

As noted earlier, moral and political philosophers have tended to theorize the distribution of protection responsibilities on the assumption that the international community will be confronted with only one mass atrocity crisis at a time. In reality, there will usually be multiple crises requiring international attention as well as several further situations requiring international engagement so as to help prevent new crises from emerging. Over the course of the Syrian crisis that has rightly commanded so much international attention since 2011, for example, the international community has also needed to attend to several other atrocity crises at once, including in the Central African Republic, the Democratic Republic of the Congo, Iraq, Mali, Myanmar, South Sudan, and Sudan, as well as numerous threats of crises emerging elsewhere. But theorists have given little thought to the question of to which situation (or situations) of concern a particular state should focus its attention and direct its resources. Or, to put it another way, whom among many vulnerable people should a particular state seek to protect? States are left with a Kantian "playroom for free choice," which is barely acknowledged much less analyzed, when it comes to the question of where they should discharge their protection responsibilities. The clarification of norms and principles for determining where individual states should act is essential if the international community is to coordinate effectively to work toward optimal coverage of the plurality of threatened and actual crises that it confronts.

Certainly, some theorists have touched on this issue of determining where to act and whom to protect, drawing particular attention to the question of how states can justify intervening militarily in response to one crisis but not another. Chris Brown puts it bluntly, "How can it be *morally* acceptable for the interveners to be so selective in their approach to intervention?"[96] Mark Evans elaborates, "Why did Kosovo merit military intervention whilst Chechnya was left to the mercy of the Russians and Rwanda was abandoned to drown in the blood of one of the worst genocides since World War Two?"[97] An initial response often given is that while no state has the capacity to relieve suffering everywhere, this should not prevent it from providing relief somewhere. Indeed, failure to do so would constitute a violation of the Kantian imperfect duty. A further answer often provided is that when a state is confronted with one atrocity crisis beyond its borders that is amenable to international solution and a second crisis in which international action would be excessively costly or would risk exacerbating suffering, the state should act in the former but not the latter. This is the answer commonly given to the question of why Kosovo but not Chechnya, for example.[98] But theorists tend to neglect to answer the question of how a state should choose from among a plurality of situations in which it can make a positive contribution to the protection of vulnerable people. Brown suggests three principles that ought to guide decision making: the seriousness of the crisis, the likelihood that international intervention can improve the situation, and the material self-interests at stake. But he ultimately deploys these principles to explain how a state should decide whether to respond to a single crisis rather than how a state should decide from among multiple crises.[99] Evans, having posed the Kantian question of how a state should select from a plurality of crises, actually proceeds to offer an answer to the Vattelian question of which among many states should act in a single crisis.[100]

The only focused treatment of principles for determining when and where a state should act that I know of is that offered by Lea Brilmayer across a few pages of a 1995 article titled "What's the Matter with Selective Intervention?" Brilmayer spells out three principles: act in response to the most urgent need; act where you have the resources to make a difference; and act where it is clear what needs to be done and where there is confidence that action will not make matters worse.[101] This is useful, but more needs to be said. In particular, we need to think through how such principles should be ordered, and we also need to take into account the fact that the question of whom to protect confronts not just a single state, but many states at once.

I here propose five principles that can fruitfully guide individual states in deciding where to discharge their portion of the shared responsibility to protect and that can, in turn, inform coordination and cooperation among the collectivity of states so that optimal coverage can be provided across numerous threatened and actual atrocity crises, insofar as is possible. Some of these principles mirror those discussed earlier when considering who is best placed to respond to a single situation. Others, however, are distinct and are aimed at prompting states to consider not only what they ought to contribute to the most prominent crises, but also where else they might act to ensure more comprehensive protection of those at risk of atrocities around the world. The five principles are intentionally ordered, not to indicate their relative weight—though I make some observations about that along the way—but to suggest the sequence in which they should be considered in the pursuit of optimally fair and effective coverage.

First: Culpability. The parallels with earlier reasoning about culpability are obvious. Should a state be confronted with a plurality of situations that it might address beyond its borders, but be particularly culpable for the instability and suffering experienced in one of those situations, it has a special responsibility to work to provide redress in that situation, insofar as is appropriate. The culpability of the members of the 2003 Coalition of the

Willing for leaving Iraq's civilians vulnerable to the predations of Islamic State is again an obvious recent example. And the culpability of past colonial "masters" for the fragility of their former colonies is a widely accepted longer term example. Put plainly, states are especially bound to fix messes to which they have contributed. Again, it may not always be appropriate for culpable states to deploy personnel or to impose themselves on a population in other ways for purposes of protection. But there will usually be a range of less intrusive means of contributing to international protection efforts that culpable states can and therefore should pursue.

Second: Need. Echoing Brown and Brilmayer, I suggest that it makes intuitive sense for states to give some priority to the protection of those beyond their borders who are in greatest and most urgent need. However, we should not make too much of this. After all, taken on its own, this principle would direct all states to attend only to the worst crisis found at a given time. Certainly, when particularly horrific crises break out, such as in Rwanda (1994), Darfur (2003–5), or Syria (since 2011), all states have a contribution to make, be it as little as applying diplomatic pressure or responsibly targeted sanctions. But the enormous collective capacity of the international community is such that the law of diminishing returns will quickly set in if all states are focused solely on contributing what they can to the alleviation of a single crisis. More effective use of this collective capacity would see states coordinating with each other to address a plurality of threatened and existing crises at one time.

Third: Effectiveness. As part of the process of effective international coordination, states should give some priority to deploying their resources where they can be individually most effective. This principle will sometimes direct a state to give substantial attention to the worst crisis, but not always. It requires that the state focuses not on where the needs are greatest, but where it can make the greatest contributions, due to its material capability and social influence. Considerations of geographical proximity and ties of history and kinship will be relevant here. So too will considerations of where the state is already engaged and where it already has experience, expertise, and the trust of relevant parties. A useful, although imperfect, example of the application of this principle is US president George H. W. Bush's decision to undertake military intervention to protect vulnerable civilians in Somalia rather than Bosnia in 1992. While the story of this decision is complex, one key part of the narrative is the belief within the Bush administration that the United States could more effectively relieve suffering, and with lower risks and costs, in Somalia than in Bosnia. As acting US secretary of state Lawrence Eagleburger explained, "The fact of the matter is that a thousand people are starving to death [in Somalia] every day, that this is not going to get better if we don't do something about it, and it is in an area where we can, in fact, affect events. There are other parts of the world where things are equally tragic, but where the cost of trying to change things would be monumental—in my view, Bosnia is one of those."[102] The principle of effectiveness finds parallels in the effective altruism movement and related arguments offered by philosophers such as Peter Singer and Thomas Pogge for prioritizing cost-effectiveness in the work of humanitarian international nongovernmental organizations.[103] These arguments have been criticized by some for being inattentive to distortions that can arise from attempts to measure the consequences of international action and for leaving insufficient room for practical judgment.[104] An additional concern is that the effectiveness principle risks the neglect of vulnerable people who are the victims of particularly complex and intractable crises. This is something that we need not accept given the multiplicity of states with capacity to contribute to a range of protection efforts, and this leads to the fourth principle.

Fourth: Optimal Coverage. Thomas Aquinas advised that "since it is not possible for one individual to relieve the needs of all, we are not bound to relieve all who are in need, but only those who could not be succored if we did not succor them." Indeed, he claimed, "we sin mortally if we omit to give alms" to one in evident and urgent need who "is not likely to be succored otherwise."[105] This strong language points to the importance of an individual state giving particular attention to the protection of vulnerable foreigners who, if that state failed to act, would likely go unprotected. Such a principle is necessary if the international community is to approach full or at least optimal coverage in protecting against atrocities. The principle enjoins a given state to act when a situation of concern is neglected by others, perhaps because there are more prominent crises attracting their attention, or when other states make clear that they are unwilling to act, or when the state has a special capacity to act that is not shared by others. A troubling example of the application of this principle is the French intervention during the latter stages of the Rwandan genocide, undertaken when it became clear that no other state was willing to intervene, but focused on protecting the génocidaires as much as their victims.[106] A more responsible application, perhaps, was again the US-led intervention in Somalia, which

Bush Sr. justified in remarkably Thomist terms: "I understand the United States alone cannot right the world's wrongs, but we also know that some crises in the world cannot be resolved without American involvement, that American action is often necessary as a catalyst for broader involvement of the community of nations."[107] An alternative way of framing this principle of seeking optimal coverage is to say that rather than (only) acting where they can be most effective, states should (also) act where they are likely to be more effective than others. That is, if many states, including state A, can provide maximal protection in one situation, but only state A can provide even moderate protection in another situation, optimal coverage will be best advanced if state A pursues moderate protection in the latter situation and leaves it to others to provide maximal protection in the former.

Fifth: National Interest. Finally, all else being equal, states can choose to expend their material resources and risk the physical and mental well-being of their citizens in protecting the vulnerable beyond borders in situations where they have greatest security and economic interests at stake, providing that they do not allow their interests to compromise the conduct of the protection effort. Often, the principle of effectiveness will converge with national interest considerations. States will commonly have particular capacity to contribute to preventing atrocities within their region, and such contributions may particularly help secure their own peace and security. Alternatively, if a state might make an equally effective contribution to protection efforts across a range of situations, by, for example, providing humanitarian assistance or accepting refugees, it makes political sense to encourage the state to contribute where its interests are most at stake, so long as they are not bound by principles of culpability, need, or optimal coverage to act elsewhere. However, states should be careful not to allow considerations of self-interest to lead them to pursue costly and risky protection measures that will only marginally improve the plight of the vulnerable if they can be more effective elsewhere. And they certainly should not allow themselves to be led by self-interest to pursue parodies of human protection that only do more harm than good.

Overall, the effective performance of the shared responsibility to protect requires an iterative process of consultation among the collectivity of states. Answers to the Vattelian question of which state or states are best placed to act in a given situation and the Kantian question of which people or peoples a given state should best direct its attention to need to be woven together to generate coordinated responses to the range of threatened and actual atrocity crises confronted at a given time. States need to work together to ensure that burdens are shared and that optimal coverage in the protection of the vulnerable is provided, insofar as is possible. Flexibility is needed so that states can renegotiate the distribution of responsibilities as situations evolve and new crises emerge.

That, at least, is the ideal. In our nonideal world, of course, many states will choose to discharge a suboptimal selection of responsibilities, focusing for example on situations where they have most at stake rather than where they can do the most good, or worse they may refuse to take up their portion of global responsibility for human protection at all. In such instances, other states will need to renegotiate the allocation of responsibilities. Do these states have a responsibility to take up the slack left by others? It will be recalled that this question was a feature of parliamentary debates in 1896 concerning what Britain owed to persecuted Armenians given that the other European powers refused to contribute to, and indeed threatened to impede, a collective protection effort. It has likewise been a feature of international debates in recent years about what certain states owe to suffering Syrians given that other states have prevented the adoption of Security Council resolutions that might have helped alleviate the suffering, refused to contribute their fair share of humanitarian assistance, and closed their borders to asylum seekers.

Some, such as Miller, deny that when states fail to discharge their global responsibilities others have a responsibility to take up the slack. States, they argue, are required to do only their fair share.[108] But the very idea of international human protection is grounded in the idea of taking up the slack: when states struggle or fail to protect their populations, other states incur a responsibility to assist, pressure, or compel protection.[109] Sometimes, taking up the slack will simply involve contributing more to a protection effort than considerations of fairness require—deploying more troops, for example, or providing more humanitarian assistance, or resettling more refugees. At other times, however, such as when a permanent member of the Security Council vetoes certain measures—as has repeatedly occurred in the case of Syria—taking up the slack will involve pursuing alternative, perhaps more creative even if less optimal, means of protecting the vulnerable. If states have good reasons for thinking that they can make a positive contribution to the protection of the vulnerable, the inaction of others should not lead them to refrain from acting. Rather, it impels them to take up the slack, to take on risks and costs in excess of their fair share, and to cooperate with whichever other states are willing to cooperate, insofar as they can without doing an "essential injury" to themselves.

———

It is commonly suggested that what is ultimately required to ensure that duties of international human protection are effectively and consistently performed—in other words, what is required to "perfect" the imperfect responsibility to protect—is the establishment of international institutions, buttressed by international laws, capable of assigning duties, specifying their content, and binding states to their performance. Kok-Chor Tan, for example, claims that "the duty to institutionalize the duty to protect is one that falls on *all members* of the international community. . . . All members are obliged to *do what is necessary* to establish and support the cooperative arrangement required to carry out the duty to protect."[110] Such arguments for a duty to institutionalize and codify duties echo Kant's posited duty to work toward the establishment of a "cosmopolitan constitution" (although we saw in chapter 1 that Kant himself refrained from including positive duties of protection in his vision for a cosmopolitan order). Both the institutionalization and legalization of imperfect responsibilities have limitations that need to be thought through. I address some of the politics of institutionalized efforts at human protection, particularly with respect to the UN Security Council, in chapter 5. But it is worth saying a few things about institutionalization here to conclude the present discussion of ethics.

It is worth recognizing that some key aspects of the shared responsibility to protect are already institutionalized. Decision-making responsibility for the authorization of universal sanctions and embargos, UN peacekeeping operations, and nonconsensual military intervention are institutionalized in the Security Council, for example. Among other things, this places a special responsibility on members of the council to facilitate the adoption of resolutions authorizing international action necessary for the protection of the vulnerable (see chapter 4). Distribution of the financial costs of UN peacekeeping, moreover, is institutionalized via a complex formula approved by the General Assembly. The formula takes into account the economic wealth of each state while imposing additional costs on the permanent council members by virtue of their special responsibility for the maintenance of international peace and security.[111] States are, in turn, reimbursed for contributing personnel and equipment to these operations.

The desire for further institutionalization is certainly understandable, particularly at times when the international community fails to effectively cooperate and allocate responsibilities in response to an urgent need. However, we ought not to think that institutionalization can resolve all ethical questions, sidestep all political considerations, and obviate the need for practical judgment. Institutions never work perfectly. After all, the very reason why R2P needs to be articulated, distributed, and discharged is because the institution that is the sovereign state so often proves unwilling or unable to perform its fundamental obligation of protecting the safety of its own people. Onora O'Neill claims that universal rights are "easy to proclaim, but until there are effective institutions their proclamation may seem a bitter mockery to those who most need them."[112] But there is surely no more bitter mockery than that states, whose authority rests on the promise of protection, are so often the perpetrators of atrocities against their own citizens. And international institutions tend not to fare better. Recall how the European great powers passed the burden of responsibility for minority rights protection onto the League of Nations. Denied meaningful capacity for enforcement, the league proved largely unable to carry out its mandate. Consider also the failures of the Security Council to respond adequately to the Rwandan genocide (1994), to confront atrocities in Sri Lanka (2009), or to end the horrors of the Syrian civil war (2011–). The problem is not only that international institutions are sometimes insufficiently resourced to discharge their protection mandates, as was the case with the league. Rather, the institutionalization of responsibilities often has the effect of generating loopholes and encouraging buck passing, locking in inflexibility despite changing material and political realities, and inhibiting incremental reform necessary to sustain consensus and generate responsible action.[113] We only need to contemplate the failures of the Security Council to respond to repeated calls from the General Assembly to take more meaningful action on Syria over the past decade to recognize this.[114] Institutionalization of responsibilities can help produce more consistent and effective international protection. I discuss some of the fruits as well as the failures of institutionalized and routinized aspects of R2P in chapter 5. But institutionalization cannot fully overcome either the ongoing need for ethical judgment or the perversities of global politics. As for the possibilities and limits of furthering the performance of shared responsibilities by codifying them in law, that is the topic of the next chapter.

4

International Law

The obligation of states to protect their *own* populations from atrocities is well established in law via a range of international human rights conventions.[1] The idea that the collectivity of states *may* in certain circumstances hold individual states to account for the performance of this responsibility is also well established. Since the end of the Cold War, the United Nations (UN) Security Council has repeatedly, if far from consistently, condemned states, imposed sanctions, and authorized military interventions in response to the threat or perpetration of atrocities in accordance with the UN Charter.[2] Whether international law imposes upon states an *obligation* to take action to protect populations beyond their borders, however, is a very different question. Some commentators deliberating the legal basis for the shared responsibility to protect have been content merely to interrogate—and usually denigrate—the legal status of key international reports and resolutions on R2P.[3] But there is much more to be said on the matter. While the legal force of leading R2P statements may be weak at best, the International Court of Justice (ICJ) and the International Law Commission (ILC) have offered bold declarations in recent years that complement these statements and point toward a significant shift in the legal obligations of bystander states. These developments, however, raise as many questions as they answer—questions that arise from a failure to coherently address the various senses in which these extraterritorial obligations are imperfect. The argument of this chapter is thus twofold: extraterritorial obligations for the prevention of genocide and other atrocity crimes have become more firmly established in law in recent years than is commonly recognized, but such legal developments remain not only incomplete, but troublingly incoherent.

This chapter proceeds in four sections. The first, building on the discussion of historical practice in chapter 2, briefly traces the development of duties of extraterritorial protection in positive international law through the nineteenth and twentieth centuries. The second then briefly considers the legal status of key international reports and resolutions on R2P in the twenty-first century, concluding, as others have, that there is little ground for thinking that these reports and resolutions, by themselves, established new legal obligations. The third section then thoroughly examines contemporaneous legal developments, particularly the ICJ's 2007 *Genocide* judgment and the ILC's work on the obligation to cooperate to end serious breaches of peremptory norms, demonstrating that they provide considerable legal basis for the notion that there is a shared responsibility to protect—an obligation borne by all states, but also capable of allocation to particular states in particular situations. The fourth section, however, building on the discussion of the need to "perfect" the shared responsibility to protect in chapter 3, explores several limitations to the law as it presently stands: lack of clarity or even coherence around questions of enforcement and reparation, especially in contexts where multiple states are responsible for failing to prevent atrocities; the unfair burden of obligation it places on states that have diligently cultivated capacity for extraterritorial protection; and ambiguity regarding whether a state can be obligated to respond to a particular atrocity crisis given that it will often be confronted with multiple crises at once. I conclude by contemplating what we should actually hope for from law when seeking to advance the international protection of vulnerable populations.

A brief note on terminology, before proceeding. Throughout this book, I have been varying my usage of the terms "responsibility," "duty," and "obligation" in accordance with the conventions of the theorists and practitioners with whom I am engaging. It is worth signaling here that, in the field of international law, "responsibility" refers to the consequence of failing to discharge a "duty" or "obligation." A state incurs responsibility when it violates an obligation. I deploy this legal language in this chapter, except when referring explicitly to R2P.

Extraterritorial Protection Obligations
before the Twenty-First Century

While the early modern natural law theorists examined in chapter 1 offered a range of contrasting arguments about duties beyond borders, they tended to agree that these duties were a matter of internal conscience rather than mutual covenant among states. Indeed, it was the absence of legally enforceable covenants that led Immanuel Kant to dismiss these theorists as "sorry comforters."[4] Across the eighteenth and nineteenth centuries, the law of nature and nations was gradually supplanted by positive international law, which was purportedly based on the consent of states and therefore rightfully subject to enforcement. With this turn to positive law, jurists proved increasingly reluctant to articulate binding obligations of extraterritorial protection. There were some notable exceptions. Theodore Woolsey, for example, maintained in 1872 that every state "is bound to aid in maintaining justice even outside of its own sphere, if this aid can be so rendered as to violate no higher and more permanent rules of justice."[5] But such claims were typically a product of lingering natural law reasoning rather than the agreements and customs of states. We saw in chapter 2 that some British politicians alleged that provisions for minority protection in treaties contracted with the Ottoman Empire imposed binding duties on the European great powers to ensure the protection of persecuted Christians. However, as other politicians rightly observed, such claims were usually a product of moral sentiment rather than a strict reading of the treaty provisions.

With respect to the question of military intervention, numerous positivist lawyers argued that it was a *permissible* response to manifest tyranny and religious persecution in certain circumstances. But most refrained from suggesting that it was *obligatory*.[6] There were, again, some exceptions. Edward Creasy claimed in 1876, "Intervention may be justifiable, and even a duty, in certain exceptional cases . . . [such as] in behalf of a grievously oppressed people."[7] The following century, responding in 1939 to "recent barbarities perpetrated against Jews in several European states," Ellery Stowell similarly declared that whenever a state violates "that minimum of security and justice to which every individual in a civilized community is entitled, it becomes the right and the duty of other states to intervene insofar as is practicable to prevent or lessen such severities."[8] However, in an earlier, detailed study of the law of intervention, Stowell admitted that the obligation to intervene "cannot be made absolute, but must be left to the discretion of each state." He believed that this was a problem, but insisted, "It is one which cannot be remedied until the nations are sufficiently wise to perfect their law and until they are willing whenever the occasion arises to make the sacrifices necessary to ensure its enforcement."[9]

In 1948, the UN General Assembly adopted the Convention on the Prevention and Punishment of the Crime of Genocide.[10] As we saw in chapter 2, while contracting parties declared genocide to be a crime, "which they undertake to prevent and to punish" (Article I), neither a plain reading of the text nor an analysis of the *travaux préparatoires* provided grounds for thinking that it imposed upon states a duty to take action to prevent genocide beyond their borders. However, with the development of an international human rights regime over the next few decades, and particularly with the increased activism of the Security Council after the Cold War, there emerged a belief in some quarters of the international community that the convention did bind capable states to take extraterritorial action to prevent the crime.

This belief was displayed most clearly in the context of the 1994 Rwandan genocide. The United States, in particular, consciously avoided characterizing the violence in Rwanda as "genocide" out of fear that such a determination would generate an obligation to "do something." Most American officials were concerned about the *political* implications of a genocide finding. But some were motivated by reluctance to accept the *legal* obligations that they feared would "arise in connection with the use of the term."[11] Four years later, however, David Scheffer, the US ambassador for war crimes, clarified the position of the Bill Clinton administration: rather than imposing a "specific obligation," the Genocide Convention merely provided states with an "opportunity" to choose from a range of measures, from diplomatic pressure to the use of force, that they might take when confronted with genocide beyond their borders.[12] At the close of the century, William Schabas concluded, "The obligation to prevent genocide is a blank sheet awaiting the inscriptions of State practice and case law."[13]

The Legal Status of R2P Reports and Resolutions

In 2001, the International Commission on International and State Sovereignty (ICISS), established by the Canadian government the previous year, issued its landmark report, *The Responsibility to Protect*.[14] The R2P concept was born. It was endorsed in a report by a panel of experts commissioned by UN secretary-general Kofi Annan in 2004 and then again in Annan's own report proposing an agenda for UN reform in early 2005. In September that year, member states unanimously endorsed the concept at the UN World

Summit.[15] During negotiations leading up to the summit, key provisions of the ICISS report were adapted to build consensus. Several non-Western states expressed concern that formal endorsement of the responsibility to protect would facilitate self-interested and predatory interference by powerful states in the domestic affairs of the weak. Consequently, negotiators agreed to limit the scope of responsibility to four specific crimes—genocide, war crimes, ethnic cleansing, and crimes against humanity—rather than the ICISS's more elastic notions of large-scale atrocities, and to tie international enforcement to the authority of the Security Council, rather than allowing unauthorized resort to force in exceptional circumstances as the ICISS recommended.[16]

The United States, perceiving that it would often be expected to bear much of the burden of responsibility for international protection efforts, was wary of accepting any language in the summit agreement that could constrain its freedom to decide when and where to act. An early draft had accorded the international community an "obligation" to use peaceful means and, where necessary, a "shared responsibility to take collective action" to protect populations.[17] Upon reading this draft, US ambassador to the UN John Bolton issued a communiqué insisting that it be made clear that "the responsibility of the other countries in the international community is not of the same character as the responsibility of the host." He acknowledged that the international community had a responsibility to protect in a "general and moral sense," when host states fail to do so, but firmly declared, "We do not accept that either the United Nations as a whole, or the Security Council, or individual states, have an obligation to intervene under international law." The determination of how to respond to atrocities "cannot be predetermined in the abstract but should remain a decision within the purview of the Security Council," he insisted. Member states should therefore "avoid language that focuses on the obligation or responsibility of the international community and instead assert that we are prepared to take action."[18] Bolton was successful in having the language watered down. In place of an "obligation" to use peaceful means, states accepted a "responsibility" to do so, and in place of a "shared responsibility to take collective action," states merely declared that they were "prepared to take collective action . . . on a case-by-case basis."[19]

The General Assembly adopted the World Summit agreement as Resolution 60/1 on September 16, 2005. In the years since, the Security Council has repeatedly reaffirmed the R2P provisions of the agreement in thematic resolutions concerning the protection of civilians, small arms and light

weapons, the prevention of genocide, and conflict prevention, and in a resolution concerning atrocities committed in Darfur, Sudan.[20] In January 2009,
UN secretary-general Ban Ki-moon released a report, "Implementing the
Responsibility to Protect," outlining a three-pillar strategy for advancing
the R2P agenda.[21] When discussing the third pillar, which is concerned with
the need for timely and decisive collective action when states are failing
to protect their populations, the secretary-general reinserted the language
of "responsibility" that Bolton had removed from the draft summit agreement. Neither the United States nor any other state objected to this move.
Ban and his successor, António Guterres, retained this language of pillar 3
"responsibility" in all but one of the annual reports on R2P issued over the
next decade.

Whatever their political impact (which I discuss in chapter 5), none of the
various international reports and resolutions on R2P, from the ICISS report
onward, should be treated as generating binding legal obligations under the
classic sources of international law delineated in Article 38 of the statute of
the ICJ: international conventions, international custom, and general principles of law.[22] Some scholars accept that General Assembly and Security
Council resolutions and, to a lesser extent, reports by the secretary-general
and expert panels can contribute to the determination and interpretation of
law.[23] But, even so, the most authoritative international statement on R2P,
the 2005 World Summit agreement adopted by the General Assembly, is
also the one that outlines the principle of international responsibility most
tentatively. Analysis of that agreement and the negotiations that preceded
it provides no ground for concluding that states intended to establish new
legal obligations for the protection of populations beyond borders.

However, while the key documents on R2P have in no way established
legally binding obligations of extraterritorial protection in any strictly positivist sense, contemporaneous developments in international case law and
the work of the ILC do provide legal grounds upon which the shared responsibility to protect can be understood to rest, at least to some degree. It is to
these developments that we now turn.

Codifying the Shared Responsibility to Protect

On February 26, 2007, the ICJ handed down its judgment in the *Case Concerning Application of the Convention on the Prevention and Punishment of
the Crime of Genocide (Bosnia and Herzegovina v. Serbia and Montenegro)*,
hereinafter referred to as the *Genocide* judgment.[24] Let us take this judgment

as our starting point before drawing on other case law and the ILC's work to paint a picture of twenty-first-century legal developments regarding extraterritorial duties of protection. The ICJ found that while the state of Serbia was neither directly responsible for nor complicit in the perpetration of the 1995 Srebrenica genocide, Serbia *was* responsible for failing to discharge its obligation to *prevent* the genocide. In order to justify its finding, the court addressed the scope of the obligation to prevent found in Article I of the Genocide Convention. The obligation to prevent genocide, the court declared, extends beyond Article VIII's provision that states may call upon the competent organs of the United Nations to take such action as they consider appropriate. "Even if and when these organs have been called upon," the court explained, "this does not mean that the States parties to the Convention are relieved of the obligation to take such action as they can to prevent genocide from occurring."[25]

This claim that states have an obligation "to take such action as they can to prevent genocide" seems demanding. But it was one that the court repeated in a remarkable passage, paragraph 430, which further expounded the nature of the obligation. The obligation to prevent is "one of conduct and not one of result," the court explained. A state cannot be under an obligation to succeed in preventing genocide regardless of the circumstances. Rather, the obligation of states is "to employ all means reasonably available to them, so as to prevent genocide so far as possible." The court elaborated, "A State does not incur responsibility simply because the desired result is not achieved; responsibility is however incurred if the State manifestly failed to take all measures to prevent genocide which were within its power, and which might have contributed to preventing the genocide." This is a duty of "due diligence," which requires "an assessment *in concreto*."[26] The court then outlined a number of parameters for assessing whether a state has discharged its obligation in a given situation:

> The first, which varies greatly from one State to another, is clearly the capacity to influence effectively the action of persons likely to commit, or already committing, genocide. This capacity itself depends, among other things, on the geographical distance of the State concerned from the scene of the events, and on the strength of the political links, as well as links of all other kinds, between the authorities of that State and the main actors in the events. The State's capacity to influence must also be assessed by legal criteria, since it is clear that every State may only act within the limits permitted by international law; seen thus, a State's

capacity to influence may vary depending on its particular legal position vis-à-vis the situations and persons facing the danger, or the reality, of genocide.[27]

The court then returned to the idea with which it began the paragraph, declaring that it is irrelevant whether a state actually had the capacity to prevent the commission of genocide since the obligation is one of conduct rather than result. And "the more so since the possibility remains that the combined efforts of several States, each complying with its obligation to prevent, might have achieved the result—averting the commission of genocide— which the efforts of only one State were insufficient to produce."[28]

ALLOCATING THE OBLIGATION

Several ideas in paragraph 430 demand close scrutiny. First, consider that the court declared that the scope of a state's obligation to prevent genocide is determined by its "capacity to influence effectively" the genocidal actors, as far as is permissible under international law. Some legal scholars read this provision quite restrictively. One observer, noting that the court highlighted the unique influence that Serbia wielded over the Bosnian Serbs who committed the genocide, concludes that "the bar remains very high for establishing the sufficient level of influence necessary for the legal duty to prevent to arise."[29] Another suggests that the court assigned Serbia the duty to prevent genocide only because Serbia had "enabled" the genocide: "Having substantially enabled that conduct, Serbia could not lawfully stand by, even though other states with the capacity to restrain the Bosnian Serbs probably could . . . [Serbia's] causal connection to the abuse provides the normative justification for assigning it an obligation to protect."[30] But this is not what the court said.

Certainly the ICJ noted Serbia's influence over the Bosnian Serbs, due to their political, military, and financial ties, and added that Serbia was "bound by very specific obligations," due to the court's orders on provisional measures delivered in 1993, to ensure that genocide was not committed by those over whom it exercised influence.[31] But nowhere in paragraph 430 did the court indicate that the degree of influence needs to be as high as Serbia's was, and it certainly did not indicate that a state must have enabled a genocide for its obligation to kick in. Rather, as the ICJ made clear in a later paragraph, "the obligation to prevent the commission of the crime of genocide is imposed by the Genocide Convention on any State party which, in a given situation, has it in its power to contribute to restraining in any degree the commission of genocide."[32]

The obligation, then, would appear to be borne by every state, or at least every state party to the Genocide Convention (which includes 149 states, including the five permanent members of the Security Council), to a greater or lesser degree. A state with intimate ties to genocidal actors, as Serbia was in this case, will have a particularly weighty obligation to act. So too, presumably, will a great power possessing ability to persuade or compel persons to refrain from committing the crime. A less influential and weaker state may appropriately contribute less, and may merely cooperate with others where possible to facilitate the prevention of genocide, yet even it is not entirely free from the obligation to prevent under the convention.[33]

SHARING THE OBLIGATION

Next, consider that the ICJ indicated that diligent performance of the obligation may require "the combined efforts of several states" to successfully avert the commission of genocide.[34] This brings into focus the possibility that multiple states may be obligated to contribute to the prevention of genocide in a given case.[35] Such a suggestion accords with the preamble to the Genocide Convention, which asserts, "In order to liberate mankind from such an odious scourge, international cooperation is required." It also finds support in the Articles on Responsibility of States for International Wrongful Acts (ARSIWA), which the ILC adopted in 2001.[36] Article 41(1) of the ARSIWA provides, "States shall cooperate to bring to an end through lawful means any serious breach" of the peremptory norms of international law—norms that the ICJ has repeatedly confirmed include the prohibition of genocide.[37] In its commentary to Article 41(1), the ILC envisages the possibility of cooperation "organized in the framework of a competent international organization, in particular the United Nations," and also noninstitutionalized cooperation.[38] "What is called for in the face of serious breaches," the commentary suggests, "is a joint and coordinated effort by all States to counteract the effects of these breaches."[39] The commission acknowledged that this obligation to cooperate might not yet be well established in international law, and, as such, Article 41(1) "may reflect the progressive development of international law."[40] The ICJ's *Genocide* judgment, issued six years later, did not expressly establish such a duty of cooperation. But it certainly indicated that cooperation may be required if states are to diligently discharge their respective obligations to prevent genocide.

How should we conceive of the failure of a plurality of states to discharge their obligations to prevent genocide? Case law indicates that while multiple states may be responsible for collectively contributing to an internationally wrongful act, each state is "individually and independently responsible for their own conduct."[41] In the *Nauru* case (1992), for example, Australia argued that it could not be sued alone by Nauru for damage suffered under its administration given that there were two other states, New Zealand and the United Kingdom, which, with Australia, composed the administering authority. The ICJ dismissed this argument, declaring that there was no reason "why a claim brought against only one of the three States should be declared inadmissible *in limine litis* merely because that claim raises questions of the administration of the Territory, which was shared with two other States."[42] Appealing to this case for support, the ILC provides in Article 47(1) of the ARSIWA, "Where several States are responsible for the same internationally wrongful act, the responsibility of each State may be invoked in relation to that act." The commentary explains, "Where there is a plurality of responsible States in respect of the same wrongful act . . . each State is separately responsible for the conduct attributable to it, and that responsibility is not diminished or reduced by the fact that one or more other States are also responsible for the same act."[43]

In a 2011 case, the European Court of Human Rights (ECtHR) considered the responsibility of two states regarding the treatment of an asylum seeker. The court found the two states responsible for distinct acts of commission that contributed to mistreatment. Greece was responsible for mistreating the asylum seeker, and Belgium was responsible for returning the asylum seeker to Greece with knowledge of the potential for mistreatment.[44] Presumably, a plurality of states could be likewise responsible for distinct acts of *omission* that contribute to failure to prevent genocide. In its *Genocide* judgment, the ICJ made no mention of the responsibility of any particular state other than Serbia for failure to prevent the Srebrenica genocide. However, the ICJ's reference to the possibility that several states, "each complying with its obligation to prevent," may need to combine their efforts to prevent genocide, as well as the judgment of the Dutch Supreme Court in 2019 that the Dutch state is liable for 10 percent of the damages associated with the deaths of 350 of the men and boys killed in Srebrenica due to the failures of a Dutch battalion of UN peacekeepers to protect them, indicates that responsibility for failure to prevent the genocide need not be limited to Serbia alone.[45] This possibility of a plurality of responsible states seems appropriate, given that we know that in many instances a range of states will be required to pursue a range of measures to undertake and facilitate the successful prevention of genocide. However, as I explain later, it generates questions of responsibility distribution and reparation that are exceedingly difficult for the law to answer.

WHAT MEASURES DOES THE OBLIGATION REQUIRE?

The ICJ provided no indication in the *Genocide* judgment of what particular measures the obligation to prevent genocide requires. Rather, it found Serbia responsible for failing to take "any initiative to prevent what happened, or any action on its part to avert the atrocities which were committed."[46] By refraining from dictating particular measures, the ICJ grants states some discretion in determining how to discharge their obligation. Nevertheless, in invoking the notion of due diligence, the court makes clear that states do not have complete discretion to choose how they will act. As the ICJ declared, states must "employ all means reasonably available to them."[47] This notion of "all means reasonably available" is instructive. It rightly acknowledges that a state cannot be bound to discharge duties toward vulnerable outsiders to an extent that is unreasonably costly to itself.[48] Yet it indicates that the state should be attentive to the range of possible measures that it can pursue and be willing to do what it reasonably can to contribute to the prevention of genocide.

One commentator suggests, "The obligation never *requires* a state to use military force."[49] However, the ICJ did not provide any grounds for drawing this conclusion. Certainly, the court makes clear that the scope of obligation cannot exceed the limits of what international law permits. But in those instances where the Security Council authorizes the use of force or a host government consents to the deployment of peacekeepers, a state would seem to be under an obligation to contribute military personnel or resources if such measures are "reasonably available" to it and if there are strong grounds for thinking that this resort to arms will do good rather than harm.

WHAT ABOUT THE MEMBERS OF THE SECURITY COUNCIL?

The need for Security Council authorization of certain measures in certain circumstances, in turn, suggests that council members may bear a particular obligation to facilitate the prevention of genocide.[50] A number of commentators have suggested this in recent years, emphasizing particularly the duty of the council's permanent members not to impede the adoption of resolutions aimed at contributing to or facilitating the prevention of genocide. Louise Arbour, for example, wonders "why the exercise of a veto blocking an initiative designed to reduce the risk of, or put an end to, genocide would not constitute a violation of the vetoing States' obligations under the Genocide Convention."[51] Anne Peters suggests similarly that the exercise of a veto could "under special circumstances constitute an *abus de droit* by a permanent member."[52]

In response to such claims, Amrita Kapur and Emily Kidd White reply that the voting behaviors of states represent political decisions about the implementation of law rather than decisions that are themselves bound by law. There is no requirement for a permanent member to justify the exercise of a veto, they observe, and there are no established guidelines, much less mechanisms, to evaluate objectively the legitimacy of their exercise.[53] To suggest that the exercise of a veto may in certain circumstances be illegal, White argues, "misunderstands the political nature of the Security Council."[54] But such arguments are unpersuasive. All decisions made by states about how to respond to the threat or commission of genocide are political, regardless of whether they are made within or outside of the Security Council, but this does not mean that such decisions cannot also be bound by law. The fact that permanent members have discretion under the UN Charter as to how they exercise their veto does not mean that they cannot have also assumed obligations under other treaties, such as the Genocide Convention, that bound that discretion. Articles 58–61 of the ILC's Articles on the Responsibility of International Organizations, adopted in 2011, provide that states must not assist, direct, or coerce an international organization in the commission of an internationally wrongful act or attempt to circumvent their obligations by taking advantage of the separate legal personality of the organization. There is no obvious reason, then, why the voting behavior of a member of the Security Council, when confronted with genocide, is any less bound by law than are the actions of nonmember states who might similarly possess some capacity to influence effectively the genocidal actors.

The case law on this matter, however, is very thin. In 1993, Bosnia notified the ICJ that it intended to sue the United Kingdom for failing to prevent genocide and for complicity in genocide, on the grounds that the United Kingdom had prevented the passage of a Security Council resolution to lift an arms embargo that Bosnia claimed prevented it from defending itself against Serbian forces. When the United Kingdom pledged to increase humanitarian aid, Bosnia dropped its plan to file. Judge Lauterpacht opined at the time that Security Council Resolution 713, which originally imposed the embargo, had the effect of calling upon states to unknowingly and unwillingly support genocidal activity. He suggested that liability in this matter could attach to members of the Security Council.[55] Nevertheless, it remains that the ICJ has made no clear ruling on the obligations of states as members of the council. Moreover, by their ongoing rejection of France's proposed agreement to restrict the exercise of the veto in cases of atrocities, the United States, Russia, and China have made clear their opposition to moves to subject their actions within the council to external scrutiny.[56]

WHEN DOES THE OBLIGATION ARISE?

In its *Genocide* judgment, the ICJ invoked Article 14(3) of the ARSIWA, which provides that the obligation of a state to prevent a given event is breached the moment the event occurs. On this basis, the court declared, "a State can be held responsible for breaching the obligation to prevent genocide only if genocide was actually committed." However, it insisted, "a State's obligation to prevent, and the corresponding duty to act, arise at the instant that the State learns of, or should normally have learned of, the existence of a serious risk that genocide will be committed." From that moment onward, the state is under a duty to do what it can to deter "those suspected of preparing genocide, or reasonably suspected of harboring specific intent."[57] In other words, while the obligation to prevent genocide can be breached only when genocide actually occurs, it arises as soon as there is a known serious risk that the crime will be committed.

This provision encompasses much, though not all, of the temporal scope of the responsibilities of bystander states envisaged by R2P. It certainly includes pillar 3 responsibilities for timely and decisive responses to the perpetration of genocide. It also arguably includes pillar 2 responsibilities to try to persuade actors to refrain from initiating genocide, and perhaps also to help build capacities and to provide assistance to states under stress, at least in instances where there is knowledge of a "serious risk that genocide will be committed." However, the court's decision indicates that a state that fails to perform these pillar 2 responsibilities would be in breach of its legal obligations only if genocide is actually committed. Commentators have rightly criticized this aspect of the ICJ's judgment. Mark Gibney, for example, argues that the wrongness of a state's action should not be determined by whether or not genocide is actually carried out. Rather the wrong should be "doing nothing in the face of imminent genocide."[58] Andrea Gattini likewise asks "why it should not be possible to hold responsible a state which manifestly breached its obligation to prevent a violation of a peremptory norm of international law, even if the event was averted at the very brink owing to the intervention of third parties."[59] Moreover, the court's judgment provides no legal obligation akin to pillar 2 responsibilities to engage in day-to-day efforts to help strengthen the capacities of states and to encourage them to protect their populations in instances where a "serious risk" of genocide has not yet emerged. R2P's expansive temporality for extraterritorial protection obligations does not find support in other case law or in state practice either, and it is difficult to imagine support for its legal codification emerging in the near future.

WHAT ABOUT OTHER ATROCITY CRIMES?

The ICJ made clear in the *Genocide* judgment that it was confining itself to determining the scope of the duty to prevent in the Genocide Convention. It did not purport to establish general principles applicable to all obligations to prevent certain acts. And it certainly did not "purport to find whether . . . there is a general obligation on States to prevent the commission by other persons or entities of acts contrary to certain norms of general international law."[60] The *Genocide* judgment, therefore, does not establish an obligation to protect populations against the other atrocity crimes encompassed within R2P—war crimes, crimes against humanity, and ethnic cleansing. Nevertheless, despite refraining from ruling on such crimes, the court indicated that, in addition to the obligation to prevent genocide, states may bear other "obligations under peremptory norms, or . . . obligations which protect essential humanitarian values, and which may be owed *erga omnes*."[61] It turns out that we have good grounds for thinking that the atrocity crimes encompassed within R2P constitute breaches of peremptory norms, and their prevention may be considered obligations owed *erga omnes*.

Article 53 of the Vienna Convention on the Law of Treaties defines a peremptory norm of international law as one that is "accepted and recognized by the international community of States as a whole as a norm from which no derogation is permitted and which can be modified only by a subsequent norm of general international law having the same character."[62] The ILC suggests in the ARSIWA that peremptory norms "arise from those substantive rules of conduct that prohibit what has come to be seen as intolerable because of the threat it presents to the survival of States and their peoples and the most basic human values."[63] While the rules prohibiting war crimes, crimes against humanity, and ethnic cleansing may not be as unambiguously established as those prohibiting genocide, there is substantial evidence indicating their peremptory nature. Regarding war crimes, the ICJ declared in its *Nuclear Weapons* advisory opinion (1996) that the fundamental rules of international humanitarian law applicable in armed conflict "are to be observed by all States whether or not they have ratified the conventions that contain them, because they constitute intransgressible principles of international customary law."[64] In its *Israeli Wall* advisory opinion (2004), the court recalled that declaration and stated that these fundamental rules "incorporate obligations which are essentially of an *erga omnes* character."[65] In its commentary to the ARSIWA, the ILC includes the prohibition of crimes against humanity in a list of peremptory norms alongside the prohibitions of aggression, genocide, slavery, racial discrimination, torture, and the right of self-determination.[66] While the remaining R2P crime, ethnic cleansing, does not have a strict legal definition, "deportation or forcible transfer of population" is encompassed within the definition of crimes against humanity under the Rome Statute of the International Criminal Court (1998).[67]

A strong argument can be made that the obligation to contribute, within the bounds of international law, to ending breaches of peremptory norms falls on all states regardless of where the breaches occur. We have already seen that the ILC suggests this in Article 41(1) of the ARSIWA, which provides that states shall cooperate to bring to an end serious breaches of these norms.[68] The commission reasserts this in Conclusion 19(1) of its "draft conclusions on peremptory norms of general international law," adopted on first reading in 2019. In its commentary on these conclusions, the ILC notes that while it had expressed doubts when adopting the ARSIWA in 2001 as to whether this obligation to cooperate constituted customary international law, the obligation has since been recognized under law in the ICJ's *Israeli Wall* advisory opinion (2004) and the Inter-American Court of Human Rights' (IACtHR) judgment in the *Case of La Cantuta v. Peru* (2006), among others. The ILC adds that the obligation can be implemented in the form of collective action, undertaken through the UN (and this imposes a duty on the relevant member states to facilitate action), or other organizations such as the African Union (whose Constitutive Act provides for a right of intervention to bring to an end atrocity crimes), or noninstitutionalized cooperation that is consistent with international law, but it can also require individual states to take lawful measures to bring serious breaches of these peremptory norms to an end.[69]

If we zero in on particular atrocity crimes, we find further legal support for this shared extraterritorial obligation. Common Article 1 of the Geneva Conventions (1949), for example, binds state parties "to respect and to ensure respect for the Convention in all circumstances." While the drafters of the conventions may not have intended to oblige states to ensure that its war crimes provisions are respected by other states, this is how the duty to "ensure respect" has come to be interpreted by many legal scholars and also the International Committee of the Red Cross.[70] The ICJ endorsed this interpretation in its *Israeli Wall* advisory opinion, declaring, "Every State party to that Convention, whether or not it is a party to a specific conflict, is under an obligation to ensure that the requirements of the instruments in question are complied with," and specifying that all state parties to the fourth Geneva Convention "are under an obligation, while respecting the United Nations Charter and international law, to ensure compliance by Israel with international humanitarian law as embodied in that Convention."[71] This interpretation would seem to be further confirmed by the fact that the Additional Protocol I (1977) to the 1949 Conventions indicates that this duty to ensure respect can require that states work together when responding to war crimes: "In situations of serious violations of the Conventions or of this Protocol, the High Contracting Parties undertake to act, jointly or individually, in co-operation with the United Nations and in conformity with the United Nations Charter."[72]

There is not yet any comparable convention or case law specifically establishing an extraterritorial obligation to prevent crimes against humanity. The ILC, however, has been considering this issue for several years, and in 2019 it adopted, on second reading, a set of draft articles on prevention and punishment of crimes against humanity, recommended these draft articles to the UN General Assembly, and recommended the adoption of an international convention on the subject.[73] The draft articles replicate and expand upon the Genocide Convention's provisions for extraterritorial prevention as interpreted by the ICJ in its *Genocide* judgment. Article 3(2) declares, "Each State undertakes to prevent crimes against humanity, which are crimes under international law, whether or not committed in time of armed conflict," and Article 4 asserts, "Each State undertakes to prevent crimes against humanity, in conformity with international law, through . . . (b) cooperation with other States, relevant intergovernmental organizations, and, as appropriate, other organizations."[74] In its commentary on the draft articles, the ILC claims that the obligation to prevent crimes against humanity mirrors the obligation of due diligence borne by states with "capacity to influence" genocidal actors, described by the ICJ in the *Genocide* judgment, and the obligation to cooperate to this end.[75]

It remains to be seen whether this recommended convention on the prevention and punishment of crimes against humanity will be adopted by states. Several powerful states have expressed reservations about the ILC's framing of the obligation to prevent. China and Russia have expressed concerns that the posited obligation is too broad and too vague. Russia recommends simply stating the obligation to prevent, as per the Genocide Convention, rather than explicitly referring to extraterritorial measures and the need for cooperation among states. The United Kingdom has called for more detail on what the obligation actually requires, worrying that, if it is indeed akin to the broad duty of due diligence established in the *Genocide* judgment, this risks placing excessive burden on states, and creating disputes among states, given the "wider ranging nature" of crimes against humanity in comparison with genocide. The United States worries similarly that the obligation to prevent, as expressed in the draft articles, risks creating "an unclear array of specific requirements," which "would pose an undue burden on States in implementing the convention and could discourage States from ratifying it."[76]

Nevertheless, even in the absence of a convention on crimes against humanity, we have seen that we already have good grounds for concluding that states are legally obliged to cooperate insofar as is possible to bring to an end breaches of peremptory norms, such as the prohibition of these crimes. And while the ICJ refused to rule on the duty to prevent atrocity crimes other than genocide in the *Genocide* judgment, it seems reasonable to suggest that the parameters and requirements of the diligent discharge of the obligation to prevent crimes against humanity, and also war crimes, parallel those that the court developed with respect to genocide prevention.[77]

WHAT ABOUT OBLIGATIONS TO PROVIDE AID OR ASYLUM TO VICTIMS?

While the obligation to prevent atrocities is expansive and demanding, the obligation to assist potential and actual victims of these crimes via the provision of aid or asylum is much less well developed in law. Every state party to the 1966 International Covenant on Economic, Social, and Cultural Rights undertakes in Article 2(1) "to take steps, individually and through international assistance and cooperation, especially economic and technical, to the maximum of its available resources" in pursuit of the full realization of rights. The UN's Committee on Economic, Social, and Cultural Rights interprets this article to mean that "economically developed States parties have a special responsibility and interest to assist the poorer developing States" by providing "resources, financial and technical assistance, and . . . aid when required."[78] However, as Monica Hakimi reports, developed states have consistently resisted any suggestion that the article imposes a legal obligation to assist the vulnerable beyond their borders.[79]

Every state party to the 1951 Convention Relating to the Status of Refugees and the 1967 Protocol that augments it undertakes in Articles 31–34 of the convention to refrain from expelling refugees who enter their territories, except on grounds of national security and public order, and to facilitate their naturalization. But wealthy and powerful states have developed increasingly sophisticated legal and material means of deterring or preventing people fleeing atrocities from crossing their borders.[80] What of obligations toward victims of atrocities who remain displaced beyond one's borders? Some commentators argue that states are obliged to at least cooperate with each other to ensure that forcibly displaced people are assisted and protected. Volker Türk and Madeline Garlick, for example, suggest that such an obligation "emerges from the UN Charter, UNHCR's Statute, and subsequent relevant UNGA resolutions in conjunction with the 1951 Convention, as well as other international refugee instruments and corresponding State practice." However, they acknowledge that "a significant challenge arises in determining precisely what form and content such cooperation would take, and what States' respective contributions thereto should be."[81] And there is little reason to think that this obligation to cooperate binds any particular state to either provide financial assistance to host states or resettle refugees in their own territories. In 2018, an overwhelming majority of states voted in favor of a Global Compact on Refugees, recognizing "an urgent need for more equitable sharing of the burden and responsibility for hosting and supporting the world's refugees, while taking account of existing contributions and the differing capacities and resources among States."[82] But while states committed themselves in the compact to assist states hosting refugees, to support conditions in countries of origin for safe and dignified return, and to expand access to resettlement, they made clear that their agreement was not legally binding—and even then the United States voted against it, joined by Hungary only, insisting that the "global approach" taken in the compact "is simply not compatible with U.S. sovereignty."[83]

To summarize the state of play, judgments of the ICJ and the work of the ILC in recent years indicate that the obligation to prevent genocide is shared by every state possessing capacity to effectively influence genocidal actors, by acting either alone or in cooperation with others, including states acting in their capacity as members of the Security Council. States are charged with employing "all means reasonably available to them" to prevent genocide, an obligation that arises as soon as there is a known serious risk that genocide will be committed. Such obligations, moreover, arguably extend to the prevention of other atrocity crimes too, though the law on these crimes is less well developed. These are demanding obligations, indeed, even if they focus solely on the prevention of atrocities rather than the provision of relief or refuge to victims.

However, these momentous legal developments raise as many questions as they answer, and it remains far from clear whether these problems can or even should be subject to legal solutions. It is to these issues that we finally turn.

The Limits to Codifying Imperfect Obligations

The central limitations to contemporary efforts to codify the shared responsibility to protect in law flow from the imperfect nature of this obligation. To begin, a fundamental implication of an obligation's imperfection, as described by theorists from Samuel Pufendorf onward, is its unenforceability. We will see in a moment that, having laid out a clear judgment on Serbia's failure to prevent the Srebrenica genocide, the ICJ fumbled the issues of enforceability and reparation. The failure of the court to offer a coherent approach to enforcement in such a straightforward case of undischarged obligations as this gives little reason for confidence that more complex questions of enforcement may be answered in those many cases in which Pufendorfian, Vattelian, and Kantian senses of imperfection are more substantively in play. The remainder of this final section then lays out how these senses of imperfection reveal conceptual and practical problems that mark the developments in case law and the work of the ILC examined in this chapter: the ICJ's answer to the Vattelian question of who should act, found in its judgment that legal responsibility should be distributed among states solely on the basis of capacity, is morally problematic; and the court's answer to the Pufendorfian question of how duties should be weighed, observed in its judgment that states can be legally obliged to deploy "all measures reasonably available to them" in response to a particular atrocity crisis, risks incoherence in a world where states confront a Kantian playroom in which there are a plurality of threatened and actual crises meriting their attention at any one time.

ENFORCEMENT AND REPARATION

Some commentators bluntly declare that the responsibility to protect populations beyond borders does not constitute a legal obligation because it is not subject to enforcement. José Alvarez, for example, observes, "If there is such a thing as a responsibility to protect, the legal mind naturally assumes that a failure to exercise such responsibility is an internationally wrongful act entailing the usual panoply of potential remedies, including the legal liability of the wrongful actor and the potential for countermeasures against that actor by others." He suggests that claims that there is a legal obligation to protect in this sense are "absurdly premature."[84] Hakimi similarly suggests that the R2P concept "does not reflect a legally operative obligation to protect" since it is "essentially unenforceable and, in practice, unenforced against particular bystander states."[85] While these are valid observations, there is more to be said.

The *Genocide* judgment is again a good place to start. Recall that the ICJ found that it did not need to determine whether Serbia could have prevented the Srebrenica genocide in order to find Serbia in breach of its obligation to prevent.[86] In a later paragraph, the court insisted that the same rule did not apply with respect to the question of reparations. "Since it now has to rule on the claim for reparation," the court declared, "it must ascertain whether, and to what extent, the injury asserted by the Applicant is the consequence of wrongful conduct by the Respondent. . . . The question is whether there is a sufficiently direct and certain causal nexus between the wrongful act, the Respondent's breach of the obligation to prevent genocide, and the injury suffered by the Applicant, consisting of all damage of any type, material or moral, caused by the acts of genocide."[87]

The ICJ found that it could not conclude "with a sufficient degree of certainty that the genocide at Srebrenica would in fact have been averted if the Respondent had acted in compliance with its legal obligations." Since it could not establish a "causal nexus" between Serbia's violation of its obligation to prevent and the damage resulting from the genocide, the court found that "financial compensation is not the appropriate form of reparation for the breach."[88] Rather, the ICJ held that the form of reparation to which Bosnia was entitled was satisfaction, and the appropriate form of satisfaction was simply the court's declaration that Serbia had failed to comply with its obligation to prevent genocide.[89]

A number of commentators have rightly criticized this decision as unnecessarily restrained and logically incoherent.[90] Marko Milanović suggests that the requirement for causality with respect to reparations was "excessive."[91] He observes that the court cited no authority for its position and insists there is ample jurisprudential evidence supporting the contrary position. Both the ECtHR and the IACtHR have awarded compensation against states that failed to prevent human rights violations within their jurisdiction without requiring establishment that the violations would definitely have been prevented had the states discharged their obligations.[92] Milanović suggests that just as the scope of the obligation to prevent genocide is proportionate to the state's capacity to effectively influence the genocidal actors, so too should be the scope of reparation for failing to discharge this obligation.[93] He laments that, having interpreted the obligation to prevent genocide in a very expansive way, as an obligation of every state to do what it reasonably can, the ICJ reduced the obligation to "mere symbolism, by setting aside any truly meaningful form of reparation."[94] The court need not have been so restrained.[95]

ENFORCEMENT IN A CONTEXT OF A PLURALITY OF RESPONSIBLE STATES

However, when we consider that in most cases there will be multiple states with capacity to influence a genocidal actor, and so in the event that genocide is committed there may be multiple states responsible for failing to employ all reasonable measures available to prevent it, the issue of reparations becomes more complicated. We do not have well-developed international legal principles or formulas for distributing the costs of reparations among multiple states.[96] The principle of joint and several liability found in domestic tort law could provide some way forward.[97] Relying on this principle, a victim can recover the full amount of reparations from just one responsible actor. That actor can, in turn, seek compensation from the other responsible actors that contributed to the damage. But the international applicability of this principle is uncertain. The ICJ seemed to indicate in its judgment on Australia's preliminary objections in the *Nauru* case (1992) that joint and several liability may be internationally applicable in certain circumstances.[98] But this has not been confirmed. It is conceivable that, were joint and several liability accepted as a general principle of international law, it could be applied to some atrocity-prevention situations. When notifying the ICJ of its intention to sue the United Kingdom for preventing an arms embargo from being lifted in 1993, for example, Bosnia asserted that the United Kingdom was "jointly and severally liable for all of the harm that has been inflicted upon the People and State of Bosnia and Herzegovina because the United Kingdom is an aider and abettor to genocide under the Genocide Convention and international criminal law."[99] Bosnia, however, did not proceed with its plan to file. Moreover, even if the principle is internationally applicable and a victim is able to recover full reparations from one responsible state, we still need principles or formulas for determining how reparations should be distributed should that state seek compensation from other responsible states.

In some cases, the bulk of responsibility for failing to prevent will fall on a particular state that bears unusually substantial capacity to influence perpetrators of atrocities, such as was the case with Serbia regarding the Srebrenica genocide. However, as the ICJ acknowledged, even in this case there were other states that could have cooperated with Serbia to prevent the genocide and that could presumably be held responsible for failing to do so. And, as noted earlier, the Dutch Supreme Court has found the Dutch state liable for a portion of the damages associated with the deaths of *some* of those killed in Srebrenica, due to the failures of Dutch peacekeepers to provide protection. It is far from clear how responsibility ought to be distributed between Serbia, the Netherlands, and those many other states that could have contributed, in one way or another, and over the short or longer term, to preventing the atrocities.

Likewise, in some cases a state may bear a particularly large portion of the shared responsibility for failing to prevent because they actively impede an effective international response. They may veto a Security Council resolution that would have authorized action that could have helped end the crisis, for example. Leaving aside the difficulty of being certain in a given situation of the effectiveness of the kinds of actions that require council authorization, such as economic sanctions and military interventions, it will usually be the case that, in the absence of such authorization, there will remain a variety of other measures that other states can legally undertake to contribute to prevention efforts, such as the application of diplomatic pressure or the imposition of unilateral sanctions. Should some states fail to make use of their capacity to influence in this way, the question of how to distribute responsibility remains. Perhaps one case in which the number of potentially responsible states is more clearly limited is the Rwandan genocide. In this case, a few Western powers including the United States, the United Kingdom, and France impeded an effective international response by intentionally misrepresenting the crisis and failing to share with other states their knowledge of its genocidal nature.[100] Other states cannot be held responsible for failing to contribute to the prevention of atrocities that they did not know were occurring. Even in this case, however, should these few Western powers be found liable for failing to prevent the genocide, the question of how to distribute responsibility among them would still need to be answered.

In short, the extraterritorial prevention of atrocities is a complex task that in most instances requires the contribution of a plurality of states with a range of capacities, coordinating with each other to implement a range of measures at various stages of the crisis. As Peters observes, the obligations of bystander states in a given case "might be parallel, joint, or staggered."[101] In most instances, therefore, it will be difficult to point to or even to conceive of principles or formulas for distributing responsibility that could be considered legally binding. In the absence of such principles or formulas, the law of reparations remains not only underdeveloped but incoherent.

QUESTIONING THE NORMATIVE GROUNDS FOR DISTRIBUTION

Even if we put these reparation issues to one side, it is difficult to conceive how the questions of which states in particular should act in a given case, and how much they should contribute, can be given generalizable and legally binding answers that are normatively defensible. We have seen that the ICJ proposed an answer in the *Genocide* case: the scope of each state's obligation is determined by its "capacity to influence effectively" the genocidal actors without breaching international law. However, this answer, while relatively straightforward, is ethically troubling for two reasons. Both were outlined in chapter 3.

First, grounding the distribution of obligation in the capacities of states imposes an unfair burden on those that have diligently cultivated capacity for extraterritorial protection—or, as in the case of Dutch peacekeepers in Srebrenica, those who have willingly put themselves in a position where they are better placed to prevent atrocities—and creates disincentives for others to do the same, thus amplifying an already existing problem of free-riding.[102] Second, it neglects to account for other important ethical principles that should inform the distribution of obligation. Most importantly, it ignores the possibility that particular states may bear a particular obligation to respond to a particular crisis on the grounds that, while they may not be legally liable for *causing* the atrocities, they are culpable for contributing to the establishment of conditions that left people vulnerable to the perpetration of such crimes. This may take the form of long-term culpability, such as that of a former colonial power, or short-term culpability, such as that of those who invaded Iraq in 2003 and contributed to the vulnerability of Iraqi citizens to Islamic State's genocidal plans, or even the systemic culpability of wealthy and powerful states that have developed and benefited from global practices of economic exploitation and climate destruction that heighten the risk of atrocity crises in poorer and weaker states. Surely considerations of capacity need to be weighed against considerations of culpability when distributing the obligation to prevent atrocities among states in any given instance. Indeed, we saw in chapter 3 that states can and indeed often already do weigh their obligations in this way when deliberating who should contribute what in response to a particular crisis. However, it is highly doubtful whether such principles of distribution could be made subject to legally enforceable formulas that would command widespread support.

CONCEIVING OBLIGATIONS IN KANT'S PLAYROOM

A further obstacle confronting the establishment in law of extraterritorial obligations for the prevention of atrocities is that states are rightly understood as bearing such obligations in what Kant described as a "playroom for free choice." In every instance where a state has an opportunity to contribute to an international effort to prevent atrocities, that state must weigh what they owe to the potential victims of those crimes against not only what they owe their own citizens, but also what they owe other people at risk of atrocities or other forms of suffering elsewhere in the world. It is not enough to say that a state ought to take "all measures . . . within its power," as the ICJ put it in the *Genocide* case. That speaks to the Pufendorfian sense of imperfection (how should extraterritorial duties be weighed against domestic duties?), but it leaves the Kantian sense of imperfection (which extraterritorial crisis?) unaddressed. And as the comments by the United States and the United Kingdom on the ILC's draft articles on prevention and punishment of crimes against humanity reveal, powerful states with substantial capacity to contribute to extraterritorial protection efforts are already uncomfortable with the demands that the ICJ's language would seem to impose upon them.

A state will commonly be confronted at any one time with a plurality of threatened and actual atrocity crises beyond its borders that require international engagement, in addition to an enduring need to care for the well-being of its own people. Certainly, we have in hand a range of principles that can fruitfully guide states in ordering and weighing competing duties and deciding where in particular to discharge their portion of the shared responsibility to protect. I expounded such principles in chapter 3 in the hope that this can inform coordination and cooperation among the collectivity of states. But, as I emphasized, this process of ordering and weighing where to risk blood and expend treasure is an imperfect art that, even with guiding principles in hand, requires the careful exercise of practical judgment. It is hard to conceive how such judgment could be made subject to law.

Certainly, in some instances a state will have a particularly clear opportunity to contribute to the prevention of atrocities at little risk or cost to itself and in a manner that does not reduce its capacity to also contribute to an international response to other crises. Serbia had such an opportunity with respect to the Srebrenica genocide due to the unique influence that it wielded over the Bosnian Serb genocidal actors. It is good that the ICJ judged Serbia responsible for failing to discharge its obligation to prevent in that instance. In other instances, a member of the Security Council may be understood to have a clear obligation to refrain from blocking a resolution aimed at averting atrocities, again at minimal risk or cost to itself. However, it is difficult to imagine how international law might be coherently constructed such that a state can be legally obligated to undertake even marginally risky or costly measures—much less "all measures . . . within its power"—to prevent a particular instance of atrocities given that the state will tend to be confronted with multiple international crises and vulnerabilities to which it could justifiably direct its attention and resources. The development of such law would require far greater institutionalization of the distribution of global obligations than we have at present, such that the obligations of each state, both overall and in response to particular situations of concern, are clearly agreed upon and delineated. There exists little appetite among states for the development of such institutions.

———

We are left asking, therefore, what should we hope for from international law when seeking to encourage states to discharge their shared responsibility to protect? It is certainly important that negative duties to refrain from inciting or perpetrating atrocities continue to be codified in law and enforced where possible. We have good reasons for thinking that such laws have a positive— even if highly variable—influence on how states treat their people.[103] There is also value in having laws requiring positive action from states in situations where they have a particularly unique opportunity to contribute to international protection efforts at minimal risk or cost to themselves. The ICJ's judgment that Serbia failed in its duty in Srebrenica is a good example of the application of such laws. It would be good to see such laws developed further. We might hope, for example, for the codification of obligations of Security Council members to facilitate the passage of resolutions authorizing states to undertake demonstrably necessary measures for extraterritorial protection. However, absent further institutionalization of global duties, it is hard to conceive how the demanding obligations suggested in the judgments of the ICJ and the work of the ILC could be coherently applied to atrocity crises requiring risky and costly action from states in any but the most unique situations, much less how these laws could be further developed to require states to respond to the multiple atrocity crises that confront the international community at a given time.

I noted at the end of chapter 3 that institutionalization of duties risks generating loopholes and perverse incentives. The same is true of legalization. Scholarship on social and legal norms reveals the dangers of inscribing moral principles in strict legal terms.[104] Legalization can impede flexibility in application and hamper adaptability to change. It can lead states to perceive compliance as an unwanted burden rather than an opportunity to do good, and it can provide reluctant states with technical justifications for violation. Each of these can ultimately weaken rather than strengthen a norm. Christian Tams suggests that efforts to develop duties for the enforcement of international law are "laudatory and no doubt well-meaning, but are likely to widen further the gap between the theory and reality (or 'is' and 'ought') of law enforcement, and are probably counter-productive."[105] Peters likewise warns against spelling out the many and varied consequences of R2P in strict legal terms: "The prospects of endless chains of legal obligations might in the final analysis turn out to be counter-productive for alleviating the plight of endangered populations."[106] In short, further codification of the distribution of demanding duties of extraterritorial protection may have the unintended effect of lessening the commitment of states to the shared responsibility to protect.

What then should we hope for? After all, it is commonly assumed that some form of legalization is the optimal endpoint for a social norm. As Kenneth Abbott and Duncan Snidal rightly observe, legalization can generate a distinctive "compliance pull" on states given that it "largely disqualifies arguments based solely on interests and preferences" and instead requires "justification and persuasion in terms of applicable rules and pertinent facts."[107] And as Beth Simmons notes, legalization signals "a seriousness of intent that is difficult to replicate in other ways."[108] Constructivist international relations scholars have repeatedly shown, however, that norms need not be codified in law to influence the behavior of states. *Social* norms can have their own "compliance pull," so long as they are sufficiently determinant and coherent and accepted as legitimate.[109] And little is to be gained in codifying laws that do not command the assent of states and that facilitate or, worse, encourage norm violation. The way forward in generating positive action from states confronted with the threat or perpetration of atrocities beyond their borders, in all but the most clear-cut cases of direct influence, lies not in the further development of law but in the clarification, diffusion, and internalization of social norms for the distribution and performance of duties. It is to such political dimensions of the shared responsibility to protect that the remainder of the book turns.

5

International Politics

Since it first emerged in the early 2000s, commentators have found cause to deny the impact of the Responsibility to Protect (R2P). For some, international human protection norms simply cannot have a meaningful impact since state behavior is always driven by self-interest. Rajan Menon, whose work I described in the book's introduction, claims, "The prevailing pattern has been, and will remain, the following: States contemplating intervention to stop atrocities will weigh their interests—prospective gains, risks, and costs, as best these can be assayed—against their ethical obligations to noncitizens. Sometimes interests and ethics may complement each other. When they don't, the former prevail."[1] Such assessments take as given that states always define their interests in terms of strategic and economic gains and that the best we can hope for is the occasional coincidence of these material interests with ethical norms. But scholars of international relations have repeatedly explained that ethical norms can themselves shape how states conceive their interests. Indeed, they have detailed numerous historical examples of states reconstituting their interests in accordance with R2P-related norms of foreign aid,[2] humanitarian assistance,[3] refugee protection,[4] and humanitarian intervention.[5] The blunt claim that states act only in accordance with their interests obscures more than it reveals.

Other skeptics refrain from rejecting the possibility of normative change in general, but nevertheless insist that the R2P norm in particular has failed to alter the behavior of states. One suggests, "R2P has diminished from a high hope into an interesting collection of words lying on the table."[6] Another describes R2P as "sound and fury signifying nothing."[7] Some deny that R2P was "a major influencing factor" in the decisions of states to intervene in Libya in 2011.[8] Others conclude that the international community's failure to resolve the Syrian crisis in the years since indicates that R2P "is about to expire and its death is not avertable."[9] Such claims typically stem from a problematic understanding of how norms matter and how their impact should be interpreted. More careful analysis, I suggest, reveals that the R2P norm has in fact had a very real and readily observable impact on the behavior of states, an impact that can be detected not only in instances of compliance, but sometimes even more clearly in examples of violation.

But other commentators push too far in the other direction, exaggerating both the novelty and influence of R2P. Gareth Evans, who served as cochair of the International Commission on Intervention and State Sovereignty (ICISS), which produced the *Responsibility to Protect* report in 2001, describes R2P as "a brand new international norm of really quite fundamental ethical importance and novelty" and predicts that R2P "will over time make an ever more important contribution to making the world a safer and saner place."[10] Excessive claims of novelty ignore the long history of the construction and performance of shared protection responsibilities explored in chapter 2. They also misrepresent the international protection debates that raged through the 1990s, as I explain in a moment. And overly optimistic readings of the impact of R2P are belied by myriad examples in which states continue to fail to diligently discharge their shared protection responsibilities, examples that have been multiplying in recent years amid rising domestic populisms and international antagonisms, and they risk giving false hope to vulnerable populations crying out for assistance and relief.

This chapter tells a more balanced story of the international politics of human protection in the era of R2P. The multiple senses of imperfection that mark the responsibility to protect render it susceptible to a greater degree of uncertainty and contestation regarding what it requires of states in a given situation than tends to be the case with perfect-duty norms such as those prohibiting slave trading or the use of land mines. Violation of the imperfect duty that is R2P thus tends to be easier to deny or excuse. Nevertheless, imperfect-duty norms can still have a profound impact on state behavior. When such norms are widely embraced and institutionalized in international fora, such as R2P has been within the United Nations (UN) since 2005, the scope for contestation can narrow to the extent that recalcitrant states can be pressured to comply, or at least be forced to accept social costs that attend inexcusable violation. More powerfully, states can internalize the norm such that they discern an interest in doing what they can to discharge the duty, rather than seek opportunities for contestation and evasion. We find examples of each of these dynamics in the R2P era.

We see in the first half of the chapter that a felt imperative to protect populations from atrocities not only was pivotal to the decision to intervene in Libya, but also stalked the lamentable international response to the Syrian crisis from 2011 onward, compelling states to justify what they had done, excuse their failure to do more, and blame others for preventing them from discharging their responsibility to protect. But, of course, as chapter 2 demonstrated, states have felt a need to either comply with protection norms or defend violations of such norms on many occasions in the past. What is unique about the R2P era, and especially the period between the beginning of the Arab Spring and the end of US president Barack Obama's second term, I argue in the second half of the chapter, is that international engagement with atrocities became almost a matter of routine, such that the international community recognized a need to respond to and try to help resolve not only the most prominent crises, but also those many other situations of concern that neither attracted extensive media attention nor substantially engaged the material interests of states. However, even in this period, the international community continued to fall short in crucial ways. And things have gotten worse more recently as some Western states that have for decades provided the impetus for many international protection projects turn their backs on global responsibilities and embrace resurgent populist nationalisms, as some non-Western states with a distaste for human protection projects that seem to echo past Western imperialist practices assume more dominant positions in global affairs, and as the exposure of great-power hypocrisies and the growth of post-truth politics undermine the potential for the imperfect duty that is R2P to shape and shove states to better care for vulnerable strangers. In recent years, then, both the possibilities and the fragilities of this imperfect duty have been plainly exposed. Before examining the politics of this era, however, let us briefly address the pervasive claim about the novelty of the idea of R2P.

Questioning the Novelty of R2P

In their landmark 2001 report, members of the ICISS made much of their intention to change the terms of international debate away from the "traditional language" of the "right to intervene" and toward the "responsibility to protect." The traditional language, they claimed, "focuses attention on the claims, rights, and prerogatives of the potentially intervening states." The proposed change in terminology "helps to shift the focus of discussion where it belongs—on the requirements of those who need or seek assistance."[11] Evans suggests that he and the other commissioners were consciously "inventing a new way of talking about 'humanitarian intervention.'"[12] This effort to focus on the needs of the vulnerable and the responsibilities of states to ensure their protection was and remains laudable, and it is undeniable that the specific language of "responsibility to protect" with its memorable acronym, R2P, has assumed particular prominence in international debate in the years since. But the notion that the international community has a responsibility to protect the vulnerable was hardly new.

We saw in chapter 2 that domestic and international debates about how states ought to respond to grave suffering beyond borders have, for centuries, been waged in languages of duties, obligations, and responsibilities. Since as early as the Peace of Westphalia, states have constructed and manipulated, distributed and contested, discharged and evaded a range of responsibilities for the protection of the vulnerable. They may have disregarded or denied such responsibilities for much of the Cold War, but by the 1980s the notion of international responsibility for the relief and rescue of those in need was resurgent. The UN General Assembly routinely affirmed its "responsibility to promote and encourage respect for human rights and fundamental freedoms for all," and French president François Mitterrand spoke plainly of a duty to interfere (*devoir d'ingérence*) to ensure the provision of humanitarian assistance to vulnerable people in the absence of governmental consent.

Appeals to international responsibilities for the protection of vulnerable populations were commonplace over the next decade. Through the 1990s, members of the UN Security Council proved increasingly willing to accept that the council's responsibility for the maintenance of international peace and security, found in Article 24(1) of the UN Charter, included responsibility for the assistance and protection of populations in crisis. In 1991, contemplating Iraqi president Saddam Hussein's treatment of Kurdish civilians in the aftermath of the Gulf War, the Soviet representative declared, "It is the duty of the Security Council and of the world community as a whole to put an end to the conditions that are forcing hundreds of thousands of peaceful inhabitants to leave their homeland and seek refuge in neighboring countries."[13] The following year, in a debate on the council's responsibilities, British prime minister John Major claimed that the plight of the Kurds "still remains our responsibility," and Russian president Boris Yeltsin claimed that the council "is called upon to underscore the civilized world's collective responsibility for the protection of human rights and freedoms."[14] Deliberating the humanitarian crisis in Somalia later that year, the Russian representative stressed "the international community's obligations to put an end to the human tragedy in that country."[15] In 1994, defending its belated and controversial intervention in Rwanda, the French representative pointed to France's "moral duty to act without delay to stop the genocide and provide immediate assistance to the threatened populations."[16] The following year, another French representative spoke of "the duty—and the honor—of the Council to react swiftly" to the Srebrenica genocide.[17]

In 1999, justifying the military intervention in Kosovo, a spokesperson for the European Union declared that its member states were "under a moral obligation" to ensure an end to the violence and the return of displaced persons to their homes. US president Bill Clinton likewise invoked a "moral imperative" to act, claiming that "America has a responsibility to stand with our allies when they are trying to save innocent lives and preserve peace, freedom and stability in Europe."[18] Speaking to the General Assembly later that year, Clinton declared that the prevention of mass atrocities requires "shared responsibility, like the one West African nations accepted when they acted to restore peace in Sierra Leone; the one 19 democracies in the North Atlantic Treaty Organization (NATO) embraced to stop ethnic cleansing in Bosnia and Kosovo; the one Asian and Pacific nations have now assumed in East Timor."[19]

This idea of shared responsibility for protection, moreover, was not mere words. While it entailed an "imperfect" duty, domestic and international expectations that certain powerful states would respond to certain atrocity crises beyond their borders carried real weight. Political leaders were at times moved, if not by their own moral sensibilities then by local and global pressures, to respond to the needs of vulnerable foreigners, despite an absence of material interests compelling them to do so. The US-led intervention in Somalia is a particularly clear example of this.[20] At other times, political leaders felt the need to manage the framing of crises or to excuse or shift blame for inaction in order to avoid paying a political cost for refusing to protect vulnerable foreigners. I noted in chapter 4 that the Clinton administration avoided describing the violence in Rwanda as "genocide" due to fear that this would generate an obligation to "do something." The concern was political as often as legal. Indeed, an internal State Department memo concluded that a finding that genocide had occurred in Rwanda "would not have any particular legal consequences" for the United States, but nevertheless warned that such a finding "could increase pressure for USG

[US government] activism in response to the crisis."[21] Efforts to minimize pressure to act, as well as the apologies later offered by Clinton and others for inaction, point to the reality of a felt imperative to protect strangers.

Certainly, the 1990s witnessed heated debates about the limits of what states and the Security Council could rightfully do in discharging their responsibilities—not unlike the logic of nineteenth-century debates about the limits of what Britain could rightfully do to discharge its responsibility to abolish the Atlantic slave trade. As early as 1991, perceiving that disagreement over the permissibility of nonconsensual intervention could undermine the enthusiasm emerging among states for discharging global responsibilities in the aftermath of the Cold War, UN secretary-general Javier Pérez de Cuéllar cautioned that the focus of attention should be on "not the right of intervention but the collective obligation of States to bring relief and redress in human rights emergencies."[22] But debates about rights of interference and intervention in sovereign affairs continued through the decade, famously coming to a head with NATO's illegal intervention in Kosovo. Russia condemned NATO's "illegal use of force," which "directly undermines the fundamental bases of the entire modern system of international relations," China warned of a return to "the rule of hegemonism" and "gunboat diplomacy" that would "wreak havoc" on international peace and security, and the Group of 77 explicitly rejected "the so-called 'right' of humanitarian intervention, which has no legal basis in the United Nations Charter or in the general principles of international law."[23] Nevertheless, those on the other side of these debates tended to still speak in terms of the need to discharge their responsibility, rather than the prerogative to exercise their right, to protect the vulnerable. This should not surprise us. It would be rather odd if we were to find that states arguing in favor of intervening in northern Iraq, Somalia, Bosnia, Kosovo, and elsewhere in the 1990s did so merely on the grounds that they had a *right* to do so, rather than that they were bound by a *responsibility* to assist and rescue vulnerable people.

The same pattern of debate can be found in the R2P era. States seeking to justify extraterritorial action aimed at preventing or stopping atrocities tend to do so in the language of responsibility. Where such action is perceived as threatening norms of sovereignty and nonintervention, those that oppose it tend to do so in the language of rights, demanding full respect for a state's "sovereignty, independence, and territorial integrity," insisting on the "non-acceptability of foreign intervention," and resisting the legitimacy of "violent regime change," as Russia and China have repeatedly done in debates about the Syrian crisis.[24]

So what, if anything, has changed since the emergence of R2P, other than the fact that states have given their assent to the particular formulation of international responsibilities negotiated at the 2005 World Summit? After all, while the collective endorsement of R2P in 2005 is historically significant, and while the Security Council has repeatedly reaffirmed this endorsement in the years since, affirmation of a principle does not necessarily translate into action. To appreciate what has changed and what has stayed the same, let us first look at the two most prominent cases of the R2P era, Libya and Syria, before considering some broader dynamics of recent years.

Libya

We considered the ethics of the 2011 Libyan intervention in chapter 3. Here we consider its politics with respect to both the decision to intervene and the intervention's subsequent controversies and failures. For all the talk of humanitarian intervention in the 1990s, each actual instance of military intervention either lacked council authorization (e.g., Kosovo) or was authorized with the consent of the host government (e.g., Resolution 929 on Rwanda), or at least the *de jure* authorities (e.g., Resolution 940 on Haiti), or in the absence of a functioning governmental authority that could provide consent (e.g., Resolution 794 on Somalia). Resolution 1973, adopted on March 17, 2011, in response to Muammar Gaddafi's repeated threats of atrocities, was the first time that the council had authorized the use of force against a functioning sovereign state, without its consent, for the purpose of protecting civilians. This was a historic decision. As noted earlier, numerous commentators deny that R2P played a significant role in the decision to intervene in Libya. But such skepticism is misplaced. The impact of a felt imperative to protect on the decision to intervene can be clearly seen both at the domestic level, in the deliberations of the Obama administration, and also at the international level, in the deliberations of the Security Council. A brief examination of this case helps give a sense of how norms—even those that compose imperfect duties—can profoundly impact state behavior.

Some international relations theory can assist us. Constructivist scholars usefully observe that norms can have two types of effects on the behavior of states: "regulative" effects that constrain or encourage states to act in certain ways in spite of their prior interests and "constitutive" effects that lead states to act in certain ways by influencing the very constitution or production of their identities and interests.[25] Norms have regulative effects as states are "socialized" to adhere to them for instrumental reasons, acting in particular ways due to pressures for legitimation, conformity, and esteem, without necessarily accepting the validity of the norms. When states resist pressures to comply with a norm, they may be subject to practices of naming and shaming that can lead them to alter their approach in the future. When they make tactical concessions and adapt their arguments to alleviate pressures to comply, they implicitly accept that the norm has some social validity. They can then become "entrapped" by their own rhetoric such that resistance becomes more difficult in the future.[26] Norms can have constitutive effects as states "internalize" norms through processes of domestic "institutionalization" and "habitualization" and thus adhere to them routinely because "it is the normal thing to do."[27] In this way, norms no longer regulate the pursuit of interests. Instead, they play a part in the constitution of those interests.[28]

Though I did not refer to them as such, we saw both regulative and constitutive effects of protection norms in play in chapter 2. Recall, for example, Britain's decision to protect its reputation by agreeing to French plans for great power intervention to protect Maronites in Syria in 1860–61 (regulative effect) as well as Britain's construction of a "Protestant interest," leading it to pursue international action to protect persecuted coreligionists in the eighteenth century (constitutive effect). In recent years, scholars have debated whether the impact of R2P stems from its use as a rallying cry for action, leading states to help protect vulnerable people beyond their borders in spite of their prior interests, or whether it serves to reshape the identities and interests of states, such that they habitually consider what can be done to protect such people.[29] In essence, they have been debating whether R2P has a regulative or constitutive effect on state behavior. Well, it turns out that R2P can and often does work in both of these ways at one time, constraining the interests of some states while constituting the interests of others. This is particularly evident in the case of Libya.

On March 15, 2011, President Obama met with his advisors to discuss the Libyan crisis. France, the United Kingdom, and Lebanon had announced plans to introduce a draft resolution to the Security Council that would authorize a no-fly zone, as the League of Arab States had requested on March 12.[30] The Pentagon suggested that Obama had two options: establish the no-fly zone or do nothing. Some advisors, including Secretary of Defense Robert Gates, cautioned against action on the grounds that core security interests of the United States were not at stake. Gates later reflected that Gaddafi "was not a threat to us anywhere. He was a threat to his own people, and that was about it."[31] However, Obama himself later recalled that he could not accept the option of not acting: "That's not who we are." But a no-fly zone was not a suitable option either: "We knew a no-fly zone would not save the people of Benghazi. . . . The no-fly zone was an expression of concern that didn't really do anything." On Obama's request, the Pentagon developed a third option: secure a Security Council resolution authorizing "all necessary measures" to protect Libyan civilians and then do what was necessary to destroy Gaddafi's forces. Obama adopted this option, and his administration quickly worked to generate sufficient international support to push Resolution 1973 through the council two days later.[32]

There were exceptional factors that made the Libyan intervention unusually feasible. Gaddafi's clear threats of atrocities, his lack of powerful allies, the explicit request of the League of Arab States for international action, and the widespread belief that the resort to force could in this instance help protect civilians combined to make the intervention a viable option.[33] But these factors do not explain why Obama chose to act rather than not act. States do not undertake military intervention just because it is feasible. After all, the intervention, while limited, was still costly. It cost the United States alone around two billion dollars, even while "leading from behind."[34] And even if the risks to the lives of intervening forces were not substantial, given the reliance on airpower rather than ground troops, the action was still politically fraught, particularly given the exhaustion of Western publics with war. Americans were polled the week before the adoption of Resolution 1973 as to whether the United States had a responsibility to do something about the fighting in Libya. While 63 percent said no, only 27 percent said yes, with 10 percent unsure. When asked whether they were in favor of the United States bombing Libyan air defenses, 77 percent said no. Only 16 percent said yes, with 7 percent unsure.[35] Given the costs and risks that attend any intervention, states do not intervene simply because the conditions make it possible. They need a reason to do so.

Given the perceived absence of core security interests and the risks and costs of action, Obama's decision to intervene is inexplicable without reference to the power of the felt obligation to protect Libyan civilians. Moreover, given the absence of substantial domestic or international pressure for a Security Council resolution authorizing not merely a no-fly zone but the use of "all necessary measures . . . to protect civilians and civilian populated areas under threat of attack," the decision would seem to indicate not merely the regulative but the constitutive effects of the R2P norm in action. (Gates suggests that while the United States did not have strategic concerns at stake in Libya, it was bound to support its allies, France and the United

Kingdom, who sought the establishment of a no-fly zone. But this cannot explain why the United States pushed for an even stronger resolution than its allies proposed.)[36] Obama had spoken of the duty to respond to atrocities on numerous occasions prior to Libya, declaring, for example, in 2009, "The international community has an obligation, even when it's inconvenient, to act when genocide is occurring."[37] By 2011, he increasingly conceived this need to act not merely in the language of America's obligation, but also in the language of its interest.

Reflecting on the March 15 White House meeting, Obama noted that the suggestion by Gates and others that the United States had no interest in intervening troubled him and he felt a need to be "calibrating our national-security interests in some new way."[38] In a speech on March 28, justifying the decision to intervene, he framed these interests in more expansive terms, claiming, "If we waited one more day, Benghazi . . . could suffer a massacre that would have reverberated across the region and stained the conscience of the world. It was not in our national interest to let that happen."[39] Five months into the intervention, Obama issued a "Presidential Study Directive on Mass Atrocities," in which he declared plainly, "Preventing mass atrocities and genocide is a core national security interest and a core moral responsibility of the United States." He directed the establishment of an interagency Atrocities Prevention Board, whose purpose was "to coordinate a whole of government approach to preventing mass atrocities and genocide."[40] The board was established in April 2012. For a time, at least, the US government was intentionally internalizing and institutionalizing R2P.[41]

If analysis of the deliberations of the Obama administration shows the constitutive impact of the R2P norm, consideration of the deliberations of Security Council members on Resolution 1973 reveals its regulative impact on other states. Having agreed to push for a resolution authorizing "all necessary measures" to protect Libyan civilians, the United States, France, the United Kingdom, and Lebanon went to work to gain the support of other states. They succeeded in pressuring reluctant states to vote in favor of or at least abstain on the resolution by warning that they would otherwise be seen as standing in the way of human protection and not acting in the interests of the Libyan people.[42] The task of acquiring support for the resolution was made easier by the fact that several regional organizations—the League of Arab States, the Gulf Cooperation Council, and the Organization of the Islamic Conference—had called for the Security Council to act in one way or another. These calls were particularly crucial in moving Russia and China to abstain rather than veto the resolution. Over the previous decade, these two permanent council members had justified refusing to authorize enforcement measures in response to crises in Darfur, Myanmar, and Zimbabwe on the grounds that it was important to respect the opinions of regional organizations that opposed such measures, since such organizations best understood the dynamics of regional crises and were best placed to know how to protect civilians and preserve regional peace and security. When regional organizations themselves called for enforcement measures to protect Libyan civilians, Russia and China found themselves rhetorically entrapped. They no longer had a plausible argument against intervention and so chose instead to abstain.[43]

The Security Council debate on Resolution 1973 proceeded on the assumption that the international community in general and the council in particular have a vital role to play in protecting civilians from atrocities. States disagreed not on whether they shared a responsibility to protect, but on how best to ensure that protection. Even the five states that abstained (Brazil, China, Germany, India, and Russia) acknowledged that the council should do what it could to protect civilians, while emphasizing pragmatic concerns about whether military intervention was the appropriate course of action.[44] Some commentators note that neither individual states nor the resolution itself explicitly invoked the notion that the international community had a "responsibility to protect" Libyan civilians. But a norm need not be enunciated to have an impact on state behavior. The felt imperative to protect clearly played an important role—if not a constitutive role for some states then at least a regulative role—in guiding ten states to vote in favor and leading the remaining five to abstain and allow the resolution to pass.

The intervention, which began on March 19 and continued for seven months, largely prevented the further commission of atrocities by government forces and eventually enabled Libyan rebels to overthrow Gaddafi. Obama celebrated that the coordinated action undertaken by members of NATO and the League of Arab States was "precisely how the international community should work, as more nations bear both the responsibility and the cost of enforcing international law."[45] Yet, as I detailed in chapter 3, after Gaddafi was defeated and killed, Libya fell into a chaotic state from which it has yet to recover. As Obama reflected toward the end of his presidency, the intervention "didn't work."[46] With Gaddafi defeated and the victorious rebels requesting that they be left to determine their future for themselves, the intervening powers failed to commit sufficiently to helping establish peace and rebuild the Libyan state and its institutions. Obama conceded, "Even as we helped the Libyan people bring an end to the reign of a tyrant, our coalition could have and should have done more to fill a vacuum left behind."[47] "Failing to plan for the day after," he lamented, was his "worst mistake" as president.[48]

The intervention was also immediately and enormously controversial, not so much because it "didn't work"—although this surely emboldened critics over time—but because of how it was conducted. Having received Security Council authorization, NATO and the League of Arab States powers proceeded to intervene as they saw fit. They repeatedly dismissed efforts of the African Union and other international actors to negotiate a ceasefire or settlement between Gaddafi and the rebels. While they had good reasons for doubting that Gaddafi would negotiate in good faith, their refusal to engage with these efforts frustrated many states.[49] As the intervention progressed, the intervening powers were increasingly criticized for blurring the line between civilian protection and regime change. The pursuit of regime change came to be widely read as a violation of the provisions of Resolution 1973. This reading went largely unchallenged and has, over time, become received wisdom. In fact, the intervening powers might have reasonably claimed that the protection of civilians from atrocities required the removal of Gaddafi's regime—as was arguably the case in the 1970s with Idi Amin in Uganda and Pol Pot in Cambodia—and thus the pursuit of regime change was consistent with their mandate to take "all necessary measures" to protect civilians. But they never bothered to make this argument and defend it against those who disagreed. Instead they maintained, awkwardly and increasingly implausibly, that while their political goals included the removal of Gaddafi, their military goal was restricted to the protection of civilians.[50] Many states were unconvinced.

In early 2012, Guatemala's representative to the UN lamented that the intervention had confirmed the worst fears of R2P's skeptics, "in the sense that invoking the protection of civilians was just a new pretext to meet darker objectives, such as intervening by force to overthrow a regime." He continued, "For some countries, the execution of resolution 1973 has been traumatic, and it must be recognized that its implementation has poisoned the environment regarding the 'responsibility to protect.'"[51] This was a fair reading of the short-term backlash against the nonconsensual-interventionist aspects of R2P. But we should not overstate the impact of Libya on the willingness of states to discharge R2P in general. We will see later that, over the next five years or so, states actually embraced and discharged their obligation to protect vulnerable populations beyond their borders more routinely than ever before—even if far from perfectly.

But what about Syria? Have not Syrians "paid the price of NATO excesses in Libya," as ICISS commissioner Ramesh Thakur claims?[52] Russia certainly made a feature of the international discontent with regime change in Libya to justify its obstructionism in Security Council deliberations on the Syrian crisis—a crisis that was rapidly worsening as the Libyan intervention was coming to an end. "The situation in Syria cannot be considered in the Council separately from the Libyan experience," Russia's representative argued in October 2011. NATO's intervention in Libya saw "a Security Council resolution turned into its opposite." Such a model of intervention "should be excluded from global practices once and for all," he said.[53] A few months later, foreign minister Sergei Lavrov declared plainly, "We would never allow the Security Council to authorize anything similar to what happened in Libya."[54] But Russia's protestations about the Libyan intervention and its use of Libya to justify its position on Syria should be treated with skepticism. After all, in May 2011, Russia had joined with the rest of the Group of Eight (G8) nations in declaring that Gaddafi had "no future in a free, democratic Libya. He must go." And yet, at the same G8 meeting, Russia was already proving intransigent on Syria, refusing to agree that the emerging crisis should be discussed by the Security Council.[55] The subsequent backlash against regime change in Libya, then, explains only so much about the international community's failure to protect Syrian civilians.[56] Much more important are the particular local, regional, and geopolitical dynamics of the horrific Syrian civil war.

Syria

Syrian civilians began demonstrating against President Bashar al-Assad's rule in March 2011. Assad responded by lifting a forty-eight-year state of emergency and promising democratic reform, but he also responded with violence. Within six months, two thousand people were killed, tens of thousands were imprisoned, protestors formed the Free Syrian Army, and the country was descending into civil war. On October 4, a draft Security Council resolution condemning human rights violations and the use of force against civilians by the Syrian government was vetoed by Russia and China.[57] Russia said it could not allow the resolution to pass given the absence of language about "the non-acceptability of foreign military intervention," which it claimed was necessary to prevent another Libya. China said it was compelled to veto given that the draft included an implicit threat of future sanctions against Syria, which violated "the principle of non-interference in the internal affairs of States."[58] By the end of 2019, Russia had vetoed fourteen draft council resolutions on Syria and had been joined by China eight times. They prevented the adoption of resolutions that would have imposed sanctions on Syrian authorities and referred the situation to the International Criminal Court—measures that they had been willing to authorize in Resolution 1970 on Libya prior to the adoption of Resolution 1973 authorizing military intervention.[59] They also stood in the way of more innocuous resolutions that would have merely condemned rights abuses and the use of chemical weapons, called for political reform, access for humanitarian agencies, and an end to violence, and renewed the mandate of the Joint Investigative Mechanism, which had been formed to determine the perpetrators of chemical weapons attacks—a mechanism that Russia itself had set up in 2015 with the United States.[60]

The civil war has raged for almost a decade. For much of this time, it has borne the marks of a proxy war, with external actors funding, training, and arming various sides and participating in military operations themselves, particularly against Islamic State, whose emergence in 2014 made a complex crisis even more intractable. The brunt of the war has been borne by civilians. More than four hundred thousand people have died. From a prewar population of twenty-two million, more than thirteen million either have fled the country as refugees or are internally displaced. Thirteen million people within Syria stand in need of humanitarian assistance. The failure of the international community to protect civilians and bring the conflict to an end has understandably led many commentators to question the relevance of R2P. One suggests, "Syria marks the death of R2P as a viable, functional concept."[61] While it may strike some as absurd to say so, and it is certainly sorry comfort to the millions of Syrians who have gone unprotected, such skepticism is again misplaced. A brief examination of this case helps give a sense of the susceptibility of imperfect duties to political contestation that facilitates violation, but also the limits to contestation when such duties are widely embraced as social norms.

To begin, it is important to calibrate expectations. Recall the observation in chapter 3 that what ought to be done to prevent or end atrocities varies from case to case. This should lead us to hesitate before equating, as some have done, the absence of a Libyan-style intervention in Syria with the death of R2P. After all, while some commentators called for the use of military force to protect the Syrian population on occasion in the first few years of the civil war,[62] most concluded that it would do more harm than good. Indeed, the available evidence suggests that even lesser measures proposed, such as the establishment of no-fly zones or safe havens, would have risked doing more harm than good.[63] And those coercive measures that states *did* take to resolve the crisis, such as funding, training, and arming factions in the conflict, (predictably) lengthened the conflict and exacerbated the atrocities, rather than improved the situation.[64] Syria has always been a more complex crisis than Libya was in 2011—in terms of local, regional, and global dynamics—and it has always been difficult to envisage how the resort to force might end the suffering. Therefore, as Jennifer Welsh, former special advisor to the UN secretary-general on R2P, rightly observes, the occurrence or otherwise of military intervention in response to each instance of atrocities should not be considered an appropriate test for the effectiveness of the R2P norm.[65] Rather, I suggest, the test is whether states *do what they can*, both individually and collectively, to protect populations from atrocities.

That said, states have clearly not *done what they can* in Syria. Even if we accept that the resort to arms was never the right means of resolving the crisis, the international community's efforts to protect Syrian civilians have been shameful. Since 2011, states have failed to cooperate to discharge their shared responsibility to end the suffering. They have never so much as coordinated to place meaningful pressure on belligerents to refrain from harming civilians, with the exception of the occasional flurry of activity in response to the Assad regime's use of chemical weapons. In this sense, the R2P norm has been violated.

But norm violation does not mean that the norm has no weight or "compliance pull," much less that the norm has died.[66] The reality is that norms are sometimes violated. The security and economic concerns of states, for example, sometimes trump even the strongest social norms. But this doesn't mean that these norms are dead, or that they do not have meaningful impact on the behavior of other states, or even those same states, in other situations. No one suggested that the norm of nonintervention was obsolete or meaningless when Russia invaded Georgia in 2008 or when it annexed Crimea in 2014.[67] And if violation of a perfect-duty norm such as nonintervention does not necessarily indicate that the norm lacks weight, how much more so violation of an imperfect-duty norm such as R2P, which by its nature is subject to greater indeterminacy regarding how it should be applied, and thus greater susceptibility to both sincere and cynical contestation and, in turn, violation justified with arguments that honor the norm (as I explain further, shortly). The material interests of states sometimes trump social norms, and they have done so with particularly tragic outcomes in the case of Syria.

The primary reason for the international community's failure to protect Syrian civilians was the intransigence of Russia and China in the Security Council. It is they who most plainly violated the norm (in addition, of course, to those committing the atrocities). For all the purported universality of R2P's principles, and the unanimity of agreement on these principles at the 2005 UN World Summit—features of R2P that clearly distinguish it from past constructions of international protection responsibilities—the international order remains sufficiently hierarchical that any of the five permanent members of the council can prevent the authorization of certain forms of coordinated, multilateral action that are sometimes necessary to help protect vulnerable people from atrocities, should they perceive an interest in doing so. Russia had important strategic interests at stake, leading it to shield the Assad regime, including fear that Islamist threats might spill over to the North Caucasus region, concern that another instance of Western-driven regime change may undermine Russia's domestic political order, a desire to preserve the material benefits of relations with the Syrian state, and nostalgic considerations of solidarity with the Syrian people.[68] China, in turn, had substantial reasons for voting with Russia in the council, including both a fear of watering down the presumption against nonconsensual interference in the affairs of sovereign states and also a hope that Russia would return the favor on matters critical to China in the future. Despite the backlash against the Libyan intervention, Russia and China were joined only by Bolivia (six times), Venezuela (twice), and Equatorial Guinea (once) in casting negative votes on draft resolutions on Syria up to the end of 2019. The intransigence of just these two powerful states prevented the kind of coordinated international response necessary to protect vulnerable civilians.

The other permanent members—the United States, the United Kingdom, and France—might be faulted for antagonizing Russia and China and entrenching their obstinacy by declaring early in the crisis that "Assad must go" and repeatedly putting before the council contentious draft resolutions that they knew would be vetoed. These actions seem to have also had the twin effect of discouraging Assad from negotiating and emboldening him to commit further atrocities.[69] But such deeds are best understood as regrettable miscalculations rather than an abdication of responsibility. The bulk of responsibility surely lies with those committing atrocities and those shielding them in the council.

Certainly, many states could have done more to protect Syrians. While neighboring states such Turkey, Lebanon, and Jordan have accepted an enormous share of international responsibility in caring for millions of civilians fleeing Syria, too many others have failed to do their fair share by providing assistance and refuge to victims of the conflict, much less taking up the slack left by unwilling others. Nothing that Russia and China have done in the Security Council has prevented states from individually discharging their responsibility to protect in this regard. However, the effective application of diplomatic pressure, carefully targeted sanctions, and other international measures aimed at compelling warring parties to end the violence in Syria has always depended on the cooperation of states—particularly the council's permanent members—and in this instance Russian and Chinese intransigence has impeded the effective implementation of R2P.

As lamentable as this is, it is not necessarily indicative of the decline, much less the death, of R2P. A little international relations theory can again prove helpful. We can recognize the impact of a norm not only in examples of compliance, but also in examples of violation. As constructivist theorists observe, the key questions to be asked in interpreting the substance of a violated norm are as follows: How do violators explain their violations? And how do others respond?[70] If states violating a supposed norm feel no need to defend their behavior, and if other states neither condemn nor sanction violations, we can conclude that the norm does not matter. But if states make an effort to conceal violations, or if they seek to justify their actions, rejecting the evaluations of others that they have violated the norm, or if they offer excuses for their actions, explaining that there are legitimate reasons for violating the norm in a particular instance, then we can begin to see that the norm matters at least to some degree and that violation is understood to have consequences that states wish to avoid. Likewise, we find evidence for the weight of a norm if other states respond to violation with moral condemnation, social sanction, or material punishment. Certainly, the fact that a state chooses to violate a norm in a given instance suggests that the norm is not so strong that it trumps all competing interests and values in all situations. And the indeterminacy of an imperfect-duty norm such as R2P can facilitate especially vigorous contestation about what should be done and supply reasonably plausible pretexts for violation in certain circumstances. But the communicative dynamics around violation can reveal much about how robust the norm is perceived to be and, in turn, what expectations we might reasonably have about compliance in other situations.[71]

Even in the shameful case of Syria, at least in the first five years of the crisis, states consistently recognized the weight of human protection norms and thus sought to justify their actions, excuse their inaction, and shift blame for the failure to prevent grave suffering in an attempt to avoid paying the social costs that attend violation. (I say more later about the shift in politics since 2016.) We can observe the impact of R2P in the acceptance of the international community, and especially the permanent members of the Security Council, that they are obliged to respond in some way to the perpetration of atrocities. Despite the obstructionism of Russia and China, the council has managed to adopt more than twenty resolutions on the crisis, including resolutions demanding unhindered access for humanitarian agencies and authorizing these agencies to provide assistance, even without the consent of the Syrian government. The UN Human Rights Council and General Assembly have also adopted dozens of further resolutions on the crisis, condemning atrocities and demanding an end to the violence against civilians.[72]

We see further impact of the R2P norm in the fact that those states that are thought to have a particular capacity to do something to ease the suffering and resolve the crisis have felt the need to justify the significance of the actions they have taken and provide excuses for their decisions not to do more. Throughout his second term, for example, Obama acknowledged that the United States had "both a moral obligation and a national security interest in . . . ending the slaughter in Syria" and explained that this was why his administration had provided humanitarian aid ($5.9 billion committed by the end of his term), assisted the opposition, and worked with the international community to isolate the Assad regime.[73] Given the complexity of the crisis and the intransigence of Russia and China, there was perhaps not much more that Obama could have done to resolve it (even if he could have done more to provide relief to victims).[74] Even so, Obama felt continued pressure to defend his policies. In response, he emphasized the difficulties of the situation and the careful consideration given by his administration to alternative policies, and he characterized the suggestion that earlier financial and military assistance to the opposition could have resolved the crisis as "magical thinking."[75] Appealing to the limits of US capabilities, he insisted that "we cannot and should not" intervene with military force "every time there's an injustice in the world" and rightly cautioned that stronger action in Syria could actually do more harm than good.[76] Seeking to shift blame, he declared, "Responsibility for this brutality lies in one place alone—with the Assad regime and its allies Russia and Iran."[77] When feeling acute pressure to justify his administration's policies, he excused the decision not to do more by framing the crisis as but one of many confronting the United States: "How do I weigh tens of thousands who've been killed in Syria versus the tens of thousands who are currently being killed in the Congo?"[78]

Russia and China, for their part, have defended their repeated use of the veto not by claiming that the Security Council had no role to play in resolving the crisis, but by insisting that measures proposed by other states will do more harm than good. Russia has charged that resolutions drafted by Western states are perniciously designed to further their own interests rather than the interests of Syrians: "These Pharisees have been pushing their own geopolitical intentions, which have nothing in common with the legitimate interests of the Syrian people."[79] Conscious of potential costs to its international reputation, China has insisted that its Syria policy is not driven by self-interest and claimed that "as a permanent member of the Council and a responsible member of the international community, China will continue to actively work for a comprehensive, lasting and proper solution of the Syrian issue as soon as possible."[80]

But the arguments of Russia and China have left many other states unconvinced. Indeed, further evidence of the weight of the R2P norm is found in the fierce condemnation meted out against these two permanent members of the council for standing in the way of a more unified and more effective international response to the crisis. We saw in chapter 4 that the imperfections of extraterritorial protection obligations make legal enforcement difficult to conceive, let alone implement. Nevertheless, we see in this case that, whatever the inadequacies of the law, the political consensus and shared expectations regarding R2P have been sufficiently strong to narrow the scope for contestation and excusable violation. Individual states have strongly criticized Russia and China for vetoing council resolutions, expressing "disgust" and "distress" at their "shameful" intransigence in the face of international efforts to stem human suffering.[81] Significantly, on three occasions in 2016 and 2017, when Russia vetoed draft resolutions that would have done little more than demand an end to indiscriminate attacks against civilians in Aleppo and condemn the use of chemical weapons across Syria, China abandoned its long-standing practice of vetoing in solidarity and merely abstained—showing just how out of line with prevailing norms Russia's stance was perceived to be.[82] In 2012, 2013, and 2016, the General Assembly responded to the council's paralysis by voting overwhelmingly in favor of resolutions "deploring" and "expressing alarm" at the council's failure to discharge its responsibility to promptly and effectively respond to atrocities.[83] All of these justifications, excuses, and condemnations, even if some have been insincere and self-serving, demonstrate shared recognition that the notion that the international community has a responsibility to do what it can to protect Syrian civilians is a powerful idea against which states need to explain their actions.

New Habits and Enduring Perversities

The weight of the felt imperative to protect populations can therefore be seen in the R2P era not only in an example of compliance (Libya), but also in an example of violation (Syria). But of course we have seen states respond to a similarly felt imperative in similar ways at other times. In the nineteenth century, for example, European great powers acted in accordance with a felt obligation to protect the vulnerable in some instances, such as Syria (1860–61), and felt the need to justify, excuse, or shift blame for refusing to do so in others, such as Armenia (1894–96). In the 1990s, coalitions of states likewise acted in accordance with a felt responsibility to protect the vulnerable in some instances, such as Somalia (1992–94), and needed to work to minimize or deflect the social costs of failing to do so in others, such as Rwanda (1994). The cases of Libya and Syria reveal much about the contemporary politics of R2P. But to appreciate what is new about these politics, we need to also consider some broader dynamics.

Confronted with atrocities in Armenia in 1894–96, the European great powers felt a need to defend their limited intercessions on behalf of the vulnerable and their failure to do more not because there was a prevailing assumption that they would intercede on behalf of vulnerable people wherever atrocities were found to occur. After all, these great powers routinely ignored atrocities elsewhere in the world, and in many instances perpetrated them themselves. Rather, they felt a need to defend their response to the Armenian atrocities due to a perception that they wielded particular capacity to influence and compel Ottoman authorities and a belief that they had particular historical and contractual obligations to protect Christian minorities within the empire. Their failure to protect was controversial not because international protection efforts were commonplace, but because of the particularities of the case. International protection efforts were more common one hundred years later, in the decade following the Cold War, but they were still far from routine. Confronted with genocide in Rwanda, the United States and other leading powers felt the need to defend the Security

Council's decision to draw down rather than bolster the existing peacekeeping operation by falsely framing the situation as a complex civil war about which little could be done, not because it was expected that the international community would effectively respond to all instances of atrocities. After all, there had been little international outcry six months earlier when the great powers failed to prevent genocide in neighboring Burundi.[84] Rather, these leading powers felt a need to manipulate the framing of the Rwandan crisis because, in this instance, the case for intervention, if it had been presented in good faith, would have been unusually clear.[85]

In contrast, the crisis in Syria since 2011 has been more complex and intractable than either Armenia or Rwanda, with evolving local, regional, and global dynamics hindering the emergence of feasible solutions. And yet powerful states have still been forced to justify, excuse, or shift blame for their inadequate efforts to protect the vulnerable. This points to the rise of an international protection norm that does not merely require a response when particular groups of people are at risk, as in Armenia, or when the potential for effective protection is unusually clear, as in Rwanda, but in *all* instances of atrocities. Importantly, while this norm has failed to generate effective protection in the exceptionally thorny crisis that is Syria, it has led states to respond almost routinely to crises in other parts of the world, in which the impediments to meaningful action have not been as strong. This has been the case with respect to not only the most prominent crises, but also situations of concern that have neither attracted extensive media attention nor substantially engaged the material interests of powerful states. Alex Bellamy describes this routinized international response as a "habit of protection."[86] The emergence of this habit is what is new about the R2P era.

While some commentators refer to the 1990s as the "decade of humanitarian intervention" and the "golden age of humanitarian diplomacy," international responses to atrocities were much more erratic then than in the era of R2P.[87] As Bellamy observes, in the 1990s, the Security Council confronted nineteen new onsets of atrocities that each resulted in five thousand or more civilian deaths. It adopted resolutions in response to only twelve. And while many of these resolutions condemned atrocities and authorized the deployment of peacekeepers and the establishment of sanctions, the council specifically mandated the protection of civilians in only three cases (Rwanda, Sierra Leone, and the Democratic Republic of the Congo [DRC]). In contrast, from the beginning of the Arab Spring in late 2010 until the end of the second Obama administration in early 2017, the council confronted six new onsets of such crimes and passed resolutions mandating efforts to protect civilians in every instance (Libya, South Sudan, Mali, the Central African Republic [CAR], Iraq, and Syria).[88] Throughout this 2010–17 period, at least one hundred thousand military, police, and civilian personnel were deployed in peacekeeping operations around the world. The majority of these personnel were explicitly charged with protecting civilians, a practice that the council introduced for the first time only in 1999. And the costs and risks accepted in providing protection were substantial. More than one hundred peacekeepers lost their lives each year.

Some of these protection efforts were particularly noteworthy. As mentioned in chapter 3, the Security Council authorized peacekeepers to "use all necessary means" to protect civilians in Côte d'Ivoire in March 2011.[89] This operation did not enjoy the consent of the de facto president, Laurent Gbagbo, but it was welcomed by Alassane Ouattara, whom the Security Council recognized as the legitimate president. The UN peacekeepers, accompanied by French troops, were remarkably successful, overcoming Gbagbo's forces and defeating him in under two weeks.[90] Three months later, the council authorized a peacekeeping operation in South Sudan with a similarly robust civilian protection mandate.[91] When civil war erupted there in December 2013, peacekeepers made use of their bases to provide shelter to civilians fleeing violence. Within a week, they had taken in thirty-five thousand civilians. Three years later, they were providing refuge to two hundred thousand civilians inside "Protection of Civilians Sites" within their bases.[92] The contrast with Srebrenica, 1995, in which Bosnian men and boys were slaughtered soon after being ordered by Dutch peacekeepers to leave their compound, is stark. In March 2013, the Security Council took the unprecedented step of establishing an offensive combat force, labeled an "intervention brigade," within its peacekeeping mission in DRC, giving the brigade responsibility to neutralize and disarm rebel groups that posed a threat to state authority and civilian security in eastern DRC.[93] The brigade played an important role in driving out the M23 rebel group later that year. In August 2014, with the consent of the Iraqi government, US forces undertook a forcible rescue of Yazidis under attack from Islamic State and trapped on Mount Sinjar. They succeeded in protecting tens of thousands of Yazidis.

The Security Council even continued its practice, inaugurated in 2011, of occasionally authorizing protection efforts without host state consent— demonstrating that the backlash over Libya did not prohibit agreement on nonconsensual protection measures. While the council has utterly failed Syria's civilians, it at least proved willing in 2014, for the first time in its history, and again in each subsequent year, to adopt resolutions demanding unhindered access for humanitarian agencies and authorizing these agencies to assist civilians without Syrian government consent.[94] Then, in the final months of the Obama administration, the United States and France successfully pushed resolutions through the council authorizing the deployment of 228 police officers in Burundi to monitor human rights violations and a four-thousand-strong Regional Protection Force (RPF) in South Sudan to prevent attacks against civilians, humanitarian actors, and UN personnel. Both resolutions were adopted without first receiving the consent of the host government. While China and Russia expressed serious reservations about such interference in sovereign affairs, they refrained from exercising their veto.[95] These examples of consensual and nonconsensual protection measures point to a commitment by the international community to take meaningful steps to protect civilians at risk of atrocities in an almost routine manner.

However, throughout this 2010–17 period, the international community continued to fall short in substantial ways. In some instances, failure to adequately protect the vulnerable can be put down to the fact that the provision of protection in complex crises is extraordinarily difficult. For example, while the Security Council authorized the provision of assistance in Syria and the deployment of police in Burundi and the RPF in South Sudan without host government consent, ongoing opposition from these governments meant that humanitarian agencies in Syria were too often unable to reach the most vulnerable, police were unable to deploy to Burundi, and the phased deployment of the RPF in South Sudan was delayed by a year. Given that coercive intervention to compel acceptance of either of these measures would likely have done more harm than good, there was little more that could have been done other than to continue to apply material and diplomatic pressure on these governments to permit their implementation.

In other instances, the international community failed to provide adequate protection because it acted too little, too late. We know that carefully coordinated efforts to prevent the outbreak of atrocities can succeed, averting the need for more costly and risky measures to bring such crimes to an end. We have seen such successes in Kenya (2008 and 2013), Guinea (2009–10), and Kyrgyzstan (2010). And yet while states repeatedly declare their support—indeed their preference—for preventive strategies, they too often fail to translate this rhetoric into action. As UN secretary-general António Guterres noted in his 2017 report on R2P, the international community continues to "spend far more time and resources responding to crises than we do on preventing them."[96] For example, while a March 2013 coup in CAR was accompanied by clear signals of the imminent perpetration of atrocities and was soon followed by credible reports of such crimes, it took the Security Council a full year to authorize the deployment of a UN peacekeeping operation mandated to protect civilians. By that time, more than a thousand civilians had been killed and a further one million (of a population of less than five million) were forcibly displaced.[97]

In some instances, moreover, the international community's failure to protect the vulnerable was particularly perverse. Between 2005 and 2017, for example, an estimated two thousand allegations of sexual abuse and exploitation were leveled at UN peacekeepers and personnel around the world. More than three hundred involved children.[98] To take another example, while the US-led coalition has justified its war in Iraq against Islamic State since 2014 at least partly on civilian protection grounds, a 2017 study found that one in every five airstrikes by the coalition had killed Iraqi civilians, generating as many as three thousand civilian deaths.[99] Consider also the crisis in Yemen. Between March 2015 and the beginning of 2017, fighting between Houthi rebels and a coalition of states led by Saudi Arabia killed ten thousand civilians and wounded forty thousand more.[100] Airstrikes by the Saudi-led coalition were the leading cause of civilian casualties.[101] By late 2017, the establishment of a blockade by the coalition had left Yemen host to what UN officials described as "the worst humanitarian crisis in the world." Of a population of twenty-eight million, more than twenty million, including eleven million children, were "in need of urgent humanitarian assistance."[102] Throughout this conflict, not only have some key Western states failed to bring sufficient pressure to bear on the Saudis to stop violating international humanitarian law, they have actively supported them. During the first two years of the conflict, the United Kingdom approved arms sales of £3.7 billion to Saudi Arabia, totaling almost half of its arms exports. France authorized arms sales worth a further €455 million.[103] The United States provided training, assistance in target selection, and midair refueling for coalition airstrikes. The Obama administration offered more than $115 billion worth of arms sales to Saudi Arabia during its two terms. As its second term was coming to an end, it announced that it would halt one planned arms sale to the kingdom. A few months later, Obama's successor, Donald Trump, announced a new arms deal worth $110 billion.[104]

Three Challenges

And things have gotten worse. Since the end of the second Obama administration, three challenges to international human protection, each of which had already begun to make their presence felt, have more fully emerged. Each feeds into the others, and each pushes against consistent and effective implementation of the shared responsibility to protect. First is the growth of post-truth politics and the exposure of the hypocrisies of Western powers, which combine to weaken the potential for proponents of human protection norms to push states toward compliance. Second is the rising power and confidence of some non-Western states that, guided in part by humiliating memories of Western imperialism, express strong reservations about Western approaches to human protection and are increasingly willing to promote their own alternative visions of international protection responsibilities. And third is the trend among key Western states, which have for years provided the impetus and accepted the responsibility for many protection efforts, to turn their backs on global obligations and pursue populist nationalist agendas.

THE DECLINE OF SHAME

In recent decades, constructivist scholars have argued persuasively that tactics of rhetorical entrapment, naming and shaming, and exposure of hypocrisy can push states toward norm compliance.[105] We saw this in the case of Libya, as Russia and China, entrapped by past rhetoric and not wanting to be seen to unjustifiably oppose civilian protection, allowed the adoption of Resolution 1973. But the world has changed since 2011. The past decade has seen the emergence of a post-truth global politics in which assertions of hypocrisy, double standards, broken promises, and plain deceit are frequently dismissed as fake news. One consequence has been that the potential for the international community to deploy rhetorical tactics to constrain reluctant states to adhere to international norms has fast deteriorated.

Certainly, states have long challenged the truth claims of others when seeking to alleviate pressure for norm compliance. Recall the infamous efforts of certain Western states to frame the 1994 Rwandan crisis as something other than genocide, so as to avoid pressure to "do something." Reaching further back, consider that in the 1870s Benjamin Disraeli sought to reduce pressure to respond to the "Bulgarian Horrors" by challenging the credibility of reports of mass killings, at one stage even claiming that the atrocities were mere "inventions."[106] But the brazen rejection of manifest evidence and expert consensus is of a magnitude greater today.

To make matters worse, the embrace of post-truth politics by norm violators has coincided with the repeated exposure of abuses and hypocrisies of the United States and other traditional champions of global norms across a range of issue areas related to human protection—including practices of extraordinary rendition and torture, mistreatment of asylum seekers and refugees, reckless drone and other air campaigns generating excessive civilian casualties, and the supply of arms to brutal regimes and rebel groups. These exposures have often been met with flimsy justifications or shameless denials, rather than contrition and change.[107] This has given license to other states to perpetrate their own abuses, such as Russia's illegal annexation of Crimea, which was justified with a concocted appeal to the need to protect Russian nationals.[108] It has also emboldened reluctant states to resist efforts to shame them into complying with R2P.

This became particularly evident during the final months of Obama's second term, and has become only more manifest in the years since as the moral authority of traditional champions of human protection has further declined. Consider the Security Council debates on atrocities committed in Aleppo, Syria, in 2016. With support from Russian airstrikes, Assad's forces undertook a brutal campaign against both rebel forces and civilians, which UN High Commissioner for Human Rights Zeid bin Ra'ad Al Hussein concluded involved "crimes of historic proportions."[109] The Security Council met to discuss the situation in December. US ambassador Samantha Power charged Russia, Iran, the Assad regime, and their affiliated militias with rejecting reality and lamented their apparent incapacity for shame:

> Denying or obfuscating the facts, as they will do today, by saying that up is down and black is white will not absolve them. . . . Their barrel bombs, mortars and airstrikes have allowed the militias in Aleppo to encircle tens of thousands of civilians in their ever-tightening noose. . . . It should shame them. Instead, by all appearances, it is emboldening them. . . . Is there literally nothing that can shame them? Is there no act of barbarism against civilians, no execution of a child that gets under their skin or just creeps them out a little bit? Is there nothing that they will not lie about or justify?[110]

Taking advantage of the post-truth politics that had gained such international currency that year, and likely encouraged by the fact that Obama's term was ending and the United States would inaugurate its own post-truth president the following month, Russian ambassador Vitaly Churkin had no difficulty responding. He plainly rejected the accounts of atrocities as "fake news" and charged Power with hypocrisy: "What I find particularly strange was the statement by the representative of the United States, who delivered her statement as if she were Mother Teresa. She should remember what country she is representing and her own country's track record. Only then can she start opining from the position of moral supremacy."[111]

This pattern of argumentation continued as Churkin's successor, Vasily Nebenzia, repeatedly responded to the shaming efforts of US ambassadors to the UN during Donald Trump's presidency, first by dismissing charges laid against Russia and its allies as misunderstandings or lies and then by reminding the Security Council of past calamities wrought upon the world by the United States and its allies. In 2017, for example, justifying Russia's decision to veto the renewal of the Joint Investigative Mechanism that was charged with investigating the use of chemical weapons, which Russia had established with the United States two years earlier, Nebenzia framed the mechanism as a US-led imposition on Syria's internal affairs, drew parallels with the United States' "monstrous experiments in Iraq and Libya," and confronted his US opponent: "Will this geopolitical laboratory never shut down?"[112]

While we saw the impact of the R2P norm in the first five years of the Syrian crisis as states felt the need to justify, excuse, and shift blame for failing to protect Syrian civilians, this rhetorical maneuvering has become increasingly meaningless as the civil war has continued. Certainly, Russia has continued to offer explanations for its behavior, but there comes a point where deceit and obfuscation no longer honors a norm in its breach, but simply signals the norm's decline. Likewise, while Western states have continued to feel the need to deny or dismiss their own hypocrisies rather than simply ignore them, there surely comes a point where hypocrisy is no longer a homage that vice pays to virtue, but simply signals virtue's decline.

In situations where the imperative to protect does not clash with other values, concerns, and interests of powerful states and does not demand excessively risky or costly action, the international community has shown that it can quite routinely agree to take meaningful measures to relieve suffering. But for now, at least, the tactic of shaming states to responsibly engage with the protection of civilians in cases where they are reluctant to does not work as it once did.

THE RISE OF NON-WESTERN POWERS

It is often suggested that the rising material and social power of non-Western states and the attendant shift to what has been termed a "post-Western world" means the R2P era "is over."[113] The argument goes that rising non-Western powers, such as China, India, Brazil, and South Africa, that have strong memories of humiliating and often brutal Western imperial interventionism, justified in the name of protecting the vulnerable, and that have been wary of the perceived reemergence of such practices and claims in recent decades, are increasingly unwilling to tolerate them, much less accept the burdens of protection themselves, as they assume more dominant positions in global affairs.[114] The argument is commonly overstated, but it is not baseless. At the very least, these rising powers clearly seek to reshape prevailing human protection norms in accordance with their respective values and interests, contesting not merely the application of these norms in particular situations, but the very content of these norms—and they do so with increasing confidence and forcefulness. The efforts of China in this regard are especially noteworthy given both its role as a permanent Security Council member and also its fast-growing material and social capacity to variously impede, enable, or contribute to protection efforts, so it is worth briefly examining China's emerging position.

China has long sought to cultivate an image of itself as a "responsible major power." For a time, this rendered it susceptible to the socialization efforts of Western powers.[115] However, as it has grown in power and influence, it has appeared increasingly confident of its own vision of great-power responsibilities and willing to assert this vision globally, shifting from the role of norm taker to norm maker. This is evident in the case of R2P.

In a 2017 speech to Communist Party elites, hailing a "new era," President Xi Jinping declared that China would be "moving closer to center stage and making greater contributions to mankind."[116] This is reflected in China's acceptance of a growing share of global protection responsibilities. Xi committed China two years earlier to establishing a permanent peacekeeping police force and standby peacekeeping force of eight thousand troops, provide $100 million to the African Union to support the establishment of their own standby force and emergency response capacity, and establish a $1 billion peace and development fund to support the work of the UN.[117] Between 2012 and 2019, China increased its contribution to the UN peacekeeping budget from less than 4 percent to more than 15 percent of the total, making it the second largest contributor after the United States.[118] China has also increased the number of military and police personnel it deploys to UN peacekeeping operations to more than twenty-five hundred, which is more than three times that of any other permanent Security Council member. And it has accepted risks and costs in contributing to peacekeeping, with ten fatalities since 2010 in operations in Mali, South Sudan, and elsewhere.[119]

As it takes on a greater share of global protection responsibilities, however, China advances its own, alternative vision of how protection should be pursued—seeking, in a sense, to reconfigure the courses of action available to the international community in Kant's playroom. This vision is marked by an insistence that sovereign states should in almost all instances be free to determine for themselves how to best care for their own populations and when and how international assistance might be received, and also by a determination to ensure that China's own human rights transgressions are not subject to international scrutiny or condemnation. For a time, this vision rested on a negative, defensive victimhood narrative that invoked China's "century of humiliation," suffered at the hands of Western and Japanese imperial powers from the First Opium War of 1839 to the establishment of the People's Republic of China in 1949. It is now grounded in a positive, heroic narrative of China's successful efforts to save its people from imperial subjugation and to lift millions out of poverty through state-led development policies. China succeeded in rescuing itself from injustice and poverty, the argument goes, and others should be allowed to do the same, choosing the "social systems and development paths" most appropriate for them.[120]

The best way for the international community to help protect people in this context, China insists, is to "follow the principle of national ownership and leadership, respect the judicial traditions and national reality of countries in distress, and avoid producing negative impact on the domestic situation in countries concerned."[121] In practical terms, this involves supporting governments, facilitating development, helping build atrocity-prevention capacities, mediating disputes, and providing assistance consensually, rather than intruding in sovereign affairs and imposing solutions on unwilling governments.[122] China supplements this vision with a critique of reckless Western militarism, noting, as Russia does, the failures, double standards, and hypocrisies of US-led interventions. But whatever the merits of China's alternative, sovereigntist vision of human protection, its potential perversities are made clear when China deploys it to shield tyrannical regimes even from noncoercive international measures aimed at protecting the vulnerable. In a 2019 Security Council debate on Syria, for example, China acknowledged, "The international community has a moral responsibility to help the Syrian people emerge from the shadow of war and lead a peaceful, stable and promising life." But justifying its decision to join Russia in vetoing a draft resolution demanding, among other things, that humanitarian agencies be given access to vulnerable people, it insisted that these agencies should instead fully respect Syria's sovereignty and coordinate closely with the Assad regime, unabashedly claiming that the regime, whose atrocities are well documented, "is actively promoting development and improving people's livelihoods."[123]

China has sought to advance its alternative vision of human protection across the whole of the UN's work, and has cultivated the support of allies to this end. While making increasingly substantial contributions to UN peacekeeping, China has worked to transform the nature of these operations, emphasizing the establishment of peace through development over the promotion of civilian protection.[124] In UN budget negotiations, China has repeatedly sought to cut funding for human rights officers in peacekeeping missions in CAR, DRC, and elsewhere.[125] It has also led a successful effort by a group of states to withhold funding from the "Human Rights Up Front" cell within the secretary-general's office, which was established in 2014 to ensure that all parts of the organization considered the human rights and atrocity prevention implications of their work.[126]

Meanwhile, China's own domestic human rights record has worsened. Most worrying is the detention in "reeducation camps" of more than one million Uighurs and other minorities in Xinjiang province and China's success in cultivating international support for these policies. A joint statement by twenty-three mostly Western states submitted to a General Assembly committee meeting in 2019, voicing concerns "regarding credible reports of mass detention . . . and other human rights violations and abuses," was met with a joint declaration from fifty-four other states—mostly African recipients of Chinese development aid and investment—insisting that "human rights are respected and protected in China" and commending "China's remarkable achievements in the field of human rights by adhering to the people centered-development philosophy." A hundred other states remained silent, unwilling to criticize the great power.[127] Both in seeking to reshape human protection norms internationally and in grievously violating them domestically, China has been emboldened by the neglect and in some instances abnegation of these norms by Western powers, not least the United States, in recent years. This is the third challenge to which we finally turn.

THE RESURGENCE OF POPULIST NATIONALISM

The resurgence of populist nationalism in the West (and elsewhere), characterized by a backlash against cosmopolitan ideals and an embrace of anti-human-rights agendas, poses a grave threat to international human protection norms. Exemplified by the Trump presidency in the United States, the resurgence of these inclinations within states that have previously supported and at times accepted the bulk of the risks and costs of international protection is bad news for R2P. More importantly, it is bad news for people at risk of atrocities.

In his 2017 inaugural address, Trump declared, "From this moment on, it's going to be America First. Every decision on trade, on taxes, on immigration, on foreign affairs, will be made to benefit American workers and American families."[128] And this was reflected in much of his administration's approach to human protection. In UN budget negotiations that year, US ambassador Nikki Haley succeeded in pushing through a cut of $600 million from UN peacekeeping, saving the United States $150 million, but weakening one of the international community's most cost-effective instruments for protecting vulnerable populations.[129] The Trump administration cut the United States' annual intake of refugees from a ceiling of 110,000 set by Obama for 2017 down to 45,000 for 2018, 30,000 for 2019, and 18,000 for 2020, significantly impairing refugee protection globally since the United States had for several decades reliably contributed between one-third and one-half of the world's resettlement total. Increases in airstrikes by US and allied forces against Islamic State forces in urban centers in Iraq and Syria contributed to a dramatic rise in civilian casualties, with as many as six thousand fatalities in 2017 alone—triple the 2016 figure.[130] And Trump abandoned numerous international institutions and mechanisms that contribute to human protection, withdrawing from the Human Rights Council, un-signing the 2013 Arms Trade Treaty, and being one of only two states to vote against the 2018 Global Compact on Refugees (Hungary was the other). These various measures have weakened US moral authority and generated a vacuum of moral leadership globally, which China eagerly seeks to fill with its alternative visions of international order and human protection.

Trump openly embraced the leaders of numerous rights-abusing states, including the Philippines, whose "war on drugs" since 2016 has killed thousands of civilians and is credibly described as an act of genocide, North Korea, which has been accused by a UN Commission of Inquiry of rights violations that may amount to crimes against humanity, and Saudi Arabia, whose reckless violations of international humanitarian law in Yemen were noted earlier—an embrace that rendered almost useless the efforts of other states to pressure these governments to refrain from atrocities.[131] Indeed, invoking common Article 1 of the Geneva Conventions and the ILC's articles on state responsibilities, a UN Group of Experts found in 2019 that the United States, along with the United Kingdom, France, and Iran, may be not only legally responsible for failing to use their influence over parties to the Yemeni conflict to end serious violations of international humanitarian law, but, in aiding and assisting parties to the conflict, legally responsible for complicity in these violations.[132] Of course, as was the case with previous international protection norms and agreements, from the Peace of Westphalia onward, so it remains today that those great powers that claim authority to hold others to account for harms done to vulnerable people also claim for themselves sufficient legal guarantees and political safeguards—not least by maintaining their veto power within the Security Council today—such that they are in little danger of being held to account for their own crimes. This is true for the United States, United Kingdom, and France in Yemen just as it is true for China in Xinjiang and Russia in Syria.

While the Trump administration's many abnegations of global duties have clearly violated and weakened R2P, however, they do not necessarily spell the death of the norm. Norms are sticky. To the extent that shared expectations of appropriate behavior become embedded in the language of domestic politics and internalized in domestic institutions, they are not easily removed—at least not totally.[133] For all the rhetoric of "America First" by the Trump administration, the impulse to protect vulnerable people beyond borders repeatedly broke through in short bursts. The United States' 2017 National Security Strategy proclaimed, "We will hold perpetrators of genocide and mass atrocities accountable. . . . Even as we expect others to share responsibility, the United States will continue to catalyze international responses to man-made and natural disasters and provide our expertise and capabilities to those in need."[134] In 2019, Trump signed into law the Elie Wiesel Genocide and Atrocity Prevention Act, which aims at enhancing US capacities to prevent, mitigate, and respond to such crimes. The act declares, "It shall be the policy of the United States to regard the prevention of atrocities as in its national interest." It commits US administrations to pursuing a government-wide strategy for prevention and to "share responsibility" with others to this end. Trump subsequently launched an interagency Atrocity Early Warning Task Force—essentially a reboot of the Obama administration's Atrocities Prevention Board—charged with supporting government efforts to accomplish the act's goals.[135]

This institutional support for protection responsibilities was at times translated into meaningful action. The Trump administration responded to the mass displacement of Rohingya by Myanmar government forces and militias in 2017 by withdrawing military assistance from the government forces and providing more than $600 million in humanitarian assistance over the next two years. Trump signed an executive order that year, "declaring a national emergency with respect to serious human rights abuse and corruption around the world and providing for the imposition of sanctions on actors engaged in these malign activities." In an annex to the order, he imposed sanctions on thirteen rights abusers and corrupt actors around the world including the Myanmar general accused of leading the campaign of atrocities against the Rohingya. This streamlined provision for the imposition of targeted sanctions was something the Obama administration's Atrocities Prevention Board had tried and failed to establish.[136] Within two years, the number of individuals sanctioned through the provision had grown to more than one hundred.[137]

But too often, when the impulse to protect vulnerable strangers managed to breach the confines of "America First," it generated actions that were sporadic, reckless, and ultimately irresponsible. Consider Trump's impulsive decisions to launch illegal airstrikes against Syrian targets, unilaterally in April 2017 and in coalition with the United Kingdom and France twelve months later, in response to chemical weapons attacks by Syrian government forces. The attacks earned widespread praise from American pundits and the approval of many allies, who had no interest in offending the unpredictable leader of the world's most powerful state. But they did little to diminish the capacity of the Assad regime to use chemical weapons or commit other atrocities, and they were not accompanied by sustained efforts to dissuade the regime from perpetrating such crimes. Eighteen months later, as the suffering of Syrian civilians continued, Trump declared that the only reason why a few hundred US troops, deployed in 2015 to fight Islamic State, remained in Syria was to secure Syrian oil for the United States: "We're keeping the oil. We have the oil. The oil is secure. We left troops behind, only for the oil."[138]

——

In situations where the desire for meaningful action is not overwhelmed by the economic or security interests of a great power or the excessive risks and costs of acting, the international community continues to respond

almost habitually to the threat or perpetration of atrocities by taking some
form of action to protect vulnerable people. States continue to deploy more
than eighty thousand peacekeepers around the world, the vast majority
of whom serve in missions whose mandates prioritize the protection of
civilians. Around a hundred peacekeepers lose their life undertaking such
missions every year in places such as CAR, DRC, Mali, and South Sudan.
When The Gambia's president Yahya Jammeh, who had in mid-2016 threatened to eliminate the Mandinka ethnic group by killing them one by one,
refused to accept the results of an election at the end of that year and transfer
power to Adama Barrow, the Economic Community of West African States
(ECOWAS), the African Union, and the UN Security Council responded
quickly. In January 2017, ECOWAS and the African Union recognized
Barrow as The Gambia's president and seven thousand ECOWAS troops
amassed at The Gambia's border, threatening to intervene if Jammeh did not
relinquish power. The Security Council unanimously adopted a resolution
expressing support for these regional efforts and reminding the Gambian
government of its responsibility to protect the civilian population. Fear of
violence had prompted more than seventy-six thousand Gambians to flee
to Senegal since the election. But the international community's rapid and
concerted response prompted Jammeh to step down peacefully and Barrow
to assume the presidency before the end of the month. The Gambia's displaced civilians were able to return home.[139] Such routinized international
responses to potential and actual large-scale rights violations set the early
twenty-first-century politics of human protection apart from earlier periods.

But there are too many exceptions. Too often, great powers protect
not those at risk of atrocities but those perpetrating them. In August 2017,
Myanmar regime forces launched "clearance operations" in Rakhine State,
killing at least ten thousand Rohingya Muslims and forcing more than
seven hundred thousand to flee to Bangladesh.[140] The UN High Commissioner for Human Rights labeled the attacks "a textbook example of ethnic
cleansing" and noted that "acts of genocide" may have taken place.[141] And
yet the Security Council failed to adopt a single resolution responding to
or even acknowledging the atrocities. Just as Russia shields Syria and the
United States shields Saudi Arabia, China, with economic interests, security
concerns, and a desire to increase its political influence all in play, shields
Myanmar.[142] Despite British, French, and US appeals to the council's "collective responsibility" to offer a meaningful response, China succeeded in
limiting the council's actions to a presidential statement in November 2017,
condemning the violence and expressing "grave concerns over reports of

human rights violations and abuses," and a press statement six months later, declaring that council members remained "gravely concerned."[143] Russia supports China on Myanmar just as China has mostly supported Russia on Syria. And while the United States (along with others) has taken unilateral measures to sanction perpetrators and aid victims, it has lacked the appetite and focus, and increasingly the moral authority, to cultivate a coalition of like-minded states to apply substantial and sustained pressure on Myanmar's leaders and their supporters to end the violence and facilitate safe return of the displaced. Asked by a Rohingya man from a refugee camp in Bangladesh in 2019, "What is the plan to help us?," Trump replied, "And where is that, exactly?"[144] It was left to The Gambia, that small West African state that had only recently narrowly avoided a human protection crisis of its own, to file a lawsuit at the International Court of Justice that year, accusing Myanmar of genocide and seeking an order for provisional measures to protect the Rohingya. Such is the politics of the shared responsibility to protect; such is the plight of people at risk of atrocities.

Conclusion

The most extreme of all early modern treatises proclaiming the duty of princes to protect persecuted people beyond their realms was perhaps *Vindiciae, Contra Tyrannos*, published in 1579 under a pseudonym and likely written by two French Huguenots, Hubert Languet and Philippe de Mornay. Written in the aftermath of the St. Bartholomew's Day massacre of 1572, the authors asked, "Whether neighboring princes may by right, or ought, to render assistance to subjects of other princes who are being persecuted on account of pure religion, or oppressed by manifest tyranny?" They answered unambiguously in the affirmative. Seeking to marshal all resources available for articulating a binding obligation to rescue oppressed peoples, the authors appealed to the authority of Scripture and the church fathers as well as drawing heavily on classical authorities and Roman law. Claiming that Christ's parable of the good Samaritan made clear that the duty to love one's neighbor amounts to a universal duty to love all people, for example, they argued that princes are obliged to assist "anyone oppressed by tyranny," insofar as they are able.[1] The authors went so far as to argue that a prince who fails to render assistance to an oppressed people is more worthy of condemnation than the tyrant himself. After all, they explained, once a ruler turns to tyranny, he is forced to continue to rule with violence for his own safety: "But since a prince who idly observes the wicked acts of a tyrant and the slaughter of innocents, which he can prevent, takes pleasure in this sort of gladiatorial show, he is more guilty than the tyrant, to the same extent as he who sets gladiators against each other is more guilty than a murdering gladiator, and as someone who kills a man for relaxation is more guilty than one who is forced to out of fear or necessity."[2]

This was an extraordinary argument that reveals the depth of the authors' desperation for assistance against tyranny more than it evinces the careful reasoning of a pair of Calvinist theorists. There is something compelling about this urgent cry for help. But it reveals how immoderate and impractical a claim for extraterritorial obligations could be when unrestrained by Thomist anxieties that the rash resort to arms can harm more innocents than it protects or by humanist precepts about the duty of the bystander prince to think also of the needs of his own people—ideas that were in wide circulation by this time. More anachronistically, it also reveals the shortcomings of arguments about duties of protection that neglect to grapple with their "imperfections"—a way of understanding duties that theorists would begin to develop a century later. Which particular prince or princes were bound to intervene on behalf of the French Huguenots? How should princes weigh the needs of these Huguenots against the needs of many other peoples enduring persecution in these years of confessional conflict within Europe? If we are to hope for more than sporadic and impulsive—or at least highly selective—responses to particular instances of suffering, we need to wrestle with the imperfections of our responsibilities and also reckon with our own imperfections.

Wrestling with Our Imperfect Responsibilities

The shared responsibility to protect populations from atrocities is an imperfect duty. In the absence of a more complete and coherent body of international law capable of guaranteeing enforcement—a body of law whose development is highly unlikely, not least because it requires institutionalized agreement on the distribution of extraterritorial protection obligations among states—the principle will always amount to a Kantian "sorry comfort" for some, whose cries for protection go unanswered. The hope and aim is that it is sorry comfort for as few people as possible.

We saw in chapter 5 that the responsibility to protect norm had an unprecedented impact on the behavior of states in the years between the beginning of the Arab Spring and the end of Obama's second term. Buttressed by certain institutional and legal developments, this period saw the fruits of the widespread diffusion and internalization of a normative expectation that states should do what they can to respond to atrocities beyond their borders, or at least that they should refrain from preventing others from doing so. Certainly, this was sorry comfort to the millions of civilians wounded, displaced, traumatized, or killed in atrocities in Syria and elsewhere. But it made a difference for many others who received meaningful international preventive and protective action.

One way to comprehend certain states' embrace of their protection responsibilities during this period is to observe how they seem to have genuinely wrestled with the responsibilities' imperfections, seeking to do what they could in spite of these imperfections and even to overcome these imperfections to a degree, rather than invoking the imperfections to justify doing nothing. US president Barack Obama's approach to international responsibilities, for example, while leaving much to be desired, appears to have been marked by such sincere engagement. He never appealed explicitly to the "imperfect" nature of the human protection responsibilities that fell to him as president. But he alluded to and, if we take him at his word, sincerely contended with the possibilities and limits inherent to each sense of imperfection examined in this book.

Obama frequently engaged with the Kantian sense of imperfection, explaining that he was faced with difficult questions about which crises among many to devote resources to and which measures to deploy in the hope of reducing human suffering. In one of his final press conferences as president, he was asked whether he felt any responsibility for the ongoing carnage in Aleppo, Syria. "I always feel responsible," he replied:

> I felt responsible when kids were being shot by snipers. I felt responsible when millions of people had been displaced. I feel responsible for murder and slaughter that's taken place in South Sudan that's not being reported on partly because there's not as much social media being generated from there. There are places around the world where horrible things are happening, and because of my office, because I'm President of the United States, I feel responsible. I ask myself every single day, is there something I could do that would save lives and make a difference and spare some child who doesn't deserve to suffer.[3]

While such rhetoric sometimes served as a tactic for deflecting pressure to do more regarding a particular crisis, the question of how to pick and choose among multiple situations of concern, given the material and political limits of American power, seems to have continually played on Obama's mind. "We can't, at any given moment, relieve all the world's misery. . . . We have to choose where we can make a real impact," he said during his final year in office. "There are going to be times where we can do something about innocent people being killed, but there are going to be times where we can't."[4] His establishment of the interagency Atrocities Prevention Board, charged with identifying and directing attention to early warnings of atrocities that might otherwise remain under the administration's radar, was a creative and sometimes productive means of working through this imperfection, helping prompt international efforts to protect civilians at risk in Burundi and the Central African Republic during his second term.[5]

Recognizing the limits of what the United States could achieve, Obama also repeatedly alluded to the Vattelian sense of imperfection, acknowledging America's unparalleled material and social power, but insisting that other states should share more of the burden of international protection. "When we have the unique capabilities to help avert a massacre, then I believe the United States of America cannot turn a blind eye," he claimed, announcing the decision to rescue Yazidis under attack from Islamic State and trapped on Mount Sinjar in 2014.[6] But regarding other situations of concern, he made clear his frustration with free-riders who refused to contribute their fair share. While the phrase "leading from behind," used to describe the US role in the Libyan intervention, may not have been Obama's, it was a fair description of his desire for other states to take more responsibility.[7] He sometimes pushed this too far. When he complained in 2014 that China was free-riding on Western efforts to defeat Islamic State in Iraq, China responded quite reasonably that it was the United States and its allies that foolishly invaded Iraq in 2003, generating much of the chaos and instability that facilitated Islamic State's emergence.[8] However, Obama was generally right to seek greater responsibility sharing on human protection, not only for reasons of fairness and effectiveness, but also, as he himself acknowledged, to regulate US hubris and soften others' well-founded suspicions of US intentions.[9]

Obama wrestled also with the Pufendorfian sense of imperfection, deliberating the ethics and politics at stake in weighing responsibilities to foreigners against responsibilities to Americans recovering from the global financial crisis and exhausted from war. In 2011, he declared atrocity prevention "a core national security interest."[10] But by 2016 he more often framed it as an ideal that had to be weighed against more conventional, material interests. "The world is a tough, complicated, messy, mean place," he observed, and so "we've got to be hardheaded at the same time as we're bighearted, and pick and choose our spots." Nevertheless, he continued to insist that "if it is possible to do good at a bearable cost, to save lives, we will do it."[11] We might wish that the United States had accepted greater costs for the sake of doing more good, welcoming larger numbers of refugees fleeing Syrian atrocities, for example, or insisting on contributing more to help rebuild the broken Libyan state after Gaddafi's defeat. We might also wish that the United States had done more to avoid facilitating the perpetration of atrocities, whether through its careless sales of arms to abusive regimes, its support for Saudi Arabia's reckless air campaign in Yemen, or its ongoing exploitative economic policies and contributions to global environmental destruction. Nevertheless, for all these inadequacies and harms, Obama appears to have sincerely wrestled with how the United States should conceive and discharge its imperfect responsibilities for the protection of people at risk of atrocities. We ought not to reduce global engagement with R2P during Obama's two terms to the efforts of him and his administrations. But these efforts surely contributed to the development and consolidation of the habitual attention given by the international community to atrocity crises for much of this period.

It is instructive to contrast Obama's efforts to grapple with imperfect responsibilities with those of his successor, Donald Trump, not to cast Obama as the ideal and again not to reduce the global politics of human protection to American foreign policy, so much as to underline the highly contingent and fickle fate of such responsibilities. We saw in chapter 5 that the stickiness of R2P was observable both in some Trump administration rhetoric and also in instances where the United States continued to respond in meaningful ways to atrocities. This lingering stickiness, however, was so often overwhelmed by the mantra of "America First"—that unambiguous answer to the question of how competing responsibilities should be weighed, which served to justify the slashing of peacekeeping budgets and refugee intakes and the shameless embrace of tyrants the world over.

Trump's populist dismissal of international responsibilities, moreover, has been replicated in numerous Western states that have previously been relied on to champion and bear much of the responsibility for global protection efforts. Rising non-Western powers, meanwhile, have shown little interest in assuming these responsibilities for themselves, at least not insofar as it involves interfering in other states' sovereign affairs. As human protection norms weaken, states that perceive little interest in protecting distant strangers feel diminishing pressure to do so and states that desire to shield perpetrators or even perpetrate atrocities themselves pay little cost for doing so. In too many atrocity crises around the world, the limits of imperfect responsibilities are being plainly exposed.

Given the nature of the present challenges to the responsibility to protect, I conclude by suggesting two complementary ways forward. Neither overcomes these challenges fully; neither "perfects" the responsibility's imperfections. Other scholars and practitioners have and will continue to propose ways to edge toward "perfecting" human protection responsibilities, via binding institutional or legal agreements such as the oft-mooted institutionalized distribution of the costs of African Union peacekeeping operations to complement the financing of UN peacekeeping operations, and the adoption of a Convention on the Prevention and Punishment of Crimes against Humanity to complement the Genocide Convention. I fully accept the value of such work.[12] But instead I propose two fundamental shifts in thinking that proponents of human protection might fruitfully promote. If future institutional or legal developments aimed at binding states to extraterritorial protection responsibilities are to generate buy-in, rather than triggering the exploitation of new loopholes and perverse incentives that such institutions and laws so often produce, it seems to me, they will need to be grounded in changed ways of thinking.

Reckoning with Our Own Imperfections

First, powerful Western states urgently need to adopt a more humble and even a more repentant global politics. Insofar as they are able to muster the willingness to pursue human protection activities, they cannot expect to successfully cajole or shame Russia and China into facilitating such projects in the UN Security Council as they once could—at least not in instances where Russia or China discern an interest in standing in the way. As China in particular assumes a more dominant position in the global order and promotes its alternative vision of the norms underpinning that order, states seeking to protect strangers will need to increasingly rely on consensual measures rather than measures that challenge state sovereignty—working *with* host states rather than *against* them to ensure that populations are protected. This is not merely necessary for the purpose of sustaining a modicum of international consensus on human protection. It is ethically warranted since powerful states have so often succumbed to temptations of hubris and abuse when undertaking nonconsensual intervention. Put plainly, proponents of human protection should stop focusing so much on questions of nonconsensual military intervention and pay more attention to the possibilities of consensual peace operations as well as the wide array of nonmilitarized protection measures that have a relatively strong record of success.

In certain rare and tragic instances, the nonconsensual resort to force may be the most credible means of protecting civilians. But the efforts of

certain Western governments and prominent Western lawyers to either
claim a right to intervene without Security Council authorization or propose
that such a right be constructed in law are unhelpful.[13] The solution to the
problem of atrocities is not more unauthorized interventions. As we saw in
chapter 3, despite all its faults and divisions, the Security Council has not
once this century refused to authorize a nonconsensual military intervention
that has stood a credible chance of protecting civilians. And when states *have*
intervened without authorization under the guise (partial or otherwise)
of protecting people from tyranny and persecution, the results have been
either disastrous for civilians (as in Iraq 2003, Georgia 2008, and Crimea
2014) or at best fairly inconsequential (as in US-led airstrikes in response
to Syrian chemical weapons use in 2017 and 2018). Only once this century
has the international community been confronted with what has appeared
a credible opportunity to save lives through nonconsensual intervention,
and in this case, Libya in 2011, the Security Council authorized the resort to
force. Whatever the merits of that decision, the intervention's failures make
clear that the solution does not lie in further expanding the legal grounds
and opportunities for resorting to force. For all its talk of sovereign consent
and the need to respect the will and leadership of host governments, and
for all its condemnations of reckless Western militarism, China continues to
acknowledge that "when all peaceful measures have been exhausted," there
may be an occasional need for "military action taken by the international
community to protect civilians . . . authorized by the Security Council."[14]
Until China (or Russia) refuses to authorize a necessary intervention even
once this century, Western claims that states need to be allowed to intervene
without council permission risk further eroding international consensus on
human protection and risk fostering foolish wars.

The case for unauthorized intervention is particularly weak, moreover,
given that the Western states that typically advance these arguments could
in every instance do more to protect vulnerable people without resorting to
force, if they wished. As noted in chapter 3, if powerful states are so intent
on protecting foreigners, as they inevitably insist they are when defending
unauthorized intervention, they will not lack opportunities to do so via other
means. Most obviously, and with little risk of doing more harm than good,
these states could resettle more refugees fleeing atrocities. While resettlement is often domestically controversial, it brings with it none of the international tensions about host state consent or Security Council authorization
that accompany numerous other protection measures. The willingness of

states to welcome vulnerable outsiders into their communities thus constitutes an especially useful test of how sincere states really are about caring for strangers.

Resettlement, moreover, is a responsibility that in many instances proceeds quite directly from the historical and contemporary culpabilities of powerful states for the vulnerabilities of civilians beyond their borders. From the wars and conquests, the enslavement and eradication, the mass migration of people out of Europe, and the inflow of natural resources into Europe that attended European imperialism, to the reckless wars, careless arms trading, exploitative economic regulations, and environmental destruction of the postcolonial era, so many Western states have accrued and continue to maintain territories and riches via practices that sustain the poverty, instability, and vulnerability of others. Tendayi Achiume speaks of "migration as decolonization," arguing persuasively that the least that those states that have contributed to the vulnerability of people via colonial rule can do is to welcome them into their territories. Others speak similarly of "asylum as reparation," focusing often on the obligations of states whose more recent injustices contributed to the displacement of others, such as those responsible for the 2003 Iraq invasion, whose horrific legacy includes the continued production of displacement-generating atrocities across the region.[15]

Recall from chapter 1, moreover, that for at least a hundred years following Francisco de Vitoria, European colonizers and their supporters proffered an enforceable duty of (indigenous) hospitality alongside a binding duty to protect innocents from tyrannical indigenous rule, among other arguments, as justification for imperial expansion. How hypocritical it is that those same powerful Western polities that forcibly claimed hospitality from weaker and more vulnerable non-Western peoples now so often deny it to them.[16] Given these histories and hypocrisies, the provision of asylum to people fleeing atrocities, among other measures of protection, might be appropriately understood as restitution and even as a step toward repentance for past wrongs.

Inspiring Protection in an Imperfect World

Second, proponents of international human protection might fruitfully reconsider how protection responsibilities are framed. So often responsibilities are cast as burdens. I have often replicated this in this book, describing how states variously accept, distribute, and share burdens of responsibility, for example, so as to reflect the languages and sentiments of the political leaders and theorists under discussion. But the act of framing the responsibility to protect as a burden risks implying that it is something to be accepted reluctantly, something to be discharged only so as to relieve oneself of the load, something to be avoided via loopholes and excuses and shifted onto others where possible. What if we were to cast the responsibility to protect not as a burden but as an opportunity?

G. W. Leibniz, whose conception of natural duties I briefly described in chapter 1, helps us begin to see what this could look like. Lambasting Samuel Pufendorf's attempt to ground duties in considerations of material utility, Leibniz proposed that moral action be instead grounded in the happiness that people gain from promoting the well-being of others.[17] Leibniz often described this in terms of "disinterested love," but he also insisted that such love has its own earthly (as well as eternal) utility: the pleasure gained from contributing to the flourishing of others. He explained, therefore, that "while love can be disinterested, it can nonetheless never be detached from our own interest, of which pleasure is an essential part."[18]

Political leaders have occasionally appealed to such sentiments to justify decisions to care for victims of atrocities and to encourage their fellow citizens to accept the sacrifices involved. "I'm happy that Germany has become a country that many people abroad associate with hope," Chancellor Angela Merkel declared as hundreds of thousands of Syrians fleeing atrocities crossed Germany's recently opened borders to request asylum in 2015.[19] Often, the sentiment that accompanies action to protect civilians is not rightly described as "pleasure," particularly when it involves solemnly interceding to stop horrific crimes. Martha Nussbaum helpfully speaks instead of "good pains," in which actors care for others with a "painful compassion" that, while not pleasurable, nevertheless contributes to one's own "real happiness."[20] We can usefully speak of "pride" in this context, too, as a description of the deep satisfaction that can accompany a decision to protect the vulnerable. When Germans responded positively to Merkel's decision to open Germany's borders and made efforts to support new arrivals, she celebrated that they had "painted a picture of Germany which can make us proud of our country."[21] The provision of peacekeepers is, likewise, a source of pride for many states, and particularly states such as Rwanda that have their own histories of atrocities and now help prevent atrocities elsewhere by contributing troops and accepting casualties well in excess of their "fair share."

We might even join with Immanuel Kant in suggesting that if the cultivation of a compassionate disposition helps incline an individual (or state) to embrace opportunities to care for strangers in need, then such cultivation is not merely a means to responsible action. It is itself a responsibility. "But while it is not in itself a duty to share the sufferings (as well as the joys) of others," Kant claimed, "it is a duty to sympathize actively in their fate, and to this end it is therefore an indirect duty to cultivate the compassionate natural (aesthetic) feeling in us."[22] Certainly, in an often dangerous and unstable world, it can be entirely appropriate for states to secure certain material interests and prioritize the well-being of their own citizens. But states and their leaders should not thereby neglect the profound opportunities they have to accept risks and costs for the sake of outsiders. They can and should be encouraged to embrace such opportunities.

Insofar as states are proving less susceptible than they once were to international efforts to shame them into compliance with human protection norms, as I suggested in chapter 5 is the case, proponents of such norms might find greater success in presenting compliance in these positive terms: as a welcome opportunity that states can and should embrace, rather than an unwanted burden whose avoidance will come at a cost; inspiring them to comply with their shared responsibilities, rather than constraining them to do so. This is easier said than done, of course. But the politics of naming and shaming and rhetorical entrapment has always had its own struggles, not least the difficulty of generating a path from episodic shame-driven compliance to sustained norm acceptance and internalization.[23]

Recent years have witnessed useful examples of both state and non-state actors successfully enticing (as opposed to entrapping) reluctant states to embrace opportunities to comply with and to promote international norms related to human protection. We have seen nongovernmental organizations successfully enticing the United Kingdom to shift from being a spoiler to a champion of an international ban on cluster munitions, for example, as well as the United Kingdom successfully encouraging other states to commit to an international norm prohibiting the use of sexual violence in conflict.[24] It might be doubted that tactics of enticement and encouragement, which aim to mobilize feelings of pleasure and pride rather than guilt and shame, could lead a powerful state such as Russia to stop facilitating the perpetration of atrocities in Syria, or the United States and United Kingdom to stop enabling the Saudi-led coalition to commit atrocities in Yemen, or China to stop shielding Myanmar from international condemnation for its atrocities against the Rohingya. But they offer a happy alternative to prevailing and often unproductive tactics of shame and entrapment.

———

The Gambia, again, provides inspiration. The Gambia knows suffering well. As Justice Minister Abubacarr Tambadou tells it, The Gambia's own experiences of human rights abuses during the twenty-two-year rule of President Jammeh motivated it to speak out against the oppression of the Rohingya and bring the case against Myanmar to the International Court of Justice (ICJ) in 2019: "We don't want others to feel our pain or our fate." Tambadou himself knows suffering well, having listened to the stories of Rohingya survivors at a refugee camp in Bangladesh and recognized parallels with survivors' stories that he had heard years earlier as prosecutor at the International Criminal Tribunal for Rwanda. The Gambia discerned that it was obliged under the Genocide Convention to do what it could to bring the ongoing atrocities against the Rohingya to an end, Tambadou said, and by taking this case to the ICJ, his country was "showing the world you don't have to have military power or economic power to denounce oppressions. Legal obligation and moral responsibility exist for all states, big or small."[25]

The Gambia's action, which was supported from the outset by the member states of the Organization of Islamic Cooperation, quickly inspired responses from other states. Canada and the Netherlands spoke out in support of The Gambia, declaring that the case before the ICJ "should concern all of humanity."[26] Two weeks after the ICJ listened to The Gambia's argument for provisional measures against Myanmar, the UN General Assembly adopted a resolution, with 134 votes in favor and only 9 against, strongly condemning the human rights abuses and calling for immediate efforts to eliminate discrimination and statelessness within Myanmar.[27] As valuable as such statements and General Assembly resolutions can be, many states could do much more, individually and collectively, to protect not only the Rohingya but also millions of other civilians around the world threatened with, suffering, or fleeing atrocities. Recognizing that it shared with the rest of the international community an imperfect responsibility to protect, The Gambia embraced the opportunity to do what it could. May such acts inspire others to do the same.

ACKNOWLEDGMENTS

I first began thinking about this book a decade ago. I recall fondly conversations with Alex Bellamy that helped shape my initial thinking about the value of examining responsibilities through multiple lenses in order to get a clearer sense of the past and present possibilities, limits, and hazards of international efforts to protect vulnerable populations. Alex has continued to be a remarkable source of encouragement and advice in the years since. I am most grateful for the support and critical engagement that he has so frequently and generously provided.

Several colleagues provided useful and extensive comments on drafts as the book developed. Special thanks are due to Alex again, and also to Cian O'Driscoll and James Pattison, each of whom read the entire manuscript at one stage or another. I learnt much from their comments, and the book is better than it would otherwise be because of their input. I am also thankful to the UNSW Canberra International Ethics Research Group—led by Toni Erskine and including Tim Aistrope, Deane-Peter Baker, Peter Balint, Tony Burke, Simon Cotton, Ned Dobos, John Dryzek, Umut Ozguk, Jonathan Pickering, and Ana Tanasoca—who workshopped three draft chapters with me across three separate evenings and contributed numerous critical insights that helped shape the book.

I was privileged to receive thoughtful feedback on drafts of individual chapters from numerous other individuals and groups. For their input on chapter 1, I thank Richard Devetak, Andrew Fitzmaurice, Ian Hall, Ian Hunter, David Lupher, and Haig Patapan, as well as participants at a seminar at Griffith University and a workshop at the University of Queensland. I was fortunate to spend a sabbatical at the University of British Columbia (UBC) where much of the draft of chapter 2 was written, and I am grateful for numerous conversations, both on this chapter and also on the book as a whole, with my gracious host, Dick Price, as well as Michael Byers, Arjun Chowdhury, Katharina Coleman, and Brian Job. I am thankful also for feedback on an early version of that chapter from participants at a seminar at UBC organized by Michael

Byers. I am grateful to Joseph Mackay, Eglantine Staunton, and Ben Zala for conversations and comments on chapter 3. Chapter 5 benefited from the generosity of numerous colleagues who discussed ideas and provided thoughtful feedback on drafts, including Ben Day, Tim Dunne, Rosemary Foot, Charlie Hunt, Cecilia Jacob, Amy King, Phil Orchard, Sarah Teitt, Wes Widmaier, and Jeremy Youde, as well as others mentioned previously. Finally, I am indebted to many of the above, and additionally to Matt Davies, Sara Davies, Bina D'Costa, Emma Hutchison, Nick Lemay-Hébert, Alana Moore, Rhiannon Neilsen, Ellen Ravndal, Scott Robertson, Andrew Ross, and Jason Sharman, as well as participants at a seminar convened by Annette Pierdziwol at the University of Notre Dame (Sydney), a public lecture organized by David Lupher and Shampa Biswas at Whitman College, and a workshop held at my home institution, the Australian National University, for feedback on ideas and arguments presented in the book's introduction and conclusion.

My editors at Princeton University Press, Eric Crahan, Eric Weitz, Priya Nelson, and Thalia Leaf, provided invaluable support and advice throughout the process of turning a book proposal into a final manuscript. I am especially grateful to Eric Crahan, who understood from the outset my hopes and intentions in writing the book and made numerous suggestions that helped shape the manuscript to those ends. I was fortunate also to have two anonymous reviewers who engaged carefully with the book and provided detailed and insightful reviews. The opportunity to wrestle with their comments has, I hope, helped strengthen several key sections of the book and enhance its overall contribution. The input of Jenny Wolkowicki, Joseph Dahm, and Mary Lou Hickey in finalizing the manuscript and seeing it through to publication is also greatly appreciated.

Early iterations of some ideas in the book have been published elsewhere. Various chapters and sections draw on material from "The Responsibility to Protect beyond Borders in the Law of Nature and Nations," *European Journal of International Law* 28, no. 4 (2017): 1069–95, published by Oxford University Press; "The Responsibility to Protect beyond Borders," *Human Rights Law Review* 12, no. 1 (2012): 1–32, published by Oxford University Press; "Does R2P Matter? Interpreting the Impact of a Norm," *Cooperation and Conflict* 51, no. 2 (2016): 184–99, published by SAGE; "The Limits of Rhetorical Entrapment in a Post-Truth Age," *Critical Studies on Security* 7, no. 2 (2019): 162–65, published by Taylor & Francis. I am grateful to the publishers for permission to use this material.

My deepest gratitude goes to my delightful wife, Clare, for her constant support and enthusiasm for my research, and our tiny little children, Arthur, Jubilee, and Micah, for being completely silly and endlessly enjoyable.

NOTES

Introduction

1. Verbatim record of *Case Concerning Application of the Convention on the Prevention and Punishment of the Crime of Genocide (The Gambia v. Myanmar)*, ICJ, December 10, 2019, 17.

2. UN General Assembly, "2005 World Summit Outcome," A/Res/60/1 (October 24, 2005), paras. 138–39; UN Security Council Resolutions 1674 (April 28, 2006), 1706 (August 31, 2006), 1894 (November 11, 2009), 2217 (September 26, 2013), 2150 (April 16, 2014), 2171 (August 21, 2014), and 2220 (May 22, 2015).

3. UN Human Rights Council, A/HRC/39/64 (September 12, 2018), 8–9.

4. This story of a sudden shift from rights to responsibilities was first told by the international commission that developed the R2P concept in 2001 and has been accepted as fact by numerous commentators and practitioners since. See, for example, ICISS (International Commission on Intervention and State Sovereignty), *The Responsibility to Protect: Report of the International Commission on Intervention and State Sovereignty* (Ottawa: International Development Research Centre, 2001), 16–18; Manuel Fröhlich, "The Responsibility to Protect: Foundation, Transformation, and Application of an Emerging Norm," in *The Emergence of Humanitarian Intervention: Ideas and Practice from the Nineteenth Century to the Present*, ed. Fabian Klose (Cambridge: Cambridge University Press, 2016), 299–330, at 303 (accepting ICISS's claim to have instituted a "substantial change in the discourse" from a right to intervene to a responsibility to protect); Fabian Klose, "The Emergence of Humanitarian Intervention: Three Centuries of 'Enforcing Humanity,'" in Klose, *Emergence of Humanitarian Intervention*, 1–28, at 27 (claiming that the 2011 intervention in Libya was "the first time that the use of military intervention was justified by the argument of an international responsibility to react").

5. A/Res/60/1, paras. 138–39.

6. For some leading contributions to this renewed and deepening engagement with responsibilities across different fields, see Kathryn Sikkink, *The Hidden Face of Rights: Toward a Politics of Responsibilities* (New Haven, CT: Yale University Press, 2020); Hannes Hansen-Magnusson and Antje Vetterlein, eds., *The Rise of Responsibility in World Politics* (Cambridge: Cambridge University Press, 2020); Samuel Moyn, "A History of Duties for an Age of Rights" (Page-Barbour Lectures, University of Virginia, 2020); and the SHARES research project on shared responsibility in international law, directed by André Nollkaemper, which has produced three edited collections with Cambridge University Press since 2014. The field of international ethics, it should be said, despite the dominance of human rights discourse over the past half century, has consistently attended to the relationship between rights and responsibilities, as seen in works by Onora O'Neill, Henry Shue, Robert Goodin, and others.

7. Rajan Menon, *The Conceit of Humanitarian Intervention* (New York: Oxford University Press, 2016).

8. Ibid., 26.

9. Ibid., 20.

10. Ibid., 13–14. The parallels between this joke and so much analysis of the ethics of intervention are noted also in Chris Brown, "What, Exactly, Is the Problem to Which the 'Five-Part Test' Is the Solution?," *International Relations* 19, no. 2 (2005): 225–29, at 225.

11. Menon, *Conceit of Humanitarian Intervention*, 60–76.

12. Ibid., 4, 129. Several of these myths and misunderstandings are repeated in Rajan Menon, "In Defense of the Conceit of Humanitarian Intervention," *Journal of Genocide Research* 21, no. 1 (2019): 120–30.

13. Carl E. Schorske, *Thinking with History: Explorations in the Passage to Modernism* (Princeton: Princeton University Press, 1998).

14. On the possibility of "useful" anachronism, see Miri Rubin, "Presentism's Useful Anachronisms," *Past and Present* 234, no. 1 (2017): 236–44. For an illuminating examination of ongoing methodological debates among historians of international law and international relations, see Andrew Fitzmaurice, "Context in the History of International Law," *Journal of the History of International Law* 20, no. 1 (2018): 5–30.

15. Ethan A. Nadelmann, "Global Prohibition Regimes: The Evolution of Norms in International Society," *International Organization* 44, no. 4 (1990): 479–526.

16. Neta C. Crawford, *Argument and Change in World Politics: Ethics, Decolonization, and Humanitarian Intervention* (Cambridge: Cambridge University Press, 2002).

17. Audie Klotz, *Norms in International Relations: The Struggle against Apartheid* (Ithaca, NY: Cornell University Press, 1995).

18. Richard M. Price, *The Chemical Weapons Taboo* (Ithaca, NY: Cornell University Press, 1997).

19. Nina Tannenwald, *The Nuclear Taboo: The United States and the Non-use of Nuclear Weapons since 1945* (Cambridge: Cambridge University Press, 2007).

20. Richard Price, "Reversing the Gun Sights: Transnational Civil Society Targets Land Mines," *International Organization* 52, no. 3 (1998): 613–44.

21. Samuel Pufendorf, *Of the Law of Nature and Nations*, trans. Basil Kennett (London, 1729), I.7.7, III.3.

22. *Hansard's Parliamentary Debates, Third Series: Commencing with the Accession of William IV*, vol. 231, *Comprising the Period from 28 July 1876 to 15 August 1876* (London: Cornelius Buck, 1876), 1146.

23. "Remarks by President Obama and President Park of South Korea in a Joint Press Conference" (Washington, DC, May 7, 2013).

24. Emer de Vattel, *The Law of Nations, Or Principles of the Law of Nature, Applied to the Conduct and Affairs of Nations and Sovereigns, with Three Early Essays on the Origin and Nature of Natural Law and on Luxury*, ed. Béla Kapossy and Richard Whatmore (Indianapolis: Liberty Fund, 2008), I.19.230.

25. The quote is Obama's, in Jeffrey Goldberg, "The Obama Doctrine," *Atlantic*, April 2016. See also Trump lamenting the lack of burden sharing regarding the UN peacekeeping budget in UN General Assembly, A/73/PV.6 (September 25, 2019), 18.

26. Immanuel Kant, "The Metaphysics of Morals (1797)," in *Practical Philosophy*, ed. Mary J. Gregor (Cambridge: Cambridge University Press, 1996), 6.390.

27. George Earle Buckle, *The Life of Benjamin Disraeli, Earl of Beaconsfield*, vol. 6 (London: John Murray, 1920), 130, quoted in Gary J. Bass, *Freedom's Battle: The Origins of Humanitarian Intervention* (New York: Knopf, 2008), 296.

28. Quoted in Franklin Foer and Chris Hughes, "Barack Obama Is Not Pleased," *New Republic*, January 27, 2013.

29. Pufendorf, *Law of Nature and Nations*, III.3.

30. See, for example, Aidan Hehir, "The Responsibility to Protect: 'Sound and Fury Signifying Nothing?,'" *International Relations* 24, no. 2 (2010): 218–39, at 234–35.

31. Rather than providing timeless and potentially anachronistic definitions, I vary my usage of the terms "responsibility," "duty," and "obligation" in this book to accord with the conventions of the theorists and practitioners with whom I am engaging at any particular moment. I clarify at the beginning of chapter 4 a particularly important distinction between these words in the field of law.

32. *Case Concerning Application of the Convention on the Prevention and Punishment of the Crime of Genocide (Bosnia and Herzegovina v. Serbia and Montenegro)*, ICJ, February 26, 2007, para. 430.

Chapter 1

1. Lynn Hunt, *Inventing Human Rights: A History* (New York: Norton, 2007); Samuel Moyn, *The Last Utopia: Human Rights in History* (Cambridge, MA: Harvard University Press, 2010); Steven L. B. Jensen, *The Making of International Human Rights: The 1960s, Decolonization, and the Reconstruction of Global Values* (Cambridge: Cambridge University Press, 2016).

2. My previous book examined the history of the responsibilities of states to ensure the safety and well-being of their own citizens. Luke Glanville, *Sovereignty and the Responsibility to Protect: A New History* (Chicago: University of Chicago Press, 2014). Others have examined historical thinking about the responsibilities of states to extend hospitality to those who, fleeing persecution, seek asylum in their territories. Georg Cavallar, *The Rights of Strangers: Theories of International Hospitality, the Global Community, and Political Justice since Vitoria* (Farnham: Ashgate, 2002); Vincent Chetail, "Sovereignty and Migration in the Doctrine of the Law of Nations: An Intellectual History of Hospitality from Vitoria to Vattel," *European Journal of International Law* 27, no. 4 (2016): 901–22.

3. Brendan Simms and D. J. B. Trim, eds., *Humanitarian Intervention: A History* (Cambridge: Cambridge University Press, 2011); Stefano Recchia and Jennifer M. Welsh, eds., *Just and Unjust Military Intervention: European Thinkers from Vitoria to Mill* (Cambridge: Cambridge University Press, 2013); Fabian Klose, ed., *The Emergence of Humanitarian Intervention: Ideas and Practice from the Nineteenth Century to the Present* (Cambridge: Cambridge University Press, 2016).

4. For a particularly valuable exception, which has substantially influenced my own reading of intellectual history, see Richard Tuck, *The Rights of War and Peace: Political Thought and the International Order from Grotius to Kant* (Oxford: Oxford University Press, 1999).

5. Anthony Pagden, *The Enlightenment: And Why It Still Matters* (Oxford: Oxford University Press, 2013), 344.

6. See, for example, Anthony Pagden, *The Fall of Natural Man: The American Indian and the Origins of Comparative Ethnology* (Cambridge: Cambridge University Press, 1982); Anthony Pagden, *Spanish Imperialism and the Political Imagination* (New Haven, CT: Yale University Press, 1990).

7. Seyla Benhabib, *The Rights of Others: Aliens, Residents and Citizens* (Cambridge: Cambridge University Press, 2004), 40–43.

8. Immanuel Kant, "Toward Perpetual Peace (1795)," in *Practical Philosophy*, ed. Mary J. Gregor (Cambridge: Cambridge University Press, 1996), 8.346. I discuss the Peace of Westphalia and the anachronistic notion of "Westphalian sovereignty" in chapter 2.

9. Brian D. Lepard, *Rethinking Humanitarian Intervention: A Fresh Legal Approach Based on Fundamental Ethical Principles in International Law and World Religions* (University Park: Pennsylvania State University Press, 2002), 39–98; Rama Mani and Thomas G. Weiss, eds., *Responsibility to Protect: Cultural Perspectives in the Global South* (Abingdon: Routledge, 2011); Jacinta O'Hagan,

"The Responsibility to Protect: A Western Idea?" in *Theorising the Responsibility to Protect*, ed. Ramesh Thakur and William Maley (Cambridge: Cambridge University Press, 2015), 285–304.

10. For a defense of the utility of "languages" for the study of intellectual history, see Anthony Pagden, ed., *The Languages of Political Theory in Early-Modern Europe* (Cambridge: Cambridge University Press, 1987). For an explanation of why it is plausible to treat Kant as a natural law theorist, see Knud Haakonssen, "German Natural Law," in *The Cambridge History of Eighteenth-Century Political Thought*, ed. Mark Goldie and Robert Wokler (Cambridge: Cambridge University Press, 2006), 249–90.

11. For examples of contextualist historians offering chapter-length studies of the development of ideas across multiple contexts, see Quentin Skinner, "The Sovereign State: A Genealogy," in *Sovereignty in Fragments: The Past, Present and Future of a Contested Concept*, ed. Hent Kalmo and Quentin Skinner (Cambridge: Cambridge University Press, 2010), 26–46; Richard Tuck, "Grotius, Hobbes, and Pufendorf on Humanitarian Intervention," in Recchia and Welsh, *Just and Unjust Military Intervention*, 96–112.

12. See, for example, Cicero, *On Duties*, ed. M. T. Griffin and E. M. Atkins (Cambridge: Cambridge University Press, 1991); Ambrose, *De Officiis*, vol. 1, ed. Ivor J. Davidson (Oxford: Oxford University Press, 2001).

13. For useful overviews of Vitoria's vision of global order, see William Bain, "Vitoria: The Law of War, Saving the Innocent, and the Image of God," in Recchia and Welsh, *Just and Unjust Military Intervention*, 70–95; Kirstin Bunge, "Francisco de Vitoria: A Redesign of Global Order on the Threshold of the Middle Ages to Modern Times," in *System, Order, and International Law: The Early History of International Legal Thought from Machiavelli to Hegel*, ed. Stefan Kadelbach, Thomas Kleinlein, and David Roth-Isigkeit (Oxford: Oxford University Press, 2017), 38–55.

14. See Thomas Aquinas, *Summa Theologica*, trans. Fathers of the Dominican Province (Notre Dame: Christian Classics, 1981), II–II.32.5, 58.11, 66.7, 79.1.

15. Ibid., II–II.58.6, 32.5. See also Stephen J. Pope, "Aquinas on Almsgiving, Justice and Charity: An Interpretation and Reassessment," *Heythrop Journal* 32, no. 2 (1991): 167–91.

16. Aquinas, *Summa Theologica*, II–II.26.8, 31.3, 32.5.

17. Francisco de Vitoria, "On the American Indians," in *Political Writings*, ed. Anthony Pagden and Jeremy Lawrance (Cambridge: Cambridge University Press, 1991), 273–74.

18. Ibid., 287–88, quoting Proverbs 24:11.

19. Bartolomé de Las Casas, *In Defense of the Indians*, trans. Stafford Poole (DeKalb: Northern Illinois University Press, 1992), 186–87.

20. Francisco de Vitoria, "On Dietary Laws, or Self-Restraint," in *Political Writings*, ed. Pagden and Lawrance, 226.

21. Melchor Cano, "De dominio Indorum," in *Corpus Hispanorum de Pace*, vol. 9, ed. Luciano Pereña (Madrid: Consejo Superior de Investigaciones Cientificas, 1982), 561–63; Domingo de Soto, "Relectio, an liceat civitates infidelium seu gentilium expugnare ob idolatriam," in Pereña, *Corpus Hispanorum de Pace*, 592.

22. Las Casas, *In Defense of the Indians*, 190.

23. Vitoria, "On the American Indians," 281.

24. Domingo de Soto, *De iustitia et iure* (Salamanca, 1553), V.3.3; Cano, "De dominio Indorum," 579.

25. Alberico Gentili, *De jure belli libri tres*, vol. 2, trans. John C. Rolfe (Oxford: Clarendon, 1933), 79–82, 86–92; Hugo Grotius, *De jure belli ac pacis libris tres*, vol. 2, ed. Francis W. Kelsey (Oxford: Clarendon, 1925), II.2. See, for discussion, Andrew Fitzmaurice, *Sovereignty, Property and Empire: 1500–2000* (Cambridge: Cambridge University Press, 2014). For thoughtful deliberations on the long-standing debate about whether Vitoria should be read as an apologist for empire, see Andrew Fitzmaurice, "The Problem of Eurocentrism in the Thought of Francisco de Vitoria,"

in *At the Origins of Modernity: Francisco de Vitoria and the Discovery of International Law*, ed. José María Beneyto and Justo Corti Varela (New York: Springer, 2017), 77–93.

26. On the scholastic-humanist debate, see Erika Rummel, *The Humanist-Scholastic Debate in the Renaissance and Reformation* (Cambridge, MA: Harvard University Press, 1995). On the distinct visions of international order that these two traditions produced, see Tuck, *Rights of War and Peace*, 16–77.

27. Diego Panizza, "Political Theory and Jurisprudence in Gentili's De Iure Belli: The Great Debate between 'Theological' and 'Humanist' Perspectives from Vitoria to Grotius" (IILJ Working Paper 2005/15, Institute for International Law and Justice, New York University School of Law, 2005); Pärtel Piirimäe, "Alberico Gentili's Doctrine of Defensive War and its Impact on Seventeenth-Century Normative Views," in *The Roman Foundations of the Law of Nations: Alberico Gentili and the Justice of Empire*, ed. Benedict Kingsbury and Benjamin Straumann (New York: Oxford University Press, 2010), 187–209.

28. Gentili, *De jure belli*, 59.

29. Francisco de Vitoria, "On the Law of War," in *Political Writings*, ed. Pagden and Lawrance, 297.

30. Gentili, *De jure belli*, 61–66, 83–85.

31. Ibid., 67.

32. Ibid., 67–73.

33. Ibid., 74.

34. Vitoria, "On Dietary Laws," 227–28.

35. Gentili, *De jure belli*, 67.

36. Ibid., 77–78.

37. Ibid., 70.

38. Jean Barbeyrac, "An Historical and Critical Account of the Science of Morality," in Samuel Pufendorf, *Of the Law of Nature and Nations*, trans. Basil Kennett (London, 1729), 79. Barbeyrac was a French jurist and an influential translator and commentator of both Grotius and Pufendorf.

39. Ibid., 80–85.

40. Brian Tierney, *The Idea of Natural Rights: Studies on Natural Rights, Natural Law, and Church Law, 1150–1625* (Atlanta: Scholars Press, 1997), 316–42; Peter Haggenmacher, "Grotius and Gentili: A Reassessment of Thomas E. Holland's Inaugural Lecture," in *Hugo Grotius and International Relations*, ed. Hedley Bull, Benedict Kingsbury, and Adam Roberts (Oxford: Clarendon, 1990), 133–76.

41. Benjamin Straumann, *Roman Law in the State of Nature: The Classical Foundations of Hugo Grotius' Natural Law* (Cambridge: Cambridge University Press, 2015), 83–129. See also Richard Tuck, "The 'Modern' Theory of Natural Law," in Pagden, *Languages of Political Theory in Early-Modern Europe*, 99–120.

42. Tuck, *Rights of War and Peace*, 6.

43. Straumann, *Roman Law in the State of Nature*, 130–56.

44. Grotius, *De jure belli ac pacis*, Prol. 6.

45. Hugo Grotius, *Commentary on the Law of Prize and Booty*, ed. Martine Julia van Ittersum (Indianapolis: Liberty Fund, 2006), 19–50. For key contributions to ongoing debate about the relationship between self-preservation and sociability in Grotius's system, see Tuck, *Rights of War and Peace*, 78–108; Christopher Brooke, *Philosophic Pride: Stoicism and Political Thought from Lipsius to Rousseau* (Princeton: Princeton University Press, 2012), 37–58; Straumann, *Roman Law in the State of Nature*.

46. Grotius, *De jure belli ac pacis*, Prol. 8.

47. Ibid., Prol. 8, I.1.8.1, II.17.9.

48. Grotius, *Commentary on the Law of Prize and Booty*, 35–37.

49. Ibid., 433. See also 92–94, 432–35. On the context of *De jure praedae*, see Martine Julia van Ittersum, *Profit and Principle: Hugo Grotius, Natural Rights Theories and the Rise of Dutch Power in the East Indies (1595–1615)* (Leiden: Brill, 2006).

50. Grotius, *De jure belli ac pacis*, II.25.

51. Thomas Hobbes, *On the Citizen*, ed. Richard Tuck and Michael Silverthorne (Cambridge: Cambridge University Press, 1997), I.2, I.2n.

52. Thomas Hobbes, *Leviathan*, ed. J. C. A. Gaskin (Oxford: Oxford University Press, 1996), XIII.8, 12.

53. Ibid., XIV.1.

54. Noel Malcolm, *Aspects of Hobbes* (Oxford: Oxford University Press, 2002), 432–56; Theodore Christov, *Before Anarchy: Hobbes and His Critics in Modern International Thought* (New York: Cambridge University Press, 2015), 33–140.

55. Hobbes, *Leviathan*, XIII.13.

56. See, for example, Thomas Hobbes, *A Dialogue between a Philosopher and a Student of the Common Laws of England*, ed. Joseph Cropsey (Chicago: University of Chicago Press, 1971), 65, discussed in Malcolm, *Aspects of Hobbes*, 455–56.

57. Fiammetta Palladini, "Pufendorf Disciple of Hobbes: The Nature of Man and the State of Nature: The Doctrine of Socialitas," *History of European Ideas* 34, no. 1 (2008): 26. See also Fiammetta Palladini, *Samuel Pufendorf Disciple of Hobbes: For a Reinterpretation of Modern Natural Law*, trans. David Saunders (Leiden: Brill, 2020).

58. Pufendorf, *Law of Nature and Nations*, II.2–3, esp. II.3.14.

59. Ibid., II.3.15.

60. T. J. Hochstrasser, *Natural Law Theories in the Early Enlightenment* (Cambridge: Cambridge University Press, 2000), 69–70.

61. Anthony Pagden, "Stoicism, Cosmopolitanism, and the Legacy of European Imperialism," *Constellations* 7, no. 1 (2000): 3–22, at 12. See similarly Tuck, *Rights of War and Peace*, 140–65.

62. Palladini, "Pufendorf Disciple of Hobbes," 89; Christov, *Before Anarchy*, 143–210.

63. Pufendorf, *Law of Nature and Nations*, I.7.7, III.3.

64. Ibid., III.3.

65. Ibid., VIII.6.14.

66. Ibid., III.3.9.

67. On these rival visions, see Hochstrasser, *Natural Law Theories*; Ian Hunter, *Rival Enlightenments: Civil and Metaphysical Philosophy in Early Modern Germany* (Cambridge: Cambridge University Press, 2001); Haakonssen, "German Natural Law."

68. G. W. Leibniz, *Political Writings*, ed. Patrick Riley (Cambridge: Cambridge University Press, 1972), 67.

69. For a sample, see ibid., 45–84.

70. Christian Wolff, *Jus gentium methodo scientifica pertractatum*, vol. 2, ed. Joseph H. Drake (Oxford: Clarendon, 1934), II.162–63, 161, 177, 156.

71. Tuck, *Rights of War and Peace*, 191–96; Christov, *Before Anarchy*, 234–68.

72. Kant, "Toward Perpetual Peace," 8.355.

73. Emer de Vattel, *The Law of Nations, Or Principles of the Law of Nature, Applied to the Conduct and Affairs of Nations and Sovereigns, with Three Early Essays on the Origin and Nature of Natural Law and on Luxury*, ed. Béla Kapossy and Richard Whatmore (Indianapolis: Liberty Fund, 2008). For further discussion, see Luke Glanville, "Responsibility to Perfect: Vattel's Conception of Duties beyond Borders," *International Studies Quarterly* 61, no. 2 (2017): 385–95.

74. Béla Kapossy, "Introduction: Rival Histories of Emer de Vattel's Law of Nations," *Grotiana* 31, no. 1 (2010): 5–21; Christov, *Before Anarchy*, 211–68.

75. Vattel, *Law of Nations*, Prelim. §§10, 11, 16–17, 20.

76. Tuck, *Rights of War and Peace*, 191–96; David Armitage, *Foundations of Modern International Thought* (Cambridge: Cambridge University Press, 2013), 154–71.

77. Vattel, *Law of Nations*, III.13.

78. Ibid., Prelim. §20.

79. Ibid., II.1.9.

80. Ibid., Prelim. §14, II.10.131.

81. Ibid., II.1.15.

82. Ibid., II.1.6.

83. Ibid., II.1.13.

84. Ibid., I.19.230.

85. Immanuel Kant, "Groundwork of The Metaphysics of Morals (1785)," in Gregor, *Practical Philosophy*, 4.410.

86. Ibid.

87. Ibid., 4.406–45.

88. Immanuel Kant, "The Metaphysics of Morals (1797)," in Gregor, *Practical Philosophy*, 6.312.

89. Kant, "Toward Perpetual Peace," 8.355.

90. Kant, "Metaphysics of Morals," 6.350.

91. Kant, "Toward Perpetual Peace," 8.358.

92. Kant, "Metaphysics of Morals," 6.532.

93. Kant, "Toward Perpetual Peace," 8.357.

94. Ibid., 8.343–47.

95. Kant, "Metaphysics of Morals," 6.390.

96. Ibid., 6.453, 6.457. See also Nancy Sherman, *Making a Necessity of Virtue: Aristotle and Kant on Virtue* (Cambridge: Cambridge University Press, 1997), 121–86.

Chapter 2

1. Gary J. Bass, *Freedom's Battle: The Origins of Humanitarian Intervention* (New York: Alfred A. Knopf, 2008); Brendan Simms and D. J. B. Trim, eds., *Humanitarian Intervention: A History* (Cambridge: Cambridge University Press, 2011); Davide Rodogno, *Against Massacre: Humanitarian Interventions in the Ottoman Empire, 1815–1914* (Princeton: Princeton University Press, 2012); Fabian Klose, ed., *The Emergence of Humanitarian Intervention: Ideas and Practice from the Nineteenth Century to the Present* (Cambridge: Cambridge University Press, 2016).

2. Michael Barnett, *Empire of Humanity: A History of Humanitarianism* (Ithaca, NY: Cornell University Press, 2011); Bruno Cabanes, *The Great War and the Origins of Humanitarianism, 1918–1924* (Cambridge: Cambridge University Press, 2014); Keith David Watenpaugh, *Bread from Stones: The Middle East and the Making of Modern Humanitarianism* (Oakland: University of California Press, 2015); Eleanor Davey, *Idealism beyond Borders: The French Revolutionary Left and the Rise of Humanitarianism, 1954–1988* (Cambridge: Cambridge University Press, 2015); Michelle Tusan, *The British Empire and the Armenian Genocide: Humanitarianism and Imperial Politics from Gladstone to Churchill* (London: I. B. Taurus, 2017).

3. Carole Fink, *Defending the Rights of Others: The Great Powers, the Jews, and International Minority Protection, 1878–1938* (Cambridge: Cambridge University Press, 2004); Umut Özsu, *Formalizing Displacement: International Law and Population Transfers* (Oxford: Oxford University Press, 2015); Laura Robson, *States of Separation: Transfer, Partition, and the Making of the Modern Middle East* (Berkeley: University of California Press, 2017).

4. Michael R. Marrus, *The Unwanted: European Refugees from the First World War through the Cold War* (Philadelphia: Temple University Press, 2002); Phil Orchard, *A Right to Flee: Refugees,*

States, and the Construction of International Cooperation (Cambridge: Cambridge University Press, 2014); Caroline Shaw, *Britannia's Embrace: Modern Humanitarianism and the Imperial Origins of Refugee Relief* (Oxford: Oxford University Press, 2015).

5. William Bain, *Between Anarchy and Society: Trusteeship and the Obligations of Power* (Oxford: Oxford University Press, 2003); Susan Pedersen, *The Guardians: The League of Nations and the Crisis of Empire* (Oxford: Oxford University Press, 2015); Lauren Benton, Adam Clulow, and Bain Attwood, eds., *Protection and Empire: A Global History* (Cambridge: Cambridge University Press, 2018).

6. See, among a growing literature, William Gervase Clarence-Smith, *Islam and the Abolition of Slavery* (Oxford: Oxford University Press, 2006); Semih Çelik, "Between History of Humanitarianism and Humanitarianization of History: A Discussion on Ottoman Help for the Victims of the Great Irish Famine, 1845–1852," *Werkstatt Geschichte* 68 (2015): 13–27; Maria Framke, "Political Humanitarianism in the 1930s: Indian Aid for Republican Spain," *European Review of History* 23, nos. 1–2 (2016): 63–81; Esther Moeller, "The Suez Crisis of 1956 as a Moment of Transnational Humanitarian Engagement," *European Review of History* 23, nos. 1–2 (2016): 136–53; Maria Framke, "'We Must Send a Gift Worthy of India and the Congress!' War and Political Humanitarianism in Late Colonial South Asia," *Modern Asian Studies* 51, no. 6 (2017): 1969–98. See also numerous papers produced by the Overseas Development Institute's project, "Global History of Modern Humanitarian Action" (2011–15), available at https://www.odi.org/projects /2547-global-history-modern-humanitarian-action.

7. For broader discussions of the historical globalization of European international society, its practices, and its institutions, see Mark Mazower, *No Enchanted Palace: The End of Empire and the Ideological Origins of the United Nations* (Princeton: Princeton University Press, 2009); Barry Buzan and George Lawson, *The Global Transformation: History, Modernity and the Making of International Relations* (Cambridge: Cambridge University Press, 2015); Tim Dunne and Christian Reus-Smit, eds., *The Globalization of International Society* (Oxford: Oxford University Press, 2017); Adom Getachew, *Worldmaking after Empire: The Rise and Fall of Self-Determination* (Princeton: Princeton University Press, 2019).

8. Of course, non-Western efforts to resist or reshape Western practices of protection themselves have a long history, as is demonstrated, for example, in Alan Lester and Fae Dussart, *Colonization and the Origins of Humanitarian Governance: Protecting Aborigines across the Nineteenth-Century British Empire* (Cambridge: Cambridge University Press, 2014).

9. Three omissions in particular bear noting: I mention at several points, but do not piece together, a history of non-state humanitarianism and advocacy and its impact on the construction and performance of responsibilities by states and international institutions. I omit discussion of the place of ideas of responsibilities in debates about several "humanitarian interventions" that the United States undertook or refrained from undertaking in the late nineteenth and early twentieth centuries, since these debates reveal less about the politics of shared responsibilities than do the European great power interventions in the Ottoman Empire that I consider. And I do not discuss interventions by Western powers in non-Western affairs undertaken for the purpose of protecting conationals, more so than vulnerable foreigners, such as the intervention to put down the Boxer Rebellion in 1900.

10. It is worth noting that while responsibility for each mandated territory was borne by an individual power rather than shared, the negotiations among Western powers about how these responsibilities should be allocated in the first place, and especially Britain's efforts to persuade the United States to accept responsibility for the Armenians, constitute another interesting episode in the history of responsibility sharing that I have omitted from this chapter. This story is expertly told in Charlie Laderman, *Sharing the Burden: The Armenian Question, Humanitarian Intervention, and Anglo-American Visions of Global Order* (Oxford: Oxford University Press, 2019).

11. For key works demolishing the Westphalian myth, see Stephen D. Krasner, "Westphalia and All That," in *Ideas and Foreign Policy: Beliefs, Institutions, and Political Change*, ed. Judith Goldstein and Robert O. Keohane (Ithaca, NY: Cornell University Press, 1993), 235–64; Andreas Osiander, "Sovereignty, International Relations, and the Westphalian Myth," *International Organization* 55, no. 2 (2001): 251–87. For a critique of the ongoing and problematic use of the myth in R2P scholarship, see Luke Glanville, *Sovereignty and the Responsibility to Protect: A New History* (Chicago: University of Chicago Press, 2014).

12. Glanville, *Sovereignty and the Responsibility to Protect*, 49–56. In making this claim, I drew heavily on Brendan Simms, "'A False Principle in the Law of Nations': Burke, State Sovereignty, [German] Liberty, and Intervention in the Age of Westphalia," in Simms and Trim, *Humanitarian Intervention*, 89–110.

13. "Treaty of Osnabruck," in *The Consolidated Treaty Series*, vol. 1, *1648–1649*, ed. Clive Parry (Dobbs Ferry, NY: Oceana, 1969), 198–270, at §28, 228–29.

14. "Treaty of Munster," in Parry, *Consolidated Treaty Series*, 319–56, at §CXXIII–CXXIV, 354.

15. Patrick Milton, "The Early Eighteenth-Century German Confessional Crisis: The Juridification of Religious Conflict in the Reconfessionalized Politics of the Holy Roman Empire," *Central European History* 49, no. 1 (2016): 39–68. And see more broadly Patrick Milton, "Intervening against Tyrannical Rule in the Holy Roman Empire during the Seventeenth and Eighteenth Centuries," *German History* 33, no. 1 (2015): 1–29.

16. Quoted in Milton, "Early Eighteenth-Century German Confessional Crisis," 48–50, 53.

17. "A Declaration of the Causes Moving the Queen of England to Give Aid to the Defense of the People Afflicted and Oppressed in the Low Countries (1585)," in *Elizabethan and Jacobean England: Sources and Documents of the English Renaissance*, ed. Arthur F. Kinney (Malden, MA: Wiley-Blackwell, 2011), 86.

18. Andrew C. Thompson, "The Protestant Interest and the History of Humanitarian Intervention, c. 1685–c. 1756," in Simms and Trim, *Humanitarian Intervention*, 67–88, at 87–88.

19. Andrew C. Thompson, *Britain, Hanover and the Protestant Interest, 1688–1756* (Woodbridge, Suffolk: Boydell and Brewer, 2006).

20. Quoted in ibid., 72; Milton, "Early Eighteenth-Century German Confessional Crisis," 55.

21. Michael Geyer, "Humanitarianism and Human Rights: A Troubled Rapport," in Klose, *Emergence of Humanitarian Intervention*, 31–55, at 43.

22. Quoted in Mark Mazower, *Governing the World: The History of an Idea, 1815 to the Present* (New York: Penguin, 2012), 9.

23. On the great powers' joint management of the international order after 1815, see Jennifer Mitzen, *Power in Concert: The Nineteenth-Century Origins of Global Governance* (Chicago: University of Chicago Press, 2013).

24. For recent historiography, see Leslie Rogne Schumacher, "The Eastern Question as a Europe Question: Viewing the Ascent of 'Europe' through the Lens of Ottoman Decline," *Journal of European Studies* 44, no. 1 (2014): 64–80.

25. See especially Bass, *Freedom's Battle*.

26. Lynn Hunt, *Inventing Human Rights: A History* (New York: Norton, 2007); Richard Ashby Wilson and Richard D. Brown, eds., *Humanitarianism and Suffering: The Mobilization of Empathy* (Cambridge: Cambridge University Press, 2009); Barnett, *Empire of Humanity*.

27. Martha Finnemore, *The Purpose of Intervention: Changing Beliefs about the Use of Force* (Ithaca, NY: Cornell University Press, 2003), 52–84; Rodogno, *Against Massacre*.

28. Abigail Green, "Intervening in the Jewish Question, 1840–1878," in Simms and Trim, *Humanitarian Intervention*, 139–58.

29. The quote is from W. E. Gladstone, *Bulgarian Horrors and the Question of the East* (New York and Montreal: Lovell, Adam, Wesson & Company, 1876), 22.

30. Rodogno, *Against Massacre*.

31. Geyer, "Humanitarianism and Human Rights," 43.

32. Barbara Jelavich, *Russia's Balkan Entanglements: 1806–1914* (Cambridge: Cambridge University Press, 1991), 49–59.

33. Quoted in Arthur Wellesley, Duke of Wellington, *Despatches, Correspondence, and Memoranda of Field Marshal Arthur, Duke of Wellington, K.G.*, vol. 2 (London: John Murray, 1867), 371.

34. Mitzen, *Power in Concert*, 123–33.

35. Viscount Castlereagh, *Correspondence, Despatches, and Other Papers of Viscount Castlereagh*, vol. 12 (London: John Murray, 1853), 406.

36. Quoted in Charles K. Webster, *The Foreign Policy of Castlereagh*, vol. 2 (London: G. Bell and Sons, 1925), 377.

37. Thomas Erskine Holland, ed., *The European Concert in the Eastern Question: A Collection of Treaties and Other Public Acts* (Oxford: Clarendon, 1885), 7–9.

38. Echoing Castlereagh's acknowledgment of moral duty in 1821, Canning acknowledged in 1822 that, while Britain had no right or interest in intervening with force, "It is our right, our duty, and our inclination, to employ our utmost endeavours to induce the Porte . . . not only to grant the fullest amnesty, and proclaim the most liberal indulgence, but really and in good truth to govern their Christian subjects with a mild and equitable sway." Wellington, *Despatches, Correspondence, and Memoranda*, 372.

39. John Bew, "'From an Umpire to a Competitor': Castlereagh, Canning and the Issue of International Intervention in the Wake of the Napoleonic Wars," in Simms and Trim, *Humanitarian Intervention*, 117–38, at 136–37; Rodogno, *Against Massacre*, 88–90.

40. Holland, *European Concert*, 245–46.

41. Özsu, *Formalizing Displacement*, 27.

42. Rodogno, *Against Massacre*, 114.

43. Quoted in Bass, *Freedom's Battle*, 170, 175, 172.

44. Quoted in ibid., 188.

45. Ellery C. Stowell, *Intervention in International Law* (Washington, DC: John Byrne, 1921), 66.

46. Rodogno, *Against Massacre*, 117.

47. Ibid., 108.

48. Quoted in Bass, *Freedom's Battle*, 217.

49. Quoted in ibid., 181.

50. Quoted in ibid., 279–80. In 1822, Canning had expressed similar reservations about a potential war of religion against Turkish Muslims in defense of Christian Greeks. Wellington, *Despatches, Correspondence, and Memoranda*, 371.

51. Quoted in Bass, *Freedom's Battle*, 250.

52. I pursue this idea further in chapter 5.

53. *Hansard's Parliamentary Debates, Third Series: Commencing with the Accession of William IV*, vol. 231, *Comprising the Period from 28 July 1876 to 15 August 1876* (London: Cornelius Buck, 1876), 1131.

54. Ibid., 1126.

55. Ibid., 1136, quoting Micah 6:8.

56. Ibid., 1142.

57. Ibid., 1143.

58. Ibid., 1143.

59. Ibid., 1145–46.

60. Ibid., 1146–47.

61. Rodogno, *Against Massacre*, 154.

62. Gladstone, *Bulgarian Horrors*, 10.

63. Ibid., 13.

64. Ibid., 14–19.

65. Ibid., 27–28.

66. Ibid., 36, 33.

67. Quoted in Bass, *Freedom's Battle*, 278.

68. Ibid., 281.

69. Quoted in George Earle Buckle, *The Life of Benjamin Disraeli, Earl of Beaconsfield*, vol. 6 (New York: Macmillan, 1920), 122.

70. Quoted in Rodogno, *Against Massacre*, 164.

71. Quoted in Matthias Schulz, "The Guarantees of Humanity: The Concert of Europe and the Origins of the Russo-Ottoman War of 1877," in Simms and Trim, *Humanitarian Intervention*, 184–204, at 196.

72. Quoted in Bass, *Freedom's Battle*, 296.

73. Rodogno, *Against Massacre*, 164; Alexis Heraclides and Ada Dialla, *Humanitarian Intervention in the Long Nineteenth Century* (Manchester: Manchester University Press, 2015), 169–96.

74. "Treaty between Great Britain, Germany, Austria, France, Italy, Russia, and Turkey for the Settlement of Affairs in the East. Signed at Berlin, July 13, 1878," *American Journal of International Law* 2, no. 4, Supplement: Official Documents (1908): 401–24, including articles 4, 5, and 12 (Bulgaria), 27 and 30 (Montenegro), 35 and 39 (Serbia), 44 (Romania), and 20, 61, and 62 (Ottoman Empire).

75. Eric D. Weitz, "From the Vienna to the Paris System: International Politics and the Entangled Histories of Human Rights, Forced Deportations, and Civilizing Missions," *American Historical Review* 113, no. 5 (2008): 1313–43, at 1321.

76. Fink, *Defending the Rights of Others*, 15–38.

77. Ibid., 34.

78. Donald Bloxham, *The Great Game of Genocide: Imperialism, Nationalism, and the Destruction of the Ottoman Armenians* (Oxford: Oxford University Press, 2005), 53–54.

79. Peter Marsh, "Lord Salisbury and the Ottoman Massacres," *Journal of British Studies* 11, no. 2 (1972): 63–83, at 77–80; Rodogno, *Against Massacre*, 196–98.

80. *Hansard Parliamentary Debates, Fourth Series (1892–1908)*, vol. 37, 53–58. See also Marsh, "Lord Salisbury and the Ottoman Massacres," 80–81; Rodogno, *Against Massacre*, 198–99.

81. See similarly the speech by the previous prime minister, the Earl of Rosebery, in the House of Lords on the same day. *Hansard, Fourth Series*, vol. 37, 42–48. On Bryce's advocacy for the Armenians, see Oded Y. Steinberg, "The Confirmation of the Worst Fears: James Bryce, British Diplomacy and the Armenian Massacres of 1894–1896," *Études arméniennes contemporaines* 11 (2018): 15–39.

82. *Hansard, Fourth Series*, vol. 37, 152–55.

83. Ibid., 114–18, 161.

84. Ibid., 162.

85. Ibid., 163–64.

86. Bloxham, *Great Game of Genocide*; Laderman, *Sharing the Burden*.

87. Michael R. Marrus, "Holocaust Bystanders and Humanitarian Intervention," *Holocaust Studies* 13, no. 1 (2007): 1–18, at 9–12.

88. On the failed efforts by both Britain and also US president Woodrow Wilson to shift some Near-Eastern protection responsibilities onto the United States, see Laderman, *Sharing the Burden*.

89. See, among a growing literature, Barnett, *Empire of Humanity*, 49–94; Orchard, *Right to Flee*, 45–103; Shaw, *Britannia's Embrace*.

90. For analysis of the internationalization and ongoing development of humanitarianism and refugee protection in this period, see Marrus, *Unwanted*, 51–207; Cabanes, *Great War*;

Watenpaugh, *Bread from Stones*. On the "international turn" in this period more generally, see Glenda Sluga and Patricia Clavin, eds., *Internationalisms: A Twentieth Century History* (Cambridge: Cambridge University Press, 2017).

91. On the concurrent application of minority protection principles in mandated territories of the former Ottoman Empire, see Benjamin Thomas White, *The Emergence of Minorities in the Middle East: The Politics of Community in French Mandate Syria* (Edinburgh: Edinburgh University Press, 2011); Robson, *States of Separation*.

92. "Treaty of Peace between the United States of America, the British Empire, France, Italy, and Japan and Poland," *American Journal of International Law* 13, no. 4 Supplement: Official Documents (1919): 423–40.

93. "Letter Addressed to M. Paderewski by the President of the Conference Transmitting to Him the Treaty to Be Signed by Poland under Article 93 of the Treaty of Peace with Germany," *American Journal of International Law* 13, no. 4 Supplement: Official Documents (1919): 416–22, at 417–18.

94. Ibid., 419.

95. Fink, *Defending the Rights of Others*, 273.

96. "Letter Addressed to M. Paderewski," 420.

97. Weitz, "From the Vienna to the Paris System"; Özsu, *Formalizing Displacement*; Sarah Shields, "Forced Migration as Nation-Building: The League of Nations, Minority Protection, and the Greek-Turkish Population Exchange," *Journal of the History of International Law* 18, no. 1 (2016): 120–45.

98. James Headlam-Morley, quoted in Mark Mazower, "Minorities and the League of Nations in Interwar Europe," *Daedalus* 126, no. 2 (1997): 47–63, at 53.

99. Fink, *Defending the Rights of Others*, 267–365.

100. Adam Hochschild, *Bury the Chains: Prophets and Rebels in the Fight to Free an Empire's Slaves* (New York: Houghton Mifflin, 2005).

101. John Stuart Mill, "A Few Words on Non-Intervention (1859)," in *The Collected Works of John Stuart Mill*, vol. 21, *Essays on Equality, Law and Education* (London: Routledge and Kegan Paul, 1984), 111–24, at 112.

102. Lauren Benton and Lisa Ford, *Rage for Order: The British Empire and the Origins of International Law, 1800–1850* (Cambridge, MA: Harvard University Press, 2016), 117–31.

103. "Declaration of the Powers, on the Abolition of the Slave Trade (1815)," in *The Parliamentary Debates: From the Year 1803 to the Present Time*, ed. T. C. Hansard (London: T. C. Hansard, 1816), 32:200–201.

104. James Stephen, *An Inquiry into the Right and Duty of Compelling Spain to Relinquish Her Slave Trade in Northern Africa* (London: J. Butterworth and Son, 1816), 13, 50, 51; see also Fabian Klose, "Enforcing Abolition: The Entanglement of Civil Society Action, Humanitarian Norm-Setting, and Military Intervention," in Klose, *Emergence of Humanitarian Intervention*, 91–120, at 108–9.

105. Chaim D. Kaufmann and Robert A. Pape, "Explaining Costly International Moral Action: Britain's Sixty-Year Campaign against the Atlantic Slave Trade," *International Organization* 53, no. 4 (1999): 631–68, at 633.

106. Jenny S. Martinez, *The Slave Trade and the Origins of International Human Rights Law* (Oxford: Oxford University Press, 2012), 11–12.

107. "General Act of the Conference of Berlin (1885)," in *Archives of Empire*, vol. 2, *The Scramble for Africa*, ed. Barbara Harlow with Mia Carter (Durham, NC: Duke University Press, 2003), 28–42, at 32.

108. "Slave Trade and Importation into Africa of Firearms, Ammunition, and Spirituous Liquors (General Act of Brussels)," in *Treaties and Other International Agreements of the United*

States of America, 1776–1949, vol. 1, ed. Charles I. Bevans (Washington, DC: Government Printing Office, 1968), 134–60, at 135.

109. See also Kevin Grant, *A Civilized Savagery: Britain and the New Slaveries in Africa, 1884–1926* (New York: Routledge, 2005) (describing how, in abolishing the trade, the Berlin and Brussels Acts legitimated "new slaveries" in the form of coercive systems of labor, taxation, and indentured servitude in places such as the Congo, South Africa, and Portuguese West Africa); Richard Huzzey, *Freedom Burning: Anti-Slavery and Empire in Victorian Britain* (Ithaca, NY: Cornell University Press, 2012) (describing how antislavery passions and claims were deployed to legitimate imperial expansion).

110. Alan Lester and Fae Dussart emphasize the need to take seriously the humanitarian sensibilities of colonial officials and to resist separating settler colonialism from the history of the emergence of humanitarianism. Lester and Dussart, *Colonization and the Origins of Humanitarian Governance.*

111. See Bain, *Between Anarchy and Society*; Jennifer Pitts, *A Turn to Empire: The Rise of Imperial Liberalism in Britain and France* (Princeton: Princeton University Press, 2005).

112. See among a growing literature on the place of "protection" in European imperialism, Lester and Dussart, *Colonization and the Origins of Humanitarian Governance*; Benton, Clulow, and Attwood, *Protection and Empire*; Ann Curthoys and Jessie Mitchell, *Taking Liberty: Indigenous Rights and Settler Self-Government in Colonial Australia, 1830–1890* (Cambridge: Cambridge University Press, 2018); Christina Twomey and Katherine Ellinghaus, eds., "Protection: Global Genealogies, Local Practices," special issue, *Pacific Historical Review* 87, no. 1 (2018). On the annexation of Kandy, see Benton and Ford, *Rage for Order*, 85–116.

113. Herman Merivale, *Lectures on Colonization and Colonies*, vol. 2 (London: Longman, Brown, Green, and Longmans, 1842), 150–82 (quotes are from 150–53). See also the discussion in Duncan Bell, *Reordering the World: Essays on Liberalism and Empire* (Princeton: Princeton University Press, 2016), 41–42; Curthoys and Mitchell, *Taking Liberty*, 117–19.

114. Curthoys and Mitchell, *Taking Liberty*, 20.

115. "General Act of the Conference of Berlin (1885)," 31.

116. Quoted in Bain, *Between Anarchy and Society*, 68–69.

117. Adam Hochschild, *King Leopold's Ghost: A Story of Greed, Terror and Heroism in Colonial Africa* (New York: Mariner, 1998), 280.

118. Rodogno, *Against Massacre*, 181.

119. Pedersen, *Guardians*, 1.

120. "Covenant Text in the Treaty of Versailles," in *The Drafting of the Covenant*, vol. 2, ed. David Hunt Miller (New York: G. P. Putnam's Sons, 1928), 720–43, at 737.

121. Harold Temperley, *A History of the Peace Conference of Paris*, vol. 2, *The Settlement with Germany* (London: Oxford University Press, 1920), 236.

122. Pedersen, *Guardians*, 2.

123. Ibid., 4.

124. Priya Satia, "Guarding the Guardians: Payoffs and Perils," *Humanity* 7, no. 3 (2016): 481–98, at 485–86.

125. Susan Pedersen, "Getting Out of Iraq—In 1932: The League of Nations and the Road to Normative Statehood," *American Historical Review* 115, no. 4 (2010): 975–1000; Robson, *States of Separation*, 83–99.

126. Watenpaugh, *Bread from Stones*, 195–201; Özsu, *Formalizing Displacement*; Robson, *States of Separation*.

127. On the question of sovereignty, see Leonard V. Smith, "Sovereignty under the League of Nations Mandates: The Jurists' Debates," *Journal of the History of International Law* 21, no. 4 (2019): 563–87.

128. Bain, *Between Anarchy and Society*, 108–39.

129. Orchard, *Right to Flee*, 140–237.

130. Mark Mazower, "The Strange Triumph of Human Rights, 1933–1950," *Historical Journal* 47, no. 2 (2004): 379–98; Mark Mazower, *No Enchanted Palace*, 104–48; R. M. Douglas, *Orderly and Humane: The Expulsion of the Germans after the Second World War* (New Haven, CT: Yale University Press, 2012).

131. Quoted in Mazower, "Strange Triumph of Human Rights," 392.

132. United Nations Information Organizations, *Documents of the United Nations Conference on International Organization, San Francisco, 1945* (New York: Library of Congress, 1945), VI.324–25.

133. Glanville, *Sovereignty and the Responsibility to Protect*.

134. For a leading post–Cold War treatment of "Westphalian sovereignty," which, despite being concerned to emphasize how the concept had been breached and compromised historically, inadvertently served to reify it, see Stephen D. Krasner, *Sovereignty: Organized Hypocrisy* (Princeton: Princeton University Press, 1999).

135. Getachew, *Worldmaking after Empire*, 62–67; Jost Dülffer, "Humanitarian Intervention as Legitimation of Violence—The German Case 1937–1939," in Klose, *Emergence of Humanitarian Intervention*, 208–29.

136. Mazower, *No Enchanted Palace*, 104–48.

137. Quoted in William A. Schabas, *Genocide in International Law: The Crime of Crimes*, 2nd ed. (Cambridge: Cambridge University Press, 2009), 534.

138. Quoted in ibid., 536–37.

139. Ibid., 534–39.

140. Ibid., 85.

141. Alex J. Bellamy, *Massacres and Morality: Mass Atrocities in an Age of Civilian Immunity* (Oxford: Oxford University Press, 2012), 160–299.

142. Nicholas J. Wheeler, *Saving Strangers: Humanitarian Intervention in International Society* (Oxford: Oxford University Press, 2000), 55–110.

143. UN Security Council, S/PV.1606 (December 4, 1971), 30.

144. UN Security Council, S/PV.2110 (January 13, 1979), 7–8.

145. Wheeler, *Saving Strangers*, 197.

146. UN General Assembly, A/PV.832 (October 20, 1959), 483.

147. Ibid., 484.

148. UN General Assembly, A/PV.831 (October 20, 1959), 471; see also Bellamy, *Massacres and Morality*, 237–59.

149. UN General Assembly, A/43/PV.75 (December 23, 1988), 38, 16, 98–100.

150. On the origins and development of French thinking about the responsibility to interfere, see Davey, *Idealism beyond Borders*; Eglantine Staunton, *France, Humanitarian Intervention and the Responsibility to Protect* (Manchester: Manchester University Press, 2020) (crediting Jean-François Revel with introducing the language of *devoir d'ingérence* into French debates in 1979).

151. Mario Bettati and Bernard Kouchner, eds., *Le devoir d'ingérence: peut-on les laisser mourir?* (Paris: Denoël, 1987).

152. Staunton, *France, Humanitarian Intervention and the Responsibility to Protect*, 31–38.

Chapter 3

1. United Nations General Assembly, "2005 World Summit Outcome," A/Res/60/1 (October 24, 2005), paras. 138–39. UN Secretary-General Ban Ki-moon derived R2P's "three pillars" from the World Summit agreement and spelled them out in United Nations Secretary-General,

"Implementing the Responsibility to Protect: Report of the Secretary-General," A/63/677 (January 12, 2009). It is worth clarifying that, with respect to Chapter VII collective action, in contrast to the other elements of R2P, states declared in the 2005 agreement merely that they were "prepared" to take such action, not that they had a "responsibility" to do so. Nevertheless, in their annual reports on R2P, first issued in 2009, Ban Ki-moon and his successor, António Guterres, have repeatedly used the language of "responsibility" to describe this coercive component of the third pillar, and states have not objected to this. I discuss this further chapter 4.

2. See similarly Kok-Chor Tan, "Humanitarian Intervention as a Duty," *Global Responsibility to Protect* 7, no. 2 (2015): 121–41, at 124.

3. "Libya Protests: Defiant Gaddafi Refuses to Quit," *BBC News*, February 22, 2011.

4. Ban Ki-moon, "Statement by the Secretary-General on Libya," New York, March 17, 2011, https://www.un.org/sg/en/content/sg/statement/2011-03-17/statement-secretary-general-libya -scroll-down-arabic-version.

5. United Nations Support Mission in Libya and Office of the High Commissioner for Human Rights, "Desperate and Dangerous: Report on the Human Rights Situation of Migrants and Refugees in Libya," December 20, 2018.

6. Quoted in Jeffrey Goldberg, "The Obama Doctrine," *Atlantic*, April 2016.

7. Herman Merivale, *Lectures on Colonization and Colonies*, vol. 2 (London: Longman, Brown, Green, and Longmans, 1842), 152. I was alerted to this quote when reading Duncan Bell, *Reordering the World: Essays on Liberalism and Empire* (Princeton: Princeton University Press, 2016), 41–42.

8. Jessica Whyte, "'Always on Top?' The 'Responsibility to Protect' and the Persistence of Colonialism," in *The Postcolonial World*, ed. Jyotsna G. Singh and David D. Kim (Abingdon: Routledge, 2017), 308–24.

9. Adom Getachew, "The Limits of Sovereignty as Responsibility," *Constellations* 26, no. 2 (2019): 225–40, at 226, 229. Getachew's critique of R2P builds upon her argument for a postcolonial cosmopolitanism developed in her excellent book, *Worldmaking after Empire: The Rise and Fall of Self-Determination* (Princeton: Princeton University Press, 2019).

10. Getachew, "Limits of Sovereignty as Responsibility," 235–36; Adom Getachew, "Holding Ourselves Responsible," *Boston Review*, September 11, 2019. See similarly Anne Orford, *Reading Humanitarian Intervention: Human Rights and the Use of Force in International Law* (Cambridge: Cambridge University Press, 2003); Whyte, "'Always on Top?'"

11. On historical injustices in particular, see Catherine Lu, *Justice and Reconciliation in World Politics* (Cambridge: Cambridge University Press, 2017); Duncan Bell, ed., *Empire, Race and Global Justice* (Cambridge: Cambridge University Press, 2019). More generally, see Richard W. Miller, *Globalizing Justice: The Ethics of Poverty and Power* (Oxford: Oxford University Press, 2010); Iris Marion Young, *Responsibility for Justice* (Oxford: Oxford University Press, 2011).

12. Getachew, "Limits of Sovereignty as Responsibility," 236.

13. Brooke A. Ackerly, *Just Responsibility: A Human Rights Theory of Global Justice* (Oxford: Oxford University Press, 2018).

14. Getachew even acknowledges that there may be cases where coercive intervention needs to be considered, "as a last resort." Getachew, "Holding Ourselves Responsible." See also Getachew, "Limits of Sovereignty as Responsibility," 236.

15. Lauren Benton and Lisa Ford, *Rage for Order: The British Empire and the Origins of International Law, 1800–1850* (Cambridge, MA: Harvard University Press, 2016), 90.

16. For these eighty-plus resolutions, see Global Centre for the Responsibility to Protect, http://www.globalr2p.org/resources/335.

17. I discuss and further nuance some of the political machinations that led to and followed this Security Council resolution in chapter 5.

18. Whyte, "'Always on Top?'" 309, 313.

19. Benton and Ford, *Rage for Order*, 192.

20. See Luke Glanville, "Armed Humanitarian Intervention and the Problem of Abuse after Libya," in *The Ethics of Armed Humanitarian Intervention*, ed. Don Scheid (Cambridge: Cambridge University Press, 2014), 148–65.

21. Siddharth Mallavarapu, "Colonialism and the Responsibility to Protect," in *Theorising the Responsibility to Protect*, ed. Ramesh Thakur and William Maley (Cambridge: Cambridge University Press, 2015), 305–22, at 322. See also Whyte, "'Always on Top?'" 313.

22. Quoted in "President Obama: Libya Aftermath 'Worst Mistake' of Presidency," *BBC News*, April 11, 2016.

23. Jeanne Morefield, "Challenging Liberal Belief: Edward Said and the Critical Practice of History," in Bell, *Empire, Race and Global Justice*, 184–210, at 186.

24. For discussion, see Alex J. Bellamy, *Responsibility to Protect: The Global Effort to End Mass Atrocities* (Cambridge: Polity, 2009), 149–55.

25. An argument might be made that military intervention in the first two or three years of the Syrian conflict could have inhibited Russia from progressively ratcheting up its support for Assad, forestalled the spread of conflict throughout the region, and saved lives. But such a case for intervention emerges only in hindsight and was not credibly made at any particular moment in those early years.

26. Quoted in "President Obama."

27. "Libya's Interim Leaders Reject UN Military Personnel," *BBC News*, August 31, 2011; Derek Chollet, *The Long Game: How Obama Defied Washington and Redefined America's Role in the World* (New York: PublicAffairs, 2016), 108–12.

28. Nicholas J. Wheeler, *Saving Strangers: Humanitarian Intervention in International Society* (Oxford: Oxford University Press, 2000), 78–136.

29. Note, however, that there are important debates to be had about whether the morality of these two interventions is undermined by their illegality. For a powerful critique of the ethics of illegal intervention—and particularly interventions undertaken by great powers who themselves played leading roles in writing the laws on the use of force and continue to claim authority to punish violations of these laws—see Brad R. Roth, *Sovereign Equality and Moral Disagreement: Premises of a Pluralist International Legal Order* (New York: Oxford University Press, 2011).

30. UNSC Resolution 1975 (March 30, 2011).

31. Quantitative research indicates that military interventions tend to increase the probability that atrocities can be slowed or brought to an end. However, this research tends not to speak to the impact of important variables such as legality or host-government consent. Matthew Krain, "International Intervention and the Severity of Genocides and Politicides," *International Studies Quarterly* 49, no. 3 (2005): 363–87; Jacqueline H. R. DeMeritt, "Delegating Death: Military Intervention and Government Killing," *Journal of Conflict Resolution* 59, no. 3 (2015): 428–54; Michael P. Broache and Kate Cronin-Furman, "Does Type of Violence Matter for Interventions to Mitigate Mass Atrocities?," *Journal of Global Security Studies* (2020), https://doi.org/10.1093/jogss/ogz068. For a detailed and largely positive study of the consequences of 1990s interventions, see Taylor B. Seybolt, *Humanitarian Military Intervention: The Conditions for Success and Failure* (Oxford: Oxford University Press, 2007).

32. It is worth clarifying that the scope and purpose of each of the measures discussed in this section are not necessarily restricted to protecting populations from atrocities. Peacekeepers are typically mandated to do more than prevent atrocities, diplomatic pressure is appropriately applied not only in response to threats of atrocities, asylum is rightly provided to people fleeing not only atrocities, and so on. Nevertheless, each of these measures, when applied appropriately, can prove a vital means of discharging R2P.

33. Séverine Autesserre, *Peaceland: Conflict Resolution and the Everyday Politics of International Intervention* (Cambridge: Cambridge University Press, 2014); Jean-Marie Guéhenno, *The Fog of Peace: A Memoir of International Peacekeeping in the 21st Century* (Washington, DC: Brookings Institution Press, 2015).

34. Erik Melander, "Selected to Go where Murderers Lurk? The Preventive Effect of Peacekeeping on Mass Killing of Civilians," *Conflict Management and Peace Science* 26, no. 4 (2009): 389–406; Lisa Hultman, Jacob Kathman, and Megan Shannon, "United Nations Peacekeeping and Civilian Protection in Civil War," *American Journal of Political Science* 57, no. 4 (2013): 875–91.

35. Andrea Ruggeri, Han Dorussen, and Theodora-Ismene Gizelis, "Winning the Peace Locally: UN Peacekeeping and Local Conflict," *International Organization* 71, no. 1 (2017): 163–85; Hanne Fjelde, Lisa Hultman, and Desirée Nilsson, "Protection through Presence: UN Peacekeeping and the Costs of Targeting Civilians," *International Organization* 73, no. 1 (2019): 103–31.

36. Michael W. Doyle and Nicholas Sambanis, *Making War and Building Peace: United Nations Peace Operations* (Princeton: Princeton University Press, 2006); Virginia Page Fortna, *Does Peacekeeping Work? Shaping Belligerents' Choices after Civil War* (Princeton: Princeton University Press, 2008); Lisa Hultman, Jacob D. Kathman, and Megan Shannon, "United Nations Peacekeeping Dynamics and the Duration of Post–Civil Conflict Peace," *Conflict Management and Peace Science* 33, no. 3 (2016): 231–49.

37. Jacob D. Kathman and Reed M. Wood, "Stopping the Killing during the 'Peace': Peacekeeping and the Severity of Postconflict Civilian Victimization," *Foreign Policy Analysis* 12, no. 2 (2016): 149–69.

38. Ibid.; Hultman, Kathman, and Shannon, "United Nations Peacekeeping and Civilian Protection in Civil War."

39. United Nations Office of Internal Oversight Services, "Evaluation of the Implementation and Results of Protection of Civilians Mandates in United Nations Peacekeeping Operations," A/68/787 (March 7, 2014).

40. Lise Morjé Howard, *Power in Peacekeeping* (Cambridge: Cambridge University Press, 2019).

41. See, for example, Sonja Grover, "R2P and the Syrian Crisis: When Semantics Becomes a Matter of Life or Death," *International Journal of Human Rights* 19, no. 8 (2015): 1112–1128, at 1112.

42. United Nations Secretary-General, "Fulfilling our Collective Responsibility: International Assistance and the Responsibility to Protect: Report of the Secretary-General," A/68/947–S/2014/449 (July 11, 2014). See also Serena K. Sharma and Jennifer M. Welsh, eds., *The Responsibility to Prevent: Overcoming the Challenges to Atrocity Prevention* (Oxford: Oxford University Press, 2015); Scott Straus, *Fundamentals of Genocide and Mass Atrocity Prevention* (Washington, DC: US Holocaust Memorial Museum, 2016).

43. Katja Lindskov Jacobsen and Troels Gauslå Engell, "Conflict Prevention as Pragmatic Response to a Twofold Crisis: Liberal Interventionism and Burundi," *International Affairs* 94, no. 2 (2018): 363–80. See more generally Alex J. Bellamy and Edward C. Luck, *The Responsibility to Protect: From Promise to Practice* (Cambridge: Polity, 2018), 51, 144.

44. On the cost-effectiveness of prevention as opposed to reaction, see Hannes Mueller, "How Much is Prevention Worth?," Background Paper for Pathways for Peace: Inclusive Approaches to Preventing Conflict, United Nations–World Bank Joint Flagship Study, September 2017 (Washington, DC: World Bank, 2018).

45. For discussion of a broader range of nonforcible means of protection, see Alex J. Bellamy, "The First Response: Peaceful Means in the Third Pillar of the Responsibility to Protect," Policy Analysis (Muscatine, IA: Stanley Foundation, December 2015); James Pattison, *The Alternatives to War: From Sanctions to Nonviolence* (Oxford: Oxford University Press, 2018).

46. Jacqueline H. R. DeMeritt, "International Organizations and Government Killing: Does Naming and Shaming Save Lives?," *International Interactions* 38, no. 5 (2012): 597–621; Matthew Krain, "J'accuse! Does Naming and Shaming Perpetrators Reduce the Severity of Genocides or Politicides?," *International Studies Quarterly* 56, no. 3 (2012): 574–89.

47. Serena K. Sharma, "The 2007–8 Post-Election Crisis in Kenya: A Case of Escalation Prevention," in Sharma and Welsh, *Responsibility to Prevent*, 280–303; Naomi Kikoler, "Guinea: An Overlooked Case of the Responsibility to Prevent in Practice," in Sharma and Welsh, *Responsibility to Prevent*, 304–23.

48. Matthew Krain, "The Effect of Economic Sanctions on the Severity of Genocides or Politicides," *Journal of Genocide Research* 19, no. 1 (2017): 88–111.

49. Joy Gordon, *Invisible War: The United States and the Iraq Sanctions* (Cambridge, MA: Harvard University Press, 2010).

50. John Quigley, "State Responsibility for Ethnic Cleansing," *UC Davis Law Review* 32, no. 2 (1999): 341–87, at 375–77.

51. For empirical analysis, see Thomas J. Biersteker, Sue E. Eckert, and Marcos Tourinho, eds., *Targeted Sanctions: The Impacts and Effectiveness of United Nations Action* (Cambridge: Cambridge University Press, 2016). For a philosophical defense of limited and targeted sanctions, see Cécile Fabre, *Economic Statecraft: Human Rights, Sanctions, and Conditionality* (Cambridge, MA: Harvard University Press, 2018). For a critique of the ineffectiveness and the continued harmful consequences of targeted sanctions, see Joy Gordon, Dursun Peksen, and Idriss Jazairy, "Roundtable: Economic Sanctions and Their Consequences," *Ethics & International Affairs* 33, no. 3 (2019): 275–314.

52. Neil Narang, "Assisting Uncertainty: How Humanitarian Aid Can Inadvertently Prolong Civil War," *International Studies Quarterly* 59, no. 1 (2015): 184–95; Reed M. Wood and Christopher Sullivan, "Doing Harm by Doing Good? The Negative Externalities of Humanitarian Aid Provision during Civil Conflict," *Journal of Politics* 77, no. 3 (2015): 736–48.

53. For discussion, see Alex J. Bellamy, *The Responsibility to Protect: A Defense* (Oxford: Oxford University Press, 2015), 161–64.

54. Ibid., 150.

55. Brian Barbour and Brian Gorlick, "Embracing the 'Responsibility to Protect': A Repertoire of Measures Including Asylum for Potential Victims," *International Journal of Refugee Law* 20, no. 4 (2008): 533–66, at 533, 563, 562.

56. UNHCR, "Global Trends: Forced Displacement in 2019" (Geneva: UNHCR, June 18, 2020), 3.

57. Consider the threats used by the George W. Bush administration against states that were reluctant to join the "Coalition of the Willing" that invaded Iraq in 2003. Randall Newnham, "'Coalition of the Bribed and Bullied?' US Economic Linkage and the Iraq War Coalition," *International Studies Perspectives* 9, no. 2 (2008): 183–200.

58. Barack Obama, "Remarks by President Obama to the United Nations General Assembly," New York, September 28, 2015.

59. Barack Obama, "Remarks by the President in Address to the Nation on Libya," National Defense University, Washington, DC, March 28, 2011.

60. "Remarks by President Obama and President Park of South Korea in a Joint Press Conference," Washington, DC, May 7, 2013.

61. For more extensive discussion, see Luke Glanville, "Responsibility to Perfect: Vattel's Conception of Duties beyond Borders," *International Studies Quarterly* 61, no. 2 (2017): 385–95.

62. Emer de Vattel, *The Law of Nations, or Principles of the Law of Nature, Applied to the Conduct and Affairs of Nations and Sovereigns, with Three Early Essays on the Origin and Nature of Natural Law and on Luxury*, ed. Béla Kapossy and Richard Whatmore (Indianapolis: Liberty Fund, 2008), Prelim. §11.

63. Robert E. Goodin, "What Is So Special about Our Fellow Countrymen?," *Ethics* 98, no. 4 (1988): 663–86. The quotation is at 679 and the reference to Wolff is at 682n49. See similarly Henry Shue, "Mediating Duties," *Ethics* 98, no. 4 (1988): 687–704.

64. David Miller, *National Responsibility and Global Justice* (Oxford: Oxford University Press, 2007); Michael Walzer, "The Argument about Humanitarian Intervention," *Dissent* 49, no. 1 (2002): 29–37.

65. Vattel, *Law of Nations*, Prelim. §14, II.1.16–17.

66. Ibid., II.10.131.

67. For a classic defense, see Henry Shue, *Basic Rights: Subsistence, Affluence, and US Foreign Policy*, 2nd ed. (Princeton: Princeton University Press, 1996). More recently, see Anders Herlitz, "The Indispensability of Sufficientarianism," *Critical Review of International Social and Political Philosophy* 22, no. 7 (2019): 929–42.

68. For a defense and application of a sufficientist account of human protection duties, see Cécile Fabre, *Cosmopolitan War* (Oxford: Oxford University Press, 2012).

69. Samuel Moyn, *Not Enough: Human Rights in an Unequal World* (Cambridge, MA: Harvard University Press, 2018).

70. It might be replied that global duties are not limited to atrocity prevention and that states can justifiably choose to devote their resources to other concerns, such as the mitigation of climate change or global poverty. I would suggest, however, that unless states are in fact devoting their resources to such alternative concerns to a sufficientist extent, which they clearly are not at present, we can continue to call on them to do more to discharge their shared responsibility to protect.

71. For a defense and discussion of the international exercise of "practical judgment," see Chris Brown, *Practical Judgment in International Political Theory: Selected Essays* (London: Routledge, 2010); Mathias Albert and Anthony F. Lang Jr., eds., *The Politics of International Political Theory: Reflections on the Work of Chris Brown* (New York: Palgrave, 2019).

72. "Migrant Crisis: Merkel Warns of EU 'Failure,'" *BBC News*, August 31, 2015.

73. Goodin, "What Is So Special about Our Fellow Countrymen?," 684. See also Toni Erskine, "Moral Agents of Protection and Supplementary Responsibilities to Protect," in *The Oxford Handbook of the Responsibility to Protect*, ed. Alex J. Bellamy and Tim Dunne (Oxford: Oxford University Press, 2016), 167–86, at 175–76.

74. Robert E. Goodin, *Protecting the Vulnerable: A Reanalysis of Our Social Responsibilities* (Chicago: University of Chicago Press, 1985), 138.

75. Michael Walzer, *Just and Unjust Wars: A Moral Argument with Historical Illustrations*, 3rd ed. (New York: Basic Books, 2000), xiii.

76. Quoted in Gary J. Bass, *Freedom's Battle: The Origins of Humanitarian Intervention* (New York: Knopf, 2008), 296.

77. Quoted in Franklin Foer and Chris Hughes, "Barack Obama Is Not Pleased," *New Republic*, January 27, 2013.

78. Shue, *Basic Rights*, 166; Henry Shue, "Limiting Sovereignty," in *Humanitarian Intervention and International Relations*, ed. Jennifer M. Welsh (Oxford: Oxford University Press, 2004), 1–28, at 18; Shue, "Mediating Duties," 690.

79. Onora O'Neill, *Bounds of Justice* (Cambridge: Cambridge University Press, 2000), 103; Kok-Chor Tan, "The Duty to Protect," in *Humanitarian Intervention*, ed. Terry Nardin and Melissa S. Williams (New York: New York University Press, 2006), 84–116, at 104.

80. The discussion that follows builds on excellent work on the allocation of duties in response to a single atrocity crisis (rather than a plurality of atrocity crises—a dynamic that is almost entirely neglected and which I address in the next section), found in Michael Walzer, *Arguing about War* (New Haven, CT: Yale University Press, 2004), 67–81; David Miller, "Distributing Responsibilities," *Journal of Political Philosophy* 9, no. 4 (2001): 453–71; Tan, "Duty to Protect";

David Miller, "The Responsibility to Protect Human Rights," in *Legitimacy, Justice and Public International Law*, ed. Lucas H. Meyer (Cambridge: Cambridge University Press, 2009), 232–51; James Pattison, *Humanitarian Intervention and the Responsibility to Protect: Who Should Intervene?* (Oxford: Oxford University Press, 2010); Fabre, *Cosmopolitan War*, 187–92; Jennifer M. Welsh, "Who Should Act? Collective Responsibility and the Responsibility to Protect," in *The Routledge Handbook of the Responsibility to Protect*, ed. W. Andy Knight and Frazer Egerton (New York: Routledge, 2012), 103–14; Erskine, "Moral Agents of Protection."

81. Jason Ralph and James Souter, "A Special Responsibility to Protect: The UK, Australia and the Rise of Islamic State," *International Affairs* 91, no. 4 (2015): 709–23.

82. Quoted in ibid., 709.

83. For discussion, see Lea Ypi, Robert E. Goodin, and Christian Barry, "Associative Duties, Global Justice, and the Colonies," *Philosophy and Public Affairs* 37, no. 2 (2009): 103–35; Lu, *Justice and Reconciliation in World Politics*.

84. Miller, *Globalizing Justice*; Young, *Responsibility for Justice*.

85. Fabre, *Cosmopolitan War*, 190–91; James Souter, "Towards a Theory of Asylum as Reparation for Past Injustice," *Political Studies* 62, no. 2 (2014): 326–42; Fredrik D. Hjorthen, "Who Should Pay for Humanitarian Intervention?," *European Journal of Political Theory* 19, no. 3 (2020): 334–53.

86. Tan, "Duty to Protect," 97–99.

87. Quoted in ibid., 114n23.

88. Pattison, *Humanitarian Intervention*, 69–97.

89. Barack Obama, "Statement by the President on ISIL," Washington, DC, September 10, 2014.

90. Goldberg, "Obama Doctrine"; UN General Assembly, A/73/PV.6 (September 25, 2019), 18.

91. Quoted in Dan Halvorson, "Reputation and Responsibility in Australia's 2003 Intervention in the Solomon Islands," *Australian Journal of International Affairs* 67, no. 4 (2013): 439–55, at 450.

92. Tan, "Duty to Protect," 101–2; Welsh, "Who Should Act?," 107–8.

93. Miller, "Distributing Responsibilities," 468.

94. Ibid., 461.

95. Vattel, *Law of Nations*, II.1.13.

96. Chris Brown, "Selective Humanitarianism: In Defense of Inconsistency," in *Ethics and Foreign Intervention*, ed. Deen K. Chatterjee and Don E. Scheid (Cambridge: Cambridge University Press, 2003), 31–50, at 32.

97. Mark Evans, "Selectivity, Imperfect Obligations and the Character of Humanitarian Morality," in *Human Rights and Military Intervention*, ed. Alexander Moseley and Richard Norman (Aldershot: Ashgate, 2002), 132–49, at 132.

98. In a 1995 speech, former British prime minister Margaret Thatcher summarized, "However great our indignation, some evils which occur are truly beyond our power to solve. Nevertheless, just because we cannot intervene everywhere, it does not follow that we cannot intervene anywhere. Both conscience and calculation are required to establish our duty in any set of circumstances." Margaret Thatcher, "Managing Conflict—The Role of International Intervention," Speech to the Aspen Institute, Aspen, CO, August 4, 1995.

99. Brown, "Selective Humanitarianism."

100. Evans, "Selectivity, Imperfect Obligations."

101. Lea Brilmayer, "What's the Matter with Selective Intervention?," *Arizona Law Review* 37, no. 4 (1995): 955–70, at 966–69. See also the insightful examination of the ethics of a range of principles that guide humanitarian organizations when deciding where to deploy their resources in Jennifer C. Rubenstein, *Between Samaritans and States: The Political Ethics of Humanitarian INGOs* (Oxford: Oxford University Press, 2015), 143–70.

102. Quoted in Wheeler, *Saving Strangers*, 181.

103. Thomas Pogge, "Moral Priorities for International Human Rights NGOs," in *Ethics in Action: The Ethical Challenges of International Human Rights Nongovernmental Organizations*, ed. Daniel A. Bell and Jean-Marc Coicaud (New York: Cambridge University Press, 2006), 218–56; Peter Singer, *The Most Good You Can Do: How Effective Altruism Is Changing Ideas about Living Ethically* (New Haven, CT: Yale University Press, 2015).

104. Jennifer C. Rubenstein, "The Lessons of Effective Altruism," *Ethics & International Affairs* 30, no. 4 (2016): 511–26; Iason Gabriel, "Effective Altruism and Its Critics," *Journal of Applied Philosophy* 34, no. 4 (2017): 457–73.

105. Thomas Aquinas, *Summa Theologica*, trans. Fathers of the Dominican Province (Notre Dame, IN: Christian Classics, 1981), II–II.32.5. Goodin proposes a similar formulation: "Anyone to whom A is uniquely vulnerable (no one else will help if that person does not) has the greatest responsibilities of all." Robert E. Goodin, "Vulnerabilities and Responsibilities: An Ethical Defense of the Welfare State," in *Necessary Goods: Our Responsibilities to Meet Others' Needs*, ed. Gillian Brock (Oxford: Rowman & Littlefield, 1998), 73–94, at 79.

106. Wheeler, *Saving Strangers*, 231–37.

107. George H. W. Bush, "Address to the Nation on the Situation in Somalia," December 4, 1992.

108. Miller, it should be said, accepts that those who do their fair share might have a "humanitarian obligation" to do more. But he insists that justice requires only that they do their fair share. David Miller, "Taking Up the Slack? Responsibility and Justice in Situations of Partial Compliance," in *Responsibility and Distributive Justice*, ed. Carl Knight and Zofia Stemplowska (Oxford: Oxford University Press, 2011), 230–45. The quote is at 243. For a persuasive rebuttal of Miller's argument, as well as arguments that reject more absolutely the responsibility to take up the slack, see Zofia Stemplowska, "Doing More Than One's Fair Share," *Critical Review of International Social and Political Philosophy* 19, no. 5 (2016): 591–608.

109. See similarly Pattison, *Humanitarian Intervention*, 198.

110. Tan, "Duty to Protect," 104 (emphasis original). For a classic argument about the institutionalization of duties, see Shue, "Mediating Duties." For valuable deliberations on the institutionalization of duties of international human protection, see Heather M. Roff, *Global Justice, Kant and the Responsibility to Protect: A Provisional Duty* (Abingdon: Routledge, 2013), 110–26; Fredrik D. Hjorthen, "Humanitarian Intervention and Burden-Sharing Justice," *Political Studies* 68, no. 4 (2020): 936–53.

111. See UN General Assembly Resolution 73/272 (January 3, 2019).

112. O'Neill, *Bounds of Justice*, 105.

113. Wesley W. Widmaier and Luke Glanville, "The Benefits of Norm Ambiguity: Constructing the Responsibility to Protect across Rwanda, Iraq and Libya," *Contemporary Politics* 21, no. 4 (2015): 367–83.

114. UN General Assembly Resolutions 66/253B (August 3, 2012), 68/182 (December 18, 2013), and 71/130 (December 7, 2016).

Chapter 4

1. See, for example, the "Convention on the Prevention and Punishment of the Crime of Genocide," UN General Assembly Resolution 260 A (III) (December 9, 1948), Articles 1, 5, and 6, and the "International Covenant on Civil and Political Rights," UN General Assembly Resolution 2200A (XXI) (December 16, 1966), Articles 2 and 9.

2. See among numerous examples UN Security Council Resolutions 794 (December 3, 1992) on Somalia, 929 (June 22, 1994) on Rwanda, 1080 (November 15, 1996) on Haiti, 1264

(September 15, 1999) on East Timor, 1769 (July 31, 2007) on Darfur, 1973 (March 17, 2011) on Libya, 2127 (December 5, 2013) on the Central African Republic, and 2206 (March 3, 2016) on South Sudan.

3. See, for example, Aidan Hehir, "From Human Security to the Responsibility to Protect: The Co-option of Dissent?," *Michigan State International Law Review* 23, no. 3 (2015): 675–99, at 688 (claiming that R2P "comprises no novel legal compulsion or innovation"). Others, when considering the law as it relates to R2P, have unfortunately focused on the rather tired and largely settled question of the legal permissibility of military intervention—both authorized and unauthorized by the Security Council—rather than the more pressing and complex question of whether states are legally obligated to contribute to international protection efforts. Michael W. Doyle, "Law, Ethics, and the Responsibility to Protect," in *The Ethics of Armed Humanitarian Intervention*, ed. Don E. Scheid (Cambridge: Cambridge University Press, 2014), 187–208; Rajan Menon, *The Conceit of Humanitarian Intervention* (New York: Oxford University Press, 2016), 60–76.

4. Immanuel Kant, "Toward Perpetual Peace (1795)," in *Practical Philosophy*, ed. Mary J. Gregor (Cambridge: Cambridge University Press, 1996), 8.355.

5. Theodore D. Woolsey, *Introduction to the Study of Law*, 3rd ed. (New York: Scribner, Armstrong & Co., 1872), 86.

6. Luke Glanville, *Sovereignty and the Responsibility to Protect: A New History* (Chicago: University of Chicago Press, 2014), 81–84.

7. Edward S. Creasy, *First Platform of International Law* (London: John van Voorst, Paternoster Row, 1876), 303.

8. Ellery C. Stowell, "Humanitarian Intervention," *American Journal of International Law* 33, no. 4 (1939): 733–36, at 734.

9. Ellery C. Stowell, *Intervention in International Law* (Washington, DC: John Bryne, 1921), 49, 449–50.

10. UN General Assembly Resolution 260 A (III) (December 9, 1948).

11. See, for example, "Discussion Paper, Rwanda," Office of the Deputy Assistant Secretary of Defense for Middle East/Africa Region, Department of Defense, May 1, 1994, http://www.gwu.edu /~nsarchiv/NSAEBB/NSAEBB53/rw050194.pdf; US Department of State Daily Press Briefing, June 10, 1994, http://dosfan.lib.uic.edu/ERC/briefing/daily_briefings/1994/9406/940610db.html.

12. Quoted in William A. Schabas, *Genocide in International Law: The Crime of Crimes*, 1st ed. (Cambridge: Cambridge University Press, 2000), 496.

13. Ibid., 546.

14. ICISS, *The Responsibility to Protect: Report of the International Commission on Intervention and State Sovereignty* (Ottawa: International Development Research Centre, 2001).

15. United Nations, "A More Secure World: Our Shared Responsibility," Report of the High-Level Panel on Threats, Challenges and Change, A/59/565 (December 2, 2004), paras. 199–203; United Nations Secretary-General, "In Larger Freedom: Towards Development, Security and Human Rights for All: Report of the Secretary-General," A/59/2005 (March 21, 2005), Annex, para. 7(b); United Nations General Assembly, "2005 World Summit Outcome," A/Res/60/1 (October 24, 2005), paras. 138–39.

16. Alex J. Bellamy, *Responsibility to Protect: The Global Effort to End Mass Atrocities* (Cambridge: Polity, 2009), 66–97.

17. "Revised Draft Outcome Document of the High-Level Plenary Meeting of the General Assembly of September 2005 Submitted by the President of the General Assembly," A/59/HLP/ CRP.1/Rev.2 (August 5, 2005), para. 118.

18. John R. Bolton, "Letter from John R. Bolton, Representative of the USA to the UN, to Jean Ping, President of the UN General Assembly," August 30, 2005, http://www.responsibilitytoprotect .org/files/US_Boltonletter_R2P_30Aug05[1].pdf.

19. United Nations General Assembly, "2005 World Summit Outcome," para. 139.

20. UN Security Council Resolutions 1674 (April 28, 2006), 1706 (August 31, 2006), 1894 (November 11, 2009), 2217 (September 26, 2013), 2150 (April 16, 2014), 2171 (August 21, 2014), and 2220 (May 22, 2015).

21. United Nations Secretary-General, "Implementing the Responsibility to Protect: Report of the Secretary-General," A/63/677 (January 12, 2009).

22. Carsten Stahn, "Responsibility to Protect: Political Rhetoric or Emerging Legal Norm?" *American Journal of International Law* 101, no. 1 (2007): 99–120, at 101.

23. For discussion, see ibid.; Jennifer M. Welsh and Maria Banda, "International Law and the Responsibility to Protect: Clarifying or Expanding States' Responsibilities?," *Global Responsibility to Protect* 2, nos. 1–2 (2010): 213–31, at 229.

24. *Case Concerning Application of the Convention on the Prevention and Punishment of the Crime of Genocide (Bosnia and Herzegovina v. Serbia and Montenegro)*, ICJ, February 26, 2007 (hereinafter *Genocide* judgment).

25. Ibid., para. 427.

26. Ibid., para. 430.

27. Ibid.

28. Ibid.

29. Sheri P. Rosenberg, "Responsibility to Protect: A Framework for Prevention," in *The Responsibility to Protect and International Law*, ed. Alex J. Bellamy, Sara E. Davies, and Luke Glanville (Leiden: Martinus Nijhoff, 2011), 157–92, at 185.

30. Monica Hakimi, "State Bystander Responsibility," *European Journal of International Law* 21, no. 2 (2010): 341–85, at 364–65.

31. *Genocide* judgment, paras. 434–35.

32. Ibid., para 461.

33. Marko Milanović, "State Responsibility for Genocide: A Follow-Up," *European Journal of International Law* 18, no. 4 (2007): 669–94, at 686.

34. *Genocide* judgment, para. 430.

35. The idea of shared responsibility in international law has been the subject of an important project by André Nollkaemper and colleagues in recent years. See André Nollkaemper and Dov Jacobs, "Shared Responsibility in International Law: A Conceptual Framework," *Michigan Journal of International Law* 34, no. 2 (2013): 359–438; André Nollkaemper and Ilias Plakokefalos, eds., *Principles of Shared Responsibility in International Law: An Appraisal of the State of the Art* (Cambridge: Cambridge University Press, 2014); André Nollkaemper and Dov Jacobs, eds., *Distribution of Responsibilities in International Law* (Cambridge: Cambridge University Press, 2015); André Nollkaemper and Ilias Plakokefalos, eds., *The Practice of Shared Responsibility in International Law* (Cambridge: Cambridge University Press, 2017). See also James Crawford, *State Responsibility: The General Part* (Cambridge: Cambridge University Press, 2013), Part IV: "Collective or Ancillary Responsibility."

36. ARSIWA (Articles on Responsibility of States for International Wrongful Acts), in *Yearbook of the International Law Commission*, 2001/II(2), A/CN.4/SER.A/2001/Add.1 (Part 2) (New York: United Nations, 2007) [hereinafter ARSIWA]. The binding nature of the ILC's work on state responsibility is doubtful. The General Assembly merely took note of the articles by its Resolution 56/83 (January 28, 2002). Nevertheless, the ILC constructed the articles to reflect existing customary international law, and the ICJ has repeatedly referred to them as such.

37. ARSIWA, Article 41(1), at 113.

38. Ibid., section 2 of commentary on Article 41, at 114.

39. Ibid., section 3 of commentary on Article 41, at 114.

40. Ibid.

41. Crawford, *State Responsibility*, 334.

42. *Case Concerning Certain Phosphate Lands in Nauru (Nauru v. Australia), Preliminary Objections*, ICJ, June 26, 1992, para. 48.

43. ARSIWA, commentary on Article 47, section 1, at 124.

44. *Case of M.S.S. v. Belgium*, App. No. 30696/09, ECtHR, January 21, 2011, discussed in Nollkaemper and Jacobs, "Shared Responsibility in International Law," 380.

45. *Mothers of Srebrenica Association et al. v. The Netherlands*, Supreme Court of the Netherlands, judgment of July 19, 2019, para. 5.1.

46. *Genocide* judgment, para. 438.

47. Ibid., para. 430. See similarly para. 438, declaring that states must make "the best efforts within their power to try and prevent" the commission of genocide.

48. The ECtHR concurs, suggesting that an obligation "must be interpreted in a way which does not impose an impossible or disproportionate burden on the authorities." *Osman v. United Kingdom*, App. No. 23452/94, ECtHR, October 28, 1998, para. 116, quoted in Hakimi, "State Bystander Responsibility," 375.

49. Hakimi, "State Bystander Responsibility," 371n198, emphasis original.

50. Some scholars suggest that an obligation to prevent genocide may even be attributable to the council itself. For a thought experiment offering an intentionally progressive reading of the Security Council's obligations, see Anne Peters, "The Security Council's Responsibility to Protect," *International Organizations Law Review* 8, no. 1 (2011): 15–54, at 27–35. See also Jan Klabbers, "Reflections on Role Responsibility: The Responsibility of International Organizations for Failing to Act," *European Journal of International Law* 28, no. 4 (2017): 1133–61. Such claims find some support in ARIO (Draft Articles on the Responsibility of International Organizations, with Commentaries), adopted by the International Law Commission at its sixty-third session, in 2011, and submitted to the General Assembly as a part of the Commission's report covering the work of that session (A/66/10), especially Article 42(1) (providing a duty of states and international organizations to cooperate to bring to an end serious breaches of peremptory norms) and Article 48 (noting that a plurality of states and international organizations could be responsible for the same internationally wrongful act). For a firm critique of such thinking, see José E. Alvarez, "The Schizophrenias of R2P," in *Human Rights, Intervention, and the Use of Force*, ed. Philip Alston and Euan Macdonald (Oxford: Oxford University Press, 2008), 275–84.

51. Louise Arbour, "The Responsibility to Protect as a Duty of Care in International Law and Practice," *Review of International Studies* 34, no. 3 (2008): 445–58, at 454.

52. Anne Peters, "Humanity as the A and Ω of Sovereignty," *European Journal of International Law* 20, no. 3 (2009): 513–44, at 540. See also Peters, "Security Council's Responsibility to Protect," 38–49; John Heieck, *A Duty to Prevent Genocide: Due Diligence Obligations among the P5* (Northampton, MA: Edward Elgar, 2018); Jennifer Trahan, *Existing Legal Limits to Security Council Veto Power in the Face of Atrocity Crimes* (Cambridge: Cambridge University Press, 2020).

53. Amrita Kapur, "Humanity as the A and Ω of Sovereignty: Four Replies to Anne Peters," *European Journal of International Law* 20, no. 3 (2009): 560–67, at 564–65; Emily Kidd White, "Humanity as the A and Ω of Sovereignty: Four Replies to Anne Peters," *European Journal of International Law* 20, no. 3 (2009): 545–49, at 547–48.

54. White, "Humanity as the A and Ω of Sovereignty," 547.

55. See John Quigley, "State Responsibility for Ethnic Cleansing," *UC Davis Law Review* 32, no. 2 (1999): 341–87, at 375–77.

56. Justin Morris and Nicholas J. Wheeler, "The Responsibility Not to Veto: A Responsibility Too Far?" in *The Oxford Handbook of the Responsibility to Protect*, ed. Alex J. Bellamy and Tim Dunne (Oxford: Oxford University Press, 2016), 227–46.

57. *Genocide* judgment, para. 431.

58. Mark Gibney, "Genocide and State Responsibility," *Human Rights Law Review* 7, no. 4 (2007): 760–73, at 768–69.

59. Andrea Gattini, "Breach of the Obligation to Prevent and Reparation Thereof in the ICJ's Genocide Judgment," *European Journal of International Law* 18, no. 4 (2007): 695–713, at 701–2.

60. *Genocide* judgment, para. 429. See also para. 147.

61. Ibid., para. 147.

62. *Vienna Convention on the Law of Treaties*, concluded at Vienna on May 23, 1969.

63. ARSIWA, commentary on Article 40, section 3, at 112.

64. *Legality of the Threat or Use of Nuclear Weapons (Advisory Opinion)*, ICJ, July 8, 1996, para. 79.

65. *Legal Consequences of the Construction of a Wall in the Occupied Palestinian Territory*, ICJ, July 9, 2004, para. 157. See also ARSIWA, commentary on Article 40, section 5, at 113.

66. ARSIWA, commentary on Article 26, section 5, at 85. See also the inclusion in 2019 of the prohibition of crimes against humanity in a "non-exhaustive list" of peremptory norms in the "draft conclusions on peremptory norms of general international law (*jus cogens*) adopted by the Commission, on first reading," in *Report of the International Law Commission*, seventy-first session, A/74/10 (New York: United Nations, 2019), 146, 147.

67. Rome Statute of the International Criminal Court, circulated as document A/CONF.183/9, July 17, 1998, entered into force July 1, 2002, Article 7(1d).

68. Note, however, that the temporal scope of the obligation provided in Article 41(1) is more restrictive than the *Genocide* judgment since it requires states to act only if serious breaches of peremptory norms have been committed.

69. *Report of the International Law Commission*, A/74/10, 193–95.

70. Andrea Breslin, "A Reflection on the Legal Obligation for Third States to Ensure Respect for IHL," *Journal of Conflict & Security Law* 22, no. 1 (2017): 5–37; International Committee of the Red Cross (ICRC), *Commentary on the First Geneva Convention: Convention (I) for the Amelioration of the Condition of the Wounded and Sick in Armed Forces in the Field* (Cambridge: Cambridge University Press, 2016), 35–67. For a contrary opinion, see Verity Robson, "The Common Approach to Article 1: The Scope of Each State's Obligation to Ensure Respect for the Geneva Conventions," *Journal of Conflict & Security Law* 25, no. 1 (2020): 101–15. In its 2020 commentary on the Third Geneva Convention, the ICRC acknowledges that "there is disagreement as to the legal nature of the positive component of the duty to ensure respect by others because the content of the obligation is not clearly defined and its concretization to a large extent left to the High Contracting Parties." ICRC, "Convention (III) Relative to the Treatment of Prisoners of War. Geneva, 12 August 1949. Commentary of 2020," §202, https://ihl-databases.icrc.org/applic/ihl/ihl.nsf/Comment.xsp?action=openDocument&documentId=24FD06B3D73973D5C125858400462538#_Toc42428170.

71. *Legal Consequences of the Construction of a Wall in the Occupied Palestinian Territory*, paras. 158–59.

72. Protocol Additional to the Geneva Conventions of August 12, 1949, and relating to the Protection of Victims of International Armed Conflicts (Protocol I), June 8, 1977, Article 89.

73. For background thinking, see M. Cherif Bassiouni, "Crimes against Humanity: The Need for a Specialized Convention," *Columbia Journal of Transnational Law* 31, no. 3 (1994): 457–94; Leila Nadya Sadat, ed., *Forging a Convention for Crimes against Humanity* (Cambridge: Cambridge University Press, 2011).

74. *Report of the International Law Commission*, A/74/10, 13.

75. Ibid., 49, 60–61.

76. UN General Assembly documents A/C.6/70/SR.22 (November 23, 2015), 12 (China); A/C.6/71/SR.25 (November 22, 2016), 12 (Russia); A/C.6/70/SR.23 (November 27, 2015), 5

(Russia); A/CN.4/726 (January 21, 2019), 61 (United Kingdom); A/CN.4/726/Add.2 (May 2, 2019), 10 (United States).

77. For a similar argument, see Breslin, "Reflection on the Legal Obligation," 23, 30–36.

78. United Nations Economic and Social Council, "Substantive Issues Arising in the Implementation of the International Covenant on Economic, Social and Cultural Rights," E/C.12/2002/11 (January 20, 2003), paras. 30, 34, quoted in Monica Hakimi, "Toward a Legal Theory on the Responsibility to Protect," *Yale Journal of International Law* 39, no. 2 (2014): 247–80, at 277.

79. Hakimi, "Toward a Legal Theory on the Responsibility to Protect," 278.

80. Daniel Ghezelbash, *Refuge Lost: Asylum Law in an Interdependent World* (Cambridge: Cambridge University Press, 2018).

81. Volker Türk and Madeline Garlick, "From Burdens and Responsibilities to Opportunities: The Comprehensive Refugee Response Framework and a Global Compact on Refugees," *International Journal of Refugee Law* 28, no. 4 (2016): 656–78, at 660.

82. "Report of the United Nations High Commissioner for Refugees: Part II: Global Compact on Refugees," A/73/12 (Part II), August 2, 2018, 1.

83. Kelley Currie, "Explanation of Vote in a Meeting of the Third Committee on a UNHCR Omnibus Resolution," United States Mission to the United Nations, November 13, 2018.

84. Alvarez, "Schizophrenias of R2P," 282.

85. Hakimi, "State Bystander Responsibility," 363.

86. *Genocide* judgment, para. 430.

87. Ibid., para. 462.

88. Ibid.

89. Ibid., para. 463.

90. See, for example, Gattini, "Breach of the Obligation to Prevent," 706–12; Milanović, "State Responsibility for Genocide," 688–92; Christian Tomuschat, "Reparation in Cases of Genocide," *Journal of International Criminal Justice* 5, no. 4 (2007): 905–12.

91. Milanović, "State Responsibility for Genocide," 689.

92. Ibid., 689–90. The two cases cited by Milanović are *Case of Ilaşcu and Others v. Moldova and Russia*, ECtHR, July 8, 2004, and *Velásquez Rodriguez Case*, IACtHR, July 29, 1988.

93. Milanović, "State Responsibility for Genocide," 690–91.

94. Ibid., 694.

95. Gattini and Milanović have suggested that some responsibility may lie with the litigation strategy of Bosnia's counsel, which had emphasized Serbia's responsibility for the commission of genocide and had stated that "the most natural mode of reparation" for Serbia's breach of its duty to prevent "would be satisfaction in the form of a declaration by the Court." Gattini, "Breach of the Obligation to Prevent," 706–7; Milanović, "State Responsibility for Genocide," 692. But compare Tomuschat, "Reparation in Cases of Genocide," 909–10.

96. See Nollkaemper and Jacobs, "Shared Responsibility in International Law," 388–93; Crawford, *State Responsibility*, 355–58.

97. See Nollkaemper and Jacobs, "Shared Responsibility in International Law," 422–23.

98. *Case Concerning Certain Phosphate Lands in Nauru*, para. 48.

99. Quoted in Schabas, *Genocide in International Law*, 430.

100. See Linda Melvern, *A People Betrayed: The Role of the West in Rwanda's Genocide* (London: Zed Books, 2000).

101. Peters, "Security Council's Responsibility to Protect," 38.

102. See similarly Hakimi, "Toward a Legal Theory," 266–67.

103. Beth A. Simmons, *Mobilizing for Human Rights: International Law in Domestic Politics* (Cambridge: Cambridge University Press, 2009); Emilie M. Hafner-Burton, *Making Human Rights a Reality* (Princeton: Princeton University Press, 2013).

104. See, for example, Sarah V. Percy, "Mercenaries: Strong Norm, Weak Law," *International Organization* 61, no. 2 (2007): 367–97; Joel Quirk, *The Anti-Slavery Project: From the Slave Trade to Human Trafficking* (Philadelphia: University of Pennsylvania Press, 2011); Caroline Shaw, *Britannia's Embrace: Modern Humanitarianism and the Imperial Origins of Refugee Relief* (Oxford: Oxford University Press, 2015), 237–41; Zoltán I. Búzás, "Evading International Law: How Agents Comply with the Letter of the Law but Violate Its Purpose," *European Journal of International Relations* 23, no. 4 (2017): 857–83. Some scholars similarly speak of the benefits of "soft law" in contrast to "hard law" in this context. Kenneth W. Abbott and Duncan Snidal, "Hard and Soft Law in International Governance," *International Organization* 54, no. 3 (2000): 421–56.

105. Christian J. Tams, "Individual States as Guardians of Community Interests," in *From Bilateralism to Community Interest: Essays in Honour of Bruno Simma*, ed. Ulrich Fastenrath, Rudolf Geiger, Daniel-Erasmus Khan, Andreas Paulus, Sabine von Schorlemer, and Christoph Vedder (Oxford: Oxford University Press, 2011), 379–405, at 401.

106. Peters, "Security Council's Responsibility to Protect," 53.

107. Abbott and Snidal, "Hard and Soft Law," 428–29.

108. Simmons, *Mobilizing for Human Rights*, 5.

109. Martha Finnemore, "Are Legal Norms Distinctive?," *New York University Journal of International Law and Politics* 32, no. 3 (2000): 699–705, at 702–3.

Chapter 5

1. Rajan Menon, *The Conceit of Humanitarian Intervention* (New York: Oxford University Press, 2016), 129.

2. A. Maurits van der Veen, *Ideas, Interests and Foreign Aid* (Cambridge: Cambridge University Press, 2011).

3. Robert W. McElroy, *Morality and American Foreign Policy: The Role of Ethics in International Affairs* (Princeton: Princeton University Press, 1992), 57–87.

4. Phil Orchard, *A Right to Flee: Refugees, States, and the Construction of International Cooperation* (Cambridge: Cambridge University Press, 2014).

5. Martha Finnemore, *The Purpose of Intervention: Changing Beliefs about the Use of Force* (Ithaca, NY: Cornell University Press, 2003), 52–84.

6. Paddy Ashdown, quoted in Tom Esslemont, "As Syrian Deaths Mount, World's 'Responsibility to Protect' Takes a Hit: Experts," Reuters, October 25, 2016.

7. Aidan Hehir, "The Responsibility to Protect: 'Sound and Fury Signifying Nothing?,'" *International Relations* 24, no. 2 (2010): 218–39.

8. Justin Morris, "Libya and Syria: R2P and the Spectre of the Swinging Pendulum," *International Affairs* 89, no. 5 (2013): 1265–83, at 1272. See similarly Aidan Hehir, *Hollow Norms and the Responsibility to Protect* (New York: Palgrave, 2019), 39–40.

9. Mohammed Nuruzzaman, "Revisiting 'Responsibility to Protect' after Libya and Syria," *E-International Relations*, March 8, 2014.

10. Gareth Evans, "The Responsibility to Protect: From an Idea to an International Norm," in *Responsibility to Protect: The Global Moral Compact for the 21st Century*, ed. Richard H. Cooper and Juliette Voïnov Kohler (New York: Palgrave Macmillan, 2009), 15–30, at 16; Gareth Evans, "R2P: The Next Ten Years," in *The Oxford Handbook of the Responsibility to Protect*, ed. Alex J. Bellamy and Tim Dunne (Oxford: Oxford University Press, 2016), 913–31, at 914.

11. ICISS (International Commission on Intervention and State Sovereignty), *The Responsibility to Protect: Report of the International Commission on Intervention and State Sovereignty* (Ottawa: International Development Research Centre, 2001), 16–18.

12. Gareth Evans, *The Responsibility to Protect: Ending Mass Atrocity Crimes Once and for All* (Washington, DC: Brookings Institution Press, 2008), 39.

13. UN Security Council, S/PV.2982 (April 5, 1991), 61.

14. UN Security Council, S/PV.3046 (January 31, 1992), 117, 46

15. UN Security Council, S/PV.3145 (December 3, 1992), 27.

16. UN Security Council, S/PV.3402 (July 11, 1994), 3.

17. UN Security Council, S/PV.3612 (December 21, 1995), 13.

18. UN Security Council S/PV.3988 (March 23, 1999), 17; William J. Clinton, "Address to the Nation on Airstrikes against Serbian Targets in the Federal Republic of Yugoslavia (Serbia and Montenegro)," White House, March 24, 1999.

19. UN General Assembly, A/54/PV.6 (September 21, 1999), 4.

20. Jon Western, "Sources of Humanitarian Intervention: Beliefs, Information, and Advocacy in the US Decisions on Somalia and Bosnia," *International Security* 26, no. 4 (2002): 112–42. See more generally on this decade Nicholas J. Wheeler, *Saving Strangers: Humanitarian Intervention in International Society* (Oxford: Oxford University Press, 2000).

21. "Action Memorandum: Has Genocide Occurred in Rwanda?," May 21, 1994, https://nsarchive2.gwu.edu/NSAEBB/NSAEBB53/rw052194.pdf. See also "Discussion Paper, Rwanda," Office of the Deputy Assistant Secretary of Defense for Middle East/Africa Region, Department of Defense, May 1, 1994, http://www.gwu.edu/~nsarchiv/NSAEBB/NSAEBB53/rw050194.pdf.

22. United Nations Secretary-General, "Report of the Secretary-General on the Work of the Organization," A/46/1 (September 13, 1991), 5.

23. UN Security Council, S/PV.3989 (March 26, 1999), 5; UN General Assembly, A/54/PV.8 (September 22, 1999), 16; Group of 77, "Declaration of the South Summit," Havana, Cuba, April 10–14, 2000.

24. UN Security Council, S/PV.6627 (October 4, 2011), 4–5.

25. Audie Klotz, *Norms in International Relations: The Struggle against Apartheid* (Ithaca, NY: Cornell University Press, 1995); Peter J. Katzenstein, "Introduction: Alternative Perspectives on National Security," in *The Culture of National Security: Norms and Identity in World Politics*, ed. Peter J. Katzenstein (New York: Columbia University Press, 1996), 1–32.

26. Thomas Risse and Kathryn Sikkink, "The Socialization of International Human Rights Norms into Domestic Practices: Introduction," in *The Power of Human Rights: International Norms and Domestic Change*, ed. Thomas Risse, Stephen C. Ropp, and Kathryn Sikkink (Cambridge: Cambridge University Press, 1999), 1–38; Frank Schimmelfennig, "The Community Trap: Liberal Norms, Rhetorical Action, and the Eastern Enlargement of the European Union," *International Organization* 55, no. 1 (2001): 47–80; Ronald R. Krebs and Patrick Thaddeus Jackson, "Twisting Tongues and Twisting Arms: The Power of Political Rhetoric," *European Journal of International Relations* 13, no. 1 (2007): 35–66.

27. Risse and Sikkink, "Socialization of International Human Rights Norms," 17.

28. Klotz, *Norms in International Relations.*

29. Edward C. Luck, "The Responsibility to Protect: Growing Pains or Early Promise?," *Ethics & International Affairs* 24, no. 4 (2010): 349–65; Alex J. Bellamy, "The Responsibility to Protect: Added Value or Hot Air?," *Cooperation and Conflict* 48, no. 3 (2013): 333–57.

30. Council of the League of Arab States, "The Outcome of the Council of the League of Arab States Meeting at the Ministerial Level in its Extraordinary Session on the Implications of the Current Events in Libya and the Arab Position," Cairo, Resolution no. 7360, March 12, 2011. French president Nicolas Sarkozy and British prime minister David Cameron both appear to have been motivated by a combination of personal humanitarian concern and realization that a demonstration of such concern would be domestically popular. Some commentators have suggested that they were also motivated by an interest in protecting investments in Libya and ensuring the stability of southern Europe. But, as Christopher Chivvis observes, these goals might have been achieved

just as well by supporting rather than opposing Gaddafi. Christopher S. Chivvis, *Toppling Qaddafi: Libya and the Limits of Liberal Intervention* (New York: Cambridge University Press, 2014), 35–37.

31. Quoted in Jo Becker and Scott Shane, "Hillary Clinton, 'Smart Power' and a Dictator's Fall," *New York Times*, February 27, 2016.

32. Quotes are from Michael Lewis, "Obama's Way," *Vanity Fair*, October 2012. See also Robert M. Gates, *Duty: Memoirs of a Secretary at War* (New York: Knopf, 2014), 511–19; Samantha Power, *The Education of an Idealist* (London: William Collins, 2019), 297–308; Susan Rice, *Tough Love: My Story of the Things Worth Fighting For* (New York: Simon & Schuster, 2019), 279–87.

33. Alex J. Bellamy and Paul D. Williams, "The New Politics of Protection? Côte d'Ivoire, Libya and the Responsibility to Protect," *International Affairs* 87, no. 4 (2011): 825–50.

34. Jessica Rettig, "End of NATO's Libya Intervention Means Financial Relief for Allies," *U.S. News & World Report*, October 31, 2011.

35. Pew Research Center, "Public Wary of Military Intervention in Libya: Broad Concern that US Military Is Overcommitted," March 14, 2011.

36. Gates, *Duty*, 521.

37. "Remarks by President Obama and Chancellor Merkel of Germany in Press Availability," Dresden Castle, Germany, June 5, 2009.

38. Quoted in Lewis, "Obama's Way."

39. Barack Obama, "Remarks by the President in Address to the Nation on Libya," National Defense University, Washington, DC, March 28, 2011.

40. Barack Obama, "Presidential Study Directive on Mass Atrocities," White House, August 4, 2011.

41. For discussion, see Tessa Alleblas, Eamon Aloyo, Sarah Brockmeier, Philipp Rotmann, and Jon Western, "In the Shadow of Syria: Assessing the Obama Administration's Efforts on Mass Atrocity Prevention," Report, Hague Institute for Global Justice, April 2017; Power, *Education of an Idealist*, 266–82; Stephen Pomper, "Atrocity Prevention under the Obama Administration," in *Implementing the Responsibility to Protect: A Future Agenda*, ed. Cecilia Jacob and Martin Mennecke (London: Routledge, 2020), 61–86.

42. Rebecca Adler-Nissen and Vincent Pouliot, "Power in Practice: Negotiating the International Intervention in Libya," *European Journal of International Relations* 20, no. 4 (2014): 889–911, at 900–902.

43. See further Luke Glanville, "Intervention in Libya: From Sovereign Consent to Regional Consent," *International Studies Perspectives* 14, no. 3 (2013): 325–42.

44. UN Security Council, S/PV.6498 (March 17, 2011).

45. Barack Obama, "Remarks by the President on the Situation in Libya," White House, March 18, 2011.

46. Quoted in Jeffrey Goldberg, "The Obama Doctrine," *Atlantic*, April 2016.

47. Barack Obama, "Remarks by President Obama to the United Nations General Assembly," New York, September 28, 2015.

48. Quoted in "President Obama: Libya Aftermath 'Worst Mistake' of Presidency," *BBC News*, April 11, 2016.

49. Alex de Waal, "'My Fears, Alas, Were Not Unfounded': Africa's Responses to the Libya Conflict," in *Libya: The Responsibility to Protect and the Future of Humanitarian Intervention*, ed. Aidan Hehir and Robert Murray (New York: Palgrave, 2013), 58–82, at 65–72; Derek Chollet, *The Long Game: How Obama Defied Washington and Redefined America's Role in the World* (New York: PublicAffairs, 2016), 106–7.

50. Barack Obama, David Cameron, and Nicolas Sarkozy, "Libya's Pathway to Peace," *New York Times*, April 14, 2011.

51. "Remarks of Gert Rosenthal, Permanent Representative of Guatemala to the United Nations at the Informal Discussion on 'The Responsibility while Protecting' Organized by the Permanent

Mission of Brazil to the United Nations," February 21, 2012, http://www.responsibilitytoprotect.org/Guatemala%2021%20Feb%20RwP%20_%20english.pdf.

52. Ramesh Thakur, "R2P after Libya and Syria: Engaging Emerging Powers," *Washington Quarterly* 36, no. 2 (2013): 61–76, at 70.

53. UN Security Council, S/PV.6627, 4.

54. Sui-Lee Wee, "Russia, China Oppose 'Forced Regime Change' in Syria," Reuters, February 1, 2012.

55. Patrick Wintour and Kim Willsher, "G8 Summit: Gaddafi Isolated as Russia Joins Demand for Libyan Leader to Go," *Guardian*, May 28, 2011.

56. See similarly Alex J. Bellamy, "From Tripoli to Damascus: Lesson Learning and the Implementation of the Responsibility to Protect," *International Politics* 51, no. 1 (2014): 23–44.

57. UN Security Council, S/2011/612 (October 4, 2011).

58. UN Security Council, S/PV.6627, 4, 5.

59. UN Security Council, S/2012/538 (July 19, 2012); S/2014/348 (May 22, 2014); S/2017/172 (February 28, 2017).

60. UN Security Council, S/2012/77 (February 4, 2012); S/2016/846 (October 8, 2016); S/2016/1026 (December 5, 2016); S/2017/315 (April 12, 2017); S/2017/884, (October 24, 2017); S/2017/962 (November 16, 2017); S/2017/970 (November 17, 2017); S/2018/321 (April 10, 2018); S/2019/756 (September 19, 2019); S/2019/961 (December 20, 2019).

61. "Newton: 'R2P Is Dead and Done' Due to Response to Syria," *Vanderbilt Journal of Transnational Law Blog*, September 16, 2013.

62. See, for example, Michael Ignatieff, "With Syria, Diplomacy Needs Force," *New York Times*, February 25, 2014; Anne-Marie Slaughter, "Don't Fight in Iraq and Ignore Syria," *New York Times*, June 17, 2014.

63. This claim has been powerfully defended in a collection of papers commissioned by the US Holocaust Memorial Museum and written by Lawrence Woocher, Mona Yacoubian, Andrew Kydd, Ian Lustick, Miguel Garces, Thomas McCauley, and Daniel Solomon. The papers were for a time taken down from the museum's website for political reasons, but have since been restored. Links to the papers alongside Woocher's introduction, which has not been restored to the museum's website, can be found at Jesse Singal, "Here Is the Syria Report Withdrawn by the US Holocaust Museum," *NYMag.com*, September 7, 2017.

64. Singal, "Here Is the Syria Report"; Idean Salehyan, David Siroky, and Reed M. Wood, "External Rebel Sponsorship and Civilian Abuse: A Principal-Agent Analysis of Wartime Atrocities," *International Organization* 68, no. 3 (2014): 633–61; Katherine Sawyer, Kathleen Gallagher Cunningham, and William Reed, "The Role of External Support in Civil War Termination," *Journal of Conflict Resolution* 61, no. 6 (2017): 1174–1202.

65. Jennifer M. Welsh, "Norm Robustness and the Responsibility to Protect," *Journal of Global Security Studies* 4, no. 1 (2019): 53–72, at 58. Compare with Menon, *Conceit of Humanitarian Intervention*, 12, who admits that it would be "foolish—indeed dangerous" to insist that states intervene militarily in response to all instances of atrocities, given that some interventions only do more harm than good, but then oddly draws from this that, in situations where states do prudently intervene, "one cannot then claim that universal norms nevertheless propel humanitarian intervention. These norms are selectively applied."

66. On compliance pull, see Thomas Franck, *The Power of Legitimacy among Nations* (Oxford: Oxford University Press, 1990).

67. It is worth noting, moreover, that Russia sought to justify both interventions in the language of R2P, demonstrating that even Russia feels the need to justify actions with reference to shared norms and that it recognizes R2P as such a norm.

68. Roy Allison, "Russia and Syria: Explaining Alignment with a Regime in Crisis," *International Affairs* 89, no. 4 (2013): 795–823.

69. Jason Ralph and Jess Gifkins, "The Purpose of United Nations Security Council Practice: Contesting Competence Claims in the Normative Context Created by the Responsibility to Protect," *European Journal of International Relations* 23, no. 3 (2017): 630–53.

70. For an early example, see Friedrich Kratochwil and John Gerard Ruggie, "International Organization: A State of the Art on an Art of the State," *International Organization* 40, no. 4 (1986): 753–75, at 768.

71. On "norm contestation" generally, see Antje Wiener, *Contestation and Constitution of Norms in Global International Relations* (Cambridge: Cambridge University Press, 2018). On "norm robustness" and its relationship to contestation about how a norm should be implemented in a given situation, see Nicole Deitelhoff and Lizbeth Zimmermann, "Norms under Challenge: Unpacking the Dynamics of Norm Robustness," *Journal of Global Security Studies* 4, no. 1 (2019): 2–17. For application to R2P, see Jennifer M. Welsh, "Norm Contestation and the Responsibility to Protect," *Global Responsibility to Protect* 5, no. 4 (2013): 365–96; Welsh, "Norm Robustness and the Responsibility to Protect."

72. For Security Council, Human Rights Council, and General Assembly resolutions on Syria, see Security Council Report, "UN Documents for Syria," http://www.securitycouncilreport.org/un-documents/syria/.

73. "Remarks by President Obama and President Park of South Korea in a Joint Press Conference," Washington, DC, May 7, 2013.

74. This is the conclusion reached by the US Holocaust Museum report. See Singal, "Here Is the Syria Report."

75. David Remnick, "Going the Distance: On and Off the Road with Barack Obama," *New Yorker*, January 27, 2014.

76. Barack Obama, "Remarks by the President at the United States Holocaust Memorial Museum," Washington, DC, April 23, 2012; "Remarks by President Obama and President Park."

77. Barack Obama, "Press Conference by the President," White House, December 16, 2016.

78. Quoted in Franklin Foer and Chris Hughes, "Barack Obama Is Not Pleased," *New Republic*, January 27, 2013.

79. UN Security Council, S/PV.6810 (July 19, 2012), 8.

80. UN Security Council, S/PV.7216 (14 July 2014), 8.

81. UN Security Council, S/PV.6711 (February 4, 2012), 5.

82. UN Security Council draft resolutions, S/2016/846 (October 8, 2016), S/2017/315 (April 12, 2017), S/2017/884 (October 24, 2017).

83. UN General Assembly Resolutions 66/253B (August 3, 2012), 68/182 (December 18, 2013), and 71/130 (December 7, 2016).

84. An International Commission of Inquiry concluded in 1996 that the atrocities in Burundi amounted to genocide. UN Security Council, S/1996/682 (August 22, 1996).

85. Scott R. Feil, "Preventing Genocide: How the Early Use of Force might have Succeeded in Rwanda," Report, Carnegie Commission on Preventing Deadly Conflict, April 1998.

86. Bellamy, "Responsibility to Protect," 335.

87. Mary Kaldor, "A Decade of Humanitarian Intervention: The Role of Global Civil Society," in *Global Civil Society 2001*, ed. Helmut Anheier, Marlies Glasius, and Mary Kaldor (Oxford: Oxford University Press, 2001), 88–109; Richard Falk, "Humanitarian Intervention: A Forum," *The Nation*, June 26, 2003.

88. Alex J. Bellamy, "The Humanisation of Security? Towards an International Human Protection Regime," *European Journal of International Security* 1, no. 1 (2016): 112–33. I thank Alex Bellamy for providing additional data to extend the period of analysis to January 2017.

89. UN Security Council Resolution 1975 (March 30, 2011).

90. Bellamy and Williams, "New Politics of Protection?"

91. UN Security Council Resolution 1996 (July 8, 2011).

92. Norwegian Refugee Council, "Protection of Civilians Sites: Lessons from South Sudan for Future Operations" (Oslo: Norwegian Refugee Council, May 31, 2017).

93. UN Security Council Resolution 2098 (March 28, 2013).

94. UN Security Council Resolutions 2139 (February 22, 2014), 2165 (July 14, 2014), 2191 (December 17, 2014), 2258 (December 22, 2015), 2332 (December 21, 2016), 2393 (December 19, 2017), 2401 (24 February, 2018), 2449 (December 13, 2018), and 2504 (January 20, 2020).

95. UN Security Council Resolutions 2303 (July 29, 2016) and 2304 (August 12, 2016).

96. United Nations Secretary-General, "Implementing the Responsibility to Protect: Accountability for Prevention: Report of the Secretary-General," A/71/1016–S/2017/556 (August 10, 2017), 3.

97. UN Security Council Resolution 2049 (April 10, 2014). See also see Evan Cinq-Mars, "Too Little, Too Late: Failing to Prevent Atrocities in the Central African Republic," Occasional Paper No. 7, Global Centre for the Responsibility to Protect, September 2015; United Nations Secretary-General, "Mobilizing Collective Action: The Next Decade of the Responsibility to Protect: Report of the Secretary-General," A/70/999–S/2016/620 (July 22, 2016), 8–9.

98. Paisley Dodds, "AP Investigation: UN Troops Lured Kids into Haiti Sex Ring," AP News, April 12, 2017.

99. Azmat Khan and Anand Gopal, "The Uncounted," New York Times Magazine, November 16, 2017.

100. Ahmed al-Haj, "Top UN Official: 10,000 Civilians Killed in Yemen Conflict," AP News, January 16, 2017.

101. Zeid Ra'ad Al Hussein, "Opening Statement by Zeid Ra'ad Al Hussein, United Nations High Commissioner for Human Rights," 36th Session of the Human Rights Council, September 11, 2017. Yemen is not included in the earlier list of 2010–17 cases of atrocities resulting in more than 5,000 civilian deaths since, while some civilian deaths in Yemen are likely the product of atrocities (specifically war crimes), many are the product of a carelessness that, while certainly worthy of condemnation, likely does not amount to war crimes.

102. "UN Leaders Appeal for Immediate Lifting of Humanitarian Blockade in Yemen—Lives of Millions are at Risk," World Food Programme, November 16, 2017.

103. Anna Stavrianakis, "Playing with Words While Yemen Burns: Managing Criticism of UK Arms Sales to Saudi Arabia," Global Policy 8, no. 4 (2017): 563–68, at 564; Radhya al-Mutawakel, "I've Seen How Arms Sales Fuel Deadly Suffering in Yemen. We Must Stop Them," Guardian, September 1, 2017; Philippe Bolopion, "Will Macron Have Courage to End Arms Sales to Saudis?," Human Rights Watch, September 14, 2017.

104. While the figure that Trump announced turned out to be an exaggeration, it is significant to the extent that it reveals a lack of shame in publicizing the arming of a state that is responsible for so many civilian casualties. William D. Hartung, "U.S. Arms Transfers to Saudi Arabia and the War in Yemen," Security Assistance Monitor, September 7, 2016; Phil Stewart and Warren Strobel, "US to Halt Some Arms Sales to Saudi, Citing Civilian Deaths in Yemen Campaign," Reuters, December 14, 2016; Bruce Riedel, "The $110 Billion Arms Deal to Saudi Arabia is Fake News," Brookings Institution, June 5, 2017.

105. Thomas Risse, Stephen C. Ropp, and Kathryn Sikkink, eds., The Power of Human Rights: International Norms and Domestic Change (Cambridge: Cambridge University Press, 1999); Schimmelfennig, "Community Trap"; Daniel C. Thomas, The Helsinki Effect: International Norms, Human Rights, and the Demise of Communism (Princeton: Princeton University Press, 2001).

106. Quoted in Davide Rodogno, Against Massacre: Humanitarian Interventions in the Ottoman Empire, 1815–1914 (Princeton: Princeton University Press, 2012), 148.

107. For an engaging discussion of the exposure of American hypocrisy, which warned against precisely the kind of doubling-down seen from the Obama and Trump administrations, see Henry

Farrell and Martha Finnemore, "The End of Hypocrisy: American Foreign Policy in the Age of Leaks," *Foreign Affairs* 92, no. 6 (2013): 22–26.

108. Vladimir Putin, "Address by President of the Russian Federation," The Kremlin, Moscow, March 18, 2014.

109. UN News Centre, "'Crimes of Historic Proportions' Being Committed in Aleppo, UN Rights Chief Warns," October 21, 2016.

110. UN Security Council, S/PV.7834 (December 13, 2016), 6–7.

111. Ibid., 7.

112. UN Security Council, S/PV.8105 (November 16, 2017), 13.

113. Michael Ignatieff, "How Syria Divided the World," *New York Review of Books*, July 11, 2012. On the idea of a "post-Western world," see Stephen Hopgood, *The Endtimes of Human Rights* (Ithaca, NY: Cornell University Press, 2013); Oliver Stuenkel, *Post-Western World: How Emerging Powers Are Remaking Global Order* (Cambridge: Polity, 2016).

114. See, for example, Stephen Hopgood, "When the Music Stops: Humanitarianism in a Post-Liberal World Order," *Journal of Humanitarian Affairs* 1, no. 1 (2019): 4–14.

115. Alastair Iain Johnston, *Social States: China in International Institutions, 1980–2000* (Princeton: Princeton University Press, 2008); Courtney J. Fung, *China and Intervention at the UN Security Council: Reconciling Status* (Oxford: Oxford University Press, 2019).

116. Simon Denyer, "Move Over, America. China Now Presents Itself as the Model 'Blazing a New Trail' for the World," *Washington Post*, October 19, 2017.

117. UN General Assembly, A/70/PV.13 (September 28, 2015), 21.

118. UN General Assembly, A/67/224/Add.1 (December 27, 2012), 2; A/73/350/Add.1 (December 24, 2018), 2.

119. United Nations Peacekeeping, "Troop and Police Contributors" and "Peacekeeper Fatalities," available at https://peacekeeping.un.org.

120. UN General Assembly, A/70/PV.13, 19; Sarah Teitt, "Resistance and Accommodation in China's Approach toward R2P," in *Constructing the Responsibility to Protect: Contestation and Consolidation*, ed. Charles T. Hunt and Phil Orchard (London: Routledge, 2020), 149–67.

121. "Statement of the People's Republic of China—Informal Interactive Dialogue on R2P, 8 September 2015." See similarly UN General Assembly, A/73/PV.94 (June 27, 2019), 12.

122. Rosemary Foot, *China, the UN, and Human Protection* (Oxford: Oxford University Press, 2020); Teitt, "Resistance and Accommodation in China's Approach toward R2P."

123. UN Security Council, S/PV.8622 (September 19, 2019), 7–8.

124. Foot, *China, the UN, and Human Protection*, 61–131.

125. Louis Charbonneau, "China Pushes to Cut UN Human Rights Posts," Human Rights Watch, June 7, 2017; Rick Gladstone, "China and Russia Move to Cut Human Rights Jobs in U.N. Peacekeeping," *New York Times*, June 27, 2018.

126. Colum Lynch, "At the U.N., China and Russia Score Win in War on Human Rights," *Foreign Policy*, March 26, 2018.

127. Shannon Tiezi, "Rival Camps Clash over Xinjiang at UN Committee Session," *Diplomat*, October 31, 2019; Stephanie Fillion, "China Flexes Its Economic Might More Openly at the UN on Human Rights," *PassBlue*, November 17, 2019.

128. Donald J. Trump, "The Inaugural Address," Washington, DC, January 20, 2017.

129. Margaret Besheer, "UN Peacekeeping Budget Cut by $600 Million," *VOA News*, June 30, 2017.

130. Missy Ryan, "Civilian Deaths Tripled in U.S.-led Campaign against ISIS in 2017, Watchdog Alleges," *Washington Post*, January 19, 2018.

131. UN General Assembly, A/HRC/25/63 (February 7, 2014); Dahlia Simangan, "Is the Philippine 'War on Drugs' an Act of Genocide?," *Journal of Genocide Research* 20, no. 1 (2018): 68–89; "World Report, 2019: Events of 2018," Human Rights Watch (2019): 468–69.

132. UN Human Rights Council, A/HRC/42/CRP.1 (September 3, 2019), 216–21.

133. Most constructivist theorizing seeks to explain norm change rather than stickiness. One important treatment of the potential stickiness of normative ideas and practices is Ted Hopf, "The Logic of Habit in International Relations," *European Journal of International Relations* 16, no. 4 (2010): 539–61.

134. White House, "National Security Strategy of the United States of America," December 2017, 42.

135. "Elie Wiesel Genocide and Atrocities Prevention Act of 2018," signed into law by President Donald Trump, January 14, 2019; "Elie Wiesel Genocide and Atrocities Prevention Report," released by the White House, September 12, 2019.

136. It should be noted, though, that the establishment of this provision was facilitated by the enactment of the Global Magnitsky Human Rights Accountability Act by Congress during the final year of Obama's presidency. "United States Sanctions Human Rights Abusers and Corrupt Actors across the Globe," US Department of the Treasury Press Release, December 21, 2017; Pomper, "Atrocity Prevention under the Obama Administration," 74.

137. "Elie Wiesel Genocide and Atrocities Prevention Report."

138. "Remarks by President Trump and President Erdoğan of Turkey before Bilateral Meeting," White House, November 13, 2019.

139. See "Statement by Adama Dieng, United Nations Special Adviser on the Prevention of Genocide, on Recent Inflammatory Rhetoric by President Yahya Jammeh of the Gambia, Targeting the Mandinka Ethnic Group," United Nations press release, June 7, 2016; UN Security Council Resolution 2337 (January 19, 2017); Hélène Caux, "As Gambia Crisis Passes, Displaced Return from Senegal," *Refworld*, January 24, 2017.

140. UN Human Rights Council, A/HRC/39/64 (September 12, 2018), 8–9.

141. Quoted in Simon Adams, "The Responsibility to Protect and the Fate of the Rohingya," *Global Responsibility to Protect* 11, no. 4 (2019): 435–50, at 437.

142. "China's Role in Myanmar's Internal Conflicts," US Institute of Peace, September 14, 2018.

143. UN Security Council, S/PV.8381 (October 24, 2018), 11; S/PRST/2017/22 (November 6, 2017); SC/13331 (May 9, 2018).

144. "Awkward Exchanges as Trump Meets Religious Persecution Survivors—Video," *Guardian*, July 19, 2019.

Conclusion

1. Vindiciae, *Contra Tyrannos: or, Concerning the Legitimate Power of a Prince over the People, and of the People over a Prince*, ed. George Garnett (Cambridge: Cambridge University Press, 1994), 175, 181.

2. Ibid., 183.

3. Barack Obama, "Press Conference by the President," White House, December 16, 2016.

4. Quoted in Jeffrey Goldberg, "The Obama Doctrine," *Atlantic*, April 2016.

5. Stephen Pomper, "Atrocity Prevention under the Obama Administration," in *Implementing the Responsibility to Protect: A Future Agenda*, ed. Cecilia Jacob and Martin Mennecke (London: Routledge, 2020), 61–86.

6. Barack Obama, "Statement by the President," White House, August 7, 2014.

7. Quoted in Goldberg, "Obama Doctrine."

8. Bree Feng, "Obama's Free Rider' Comment Draws Chinese Criticism," *New York Times*, August 13, 2014.

9. Goldberg, "Obama Doctrine."

10. Barack Obama, "Presidential Study Directive on Mass Atrocities," White House, August 4, 2011.

11. Quoted in Goldberg, "Obama Doctrine."

12. Among several important contributions in recent years, see Alex J. Bellamy and Edward C. Luck, *The Responsibility to Protect: From Promise to Practice* (Cambridge: Polity, 2018); Jacob and Mennecke, *Implementing the Responsibility to Protect*.

13. See, for example, "Chemical Weapon Use by the Syrian Regime—UK Government Legal Position," August 29, 2013, http://i2.cdn.turner.com/cnn/2013/images/08/29/chemical-weapon-use-by-syrian-regime-uk-government-legal-position.pdf; Daniel Bethlehem, "Stepping Back a Moment—The Legal Basis in Favour of a Principle of Humanitarian Intervention," *EJIL: Talk!*, September 12, 2013; Harold Hongju Koh, "Remarks by Harold Hongju Koh," *Proceedings of the ASIL Annual Meeting* 111 (2017): 114–19; Harold Hongju Koh, "Humanitarian Intervention: Time for Better Law," *AJIL Unbound* 111 (2017): 287–91.

14. UN Security Council, A/73/PV.94 (June 27, 2019), 12.

15. E. Tendayi Achiume, "Migration as Decolonization," *Stanford Law Review* 71, no. 6 (2019): 1509–74; James Souter, "Towards a Theory of Asylum as Reparation for Past Injustice," *Political Studies* 62, no. 2 (2014): 326–42; Lucy Hovil, "Telling Truths about Migration," *International Journal of Transitional Justice* 13, no. 2 (2019): 199–205; Suketu Mehta, *This Land Is Our Land: An Immigrant's Manifesto* (London: Jonathan Cape, 2019).

16. See further Luke Glanville, "Hypocritical Inhospitality: The Global Refugee Crisis in the Light of History," *Ethics & International Affairs* 34, no. 1 (2020): 3–12.

17. For a sample of essays and letters in which Leibniz made this argument, see Gottfried Wilhelm Leibniz, *Political Writings*, ed. Patrick Riley (Cambridge: Cambridge University Press, 1972), 45–84.

18. Quoted, from a letter by Leibniz to Jacques-Bénigne Bossuet, in Patrick Riley, "Introduction," in Leibniz, *Political Writings*, 19.

19. Mihret Yohannes, "Angela Merkel Welcomes Refugees to Germany Despite Rising Anti-immigration Movement," *Washington Times*, September 10, 2015.

20. Martha C. Nussbaum, "Who Is the Happy Warrior? Philosophy, Happiness Research, and Public Policy," *International Review of Economics* 59, no. 4 (2012): 335–61, at 347, 349.

21. "Germany to Spend Extra €6bn to Fund Record Influx of 800,000 Refugees," *Guardian*, September 7, 2015.

22. Immanuel Kant, "The Metaphysics of Morals (1797)," in *Practical Philosophy*, ed. Mary J. Gregor (Cambridge: Cambridge University Press, 1996), 6.453.

23. Ronald R. Krebs and Patrick Thaddeus Jackson, "Twisting Tongues and Twisting Arms: The Power of Political Rhetoric," *European Journal of International Relations* 13, no. 1 (2007): 35–66, at 40.

24. Margarita H. Petrova, "Rhetorical Entrapment and Normative Enticement: How the United Kingdom Turned from Spoiler into Champion of the Cluster Munition Ban," *International Studies Quarterly* 60, no. 3 (2016): 387–99; Sara E. Davies and Jacqui True, "Norm Entrepreneurship in Foreign Policy: William Hague and the Prevention of Sexual Violence in Conflict," *Foreign Policy Analysis* 13, no. 3 (2017): 701–21.

25. Quoted in "Gambian Minister Brought Myanmar to The Hague 'In the Name of Humanity,'" *PRI.org*, December 12, 2019; "Rohingya Crisis: The Gambian Who Took Aung San Suu Kyi to the World Court," *BBC News*, January 23, 2020.

26. Quoted in Bina D'Costa, "A Pathway to Justice through Jurisdiction?," *Daily Star*, December 15, 2019.

27. "U.N. Resolution Condemns Myanmar's Abuse of Rohingya," *New York Times*, December 28, 2019.

SELECTED BIBLIOGRAPHY

History of International Thought

Armitage, David. *Foundations of Modern International Thought.* Cambridge: Cambridge University Press, 2013.

Christov, Theodore. *Before Anarchy: Hobbes and His Critics in Modern International Thought.* New York: Cambridge University Press, 2015.

Fitzmaurice, Andrew. *Sovereignty, Property and Empire: 1500–2000.* Cambridge: Cambridge University Press, 2014.

Hochstrasser, T. J. *Natural Law Theories in the Early Enlightenment.* Cambridge: Cambridge University Press, 2000.

Hunter, Ian. *Rival Enlightenments: Civil and Metaphysical Philosophy in Early Modern Germany.* Cambridge: Cambridge University Press, 2001.

Kingsbury, Benedict, and Benjamin Straumann, eds. *The Roman Foundations of the Law of Nations: Alberico Gentili and the Justice of Empire.* New York: Oxford University Press, 2010.

Malcolm, Noel. *Aspects of Hobbes.* Oxford: Oxford University Press, 2002.

Pagden, Anthony, ed. *The Languages of Political Theory in Early-Modern Europe.* Cambridge: Cambridge University Press, 1987.

Palladini, Fiammetta. *Samuel Pufendorf Disciple of Hobbes: For a Re-interpretation of Modern Natural Law.* Translated by David Saunders. Leiden: Brill, 2020.

Recchia, Stefano, and Jennifer M. Welsh, eds. *Just and Unjust Military Intervention: European Thinkers from Vitoria to Mill.* Cambridge: Cambridge University Press, 2013.

Sherman, Nancy. *Making a Necessity of Virtue: Aristotle and Kant on Virtue.* Cambridge: Cambridge University Press, 1997.

Straumann, Benjamin. *Roman Law in the State of Nature: The Classical Foundations of Hugo Grotius' Natural Law.* Cambridge: Cambridge University Press, 2015.

Tuck, Richard. *The Rights of War and Peace: Political Thought and the International Order from Grotius to Kant.* Oxford: Oxford University Press, 1999.

History of International Practice

Bass, Gary J. *Freedom's Battle: The Origins of Humanitarian Intervention.* New York: Knopf, 2008.

Bell, Duncan. *Reordering the World: Essays on Liberalism and Empire.* Princeton: Princeton University Press, 2016.

Bellamy, Alex J. *Massacres and Morality: Mass Atrocities in an Age of Civilian Immunity.* Oxford: Oxford University Press, 2012.

Benton, Lauren, Adam Clulow, and Bain Attwood, eds. *Protection and Empire: A Global History.* Cambridge: Cambridge University Press, 2018.

Benton, Lauren, and Lisa Ford. *Rage for Order: The British Empire and the Origins of International Law, 1800–1850*. Cambridge, MA: Harvard University Press, 2016.

Curthoys, Ann, and Jessie Mitchell. *Taking Liberty: Indigenous Rights and Settler Self-Government in Colonial Australia, 1830–1890*. Cambridge: Cambridge University Press, 2018.

Fink, Carole. *Defending the Rights of Others: The Great Powers, the Jews, and International Minority Protection, 1878–1938*. Cambridge: Cambridge University Press, 2004.

Getachew, Adom. *Worldmaking after Empire: The Rise and Fall of Self-Determination*. Princeton: Princeton University Press, 2019.

Klose, Fabian, ed. *The Emergence of Humanitarian Intervention: Ideas and Practice from the Nineteenth Century to the Present*. Cambridge: Cambridge University Press, 2016.

Laderman, Charlie. *Sharing the Burden: The Armenian Question, Humanitarian Intervention, and Anglo-American Visions of Global Order*. Oxford: Oxford University Press, 2019.

Lester, Alan, and Fae Dussart. *Colonization and the Origins of Humanitarian Governance: Protecting Aborigines across the Nineteenth-Century British Empire*. Cambridge: Cambridge University Press, 2014.

Martinez, Jenny S. *The Slave Trade and the Origins of International Human Rights Law*. Oxford: Oxford University Press, 2012.

Mazower, Mark. *No Enchanted Palace: The End of Empire and the Ideological Origins of the United Nations*. Princeton: Princeton University Press, 2009.

Özsu, Umut. *Formalizing Displacement: International Law and Population Transfers*. Oxford: Oxford University Press, 2015.

Pedersen, Susan. *The Guardians: The League of Nations and the Crisis of Empire*. Oxford: Oxford University Press, 2015.

Robson, Laura. *States of Separation: Transfer, Partition, and the Making of the Modern Middle East*. Berkeley: University of California Press, 2017.

Rodogno, Davide. *Against Massacre: Humanitarian Interventions in the Ottoman Empire, 1815–1914*. Princeton: Princeton University Press, 2012.

Simms, Brendan, and D. J. B. Trim, eds. *Humanitarian Intervention: A History*. Cambridge: Cambridge University Press, 2011.

Wheeler, Nicholas J. *Saving Strangers: Humanitarian Intervention in International Society*. Oxford: Oxford University Press, 2000.

Contemporary International Ethics

Bell, Duncan, ed. *Empire, Race and Global Justice*. Cambridge: Cambridge University Press, 2019.

Bellamy, Alex J. *The Responsibility to Protect: A Defense*. Oxford: Oxford University Press, 2015.

Brilmayer, Lea. "What's the Matter with Selective Intervention?" *Arizona Law Review* 37, no. 4 (1995): 955–70.

Fabre, Cécile. *Cosmopolitan War*. Oxford: Oxford University Press, 2012.

Getachew, Adom. "The Limits of Sovereignty as Responsibility." *Constellations* 26, no. 2 (2019): 225–40.

Goodin, Robert E. *Protecting the Vulnerable: A Reanalysis of Our Social Responsibilities*. Chicago: University of Chicago Press, 1985.

Lu, Catherine. *Justice and Reconciliation in World Politics*. Cambridge: Cambridge University Press, 2017.

Miller, David. *National Responsibility and Global Justice*. Oxford: Oxford University Press, 2007.

Pattison, James. *The Alternatives to War: From Sanctions to Nonviolence*. Oxford: Oxford University Press, 2018.

———. *Humanitarian Intervention and the Responsibility to Protect: Who Should Intervene?*. Oxford: Oxford University Press, 2010.

Sharma, Serena K., and Jennifer M. Welsh, eds. *The Responsibility to Prevent: Overcoming the Challenges to Atrocity Prevention*. Oxford: Oxford University Press, 2015.

Shue, Henry. *Basic Rights: Subsistence, Affluence, and US Foreign Policy*. 2nd ed. Princeton: Princeton University Press, 1996.

Tan, Kok-Chor. "The Duty to Protect." In *Humanitarian Intervention*, edited by Terry Nardin and Melissa S. Williams, 84–116. New York: New York University Press, 2006.

Thakur, Ramesh, and William Maley, eds. *Theorising the Responsibility to Protect*. Cambridge: Cambridge University Press, 2015.

Whyte, Jessica. "'Always on Top'? The 'Responsibility to Protect' and the Persistence of Colonialism." In *The Postcolonial World*, edited by Jyotsna G. Singh and David D. Kim, 308–24. Abingdon: Routledge, 2017.

Contemporary International Law

Alvarez, José E. "The Schizophrenias of R2P." In *Human Rights, Intervention, and the Use of Force*, edited by Philip Alston and Euan Macdonald, 275–84. Oxford: Oxford University Press, 2008.

Gattini, Andrea. "Breach of the Obligation to Prevent and Reparation Thereof in the ICJ's Genocide Judgment." *European Journal of International Law* 18, no. 4 (2007): 695–713.

Hakimi, Monica. "State Bystander Responsibility." *European Journal of International Law* 21, no. 2 (2010): 341–85.

———. "Toward a Legal Theory on the Responsibility to Protect." *Yale Journal of International Law* 39, no. 2 (2014): 247–80.

Milanović, Marko. "State Responsibility for Genocide: A Follow-Up." *European Journal of International Law* 18, no. 4 (2007): 669–94.

Nollkaemper, André, and Dov Jacobs, eds. *Distribution of Responsibilities in International Law*. Cambridge: Cambridge University Press, 2015.

———. "Shared Responsibility in International Law: A Conceptual Framework." *Michigan Journal of International Law* 34, no. 2 (2013): 359–438.

Nollkaemper, André, and Ilias Plakokefalos, eds. *The Practice of Shared Responsibility in International Law*. Cambridge: Cambridge University Press, 2017.

———, eds. *Principles of Shared Responsibility in International Law: An Appraisal of the State of the Art*. Cambridge: Cambridge University Press, 2014.

Peters, Anne. "The Security Council's Responsibility to Protect." *International Organizations Law Review* 8, no. 1 (2011): 15–54.

Schabas, William A. *Genocide in International Law: The Crime of Crimes*. 2nd ed. Cambridge: Cambridge University Press, 2009.

Contemporary International Politics

Bellamy, Alex J., and Tim Dunne, eds. *The Oxford Handbook of the Responsibility to Protect*. Oxford: Oxford University Press, 2016.

Bellamy, Alex J., and Edward C. Luck. *The Responsibility to Protect: From Promise to Practice*. Cambridge: Polity, 2018.

Foot, Rosemary. *China, the UN, and Human Protection: Beliefs, Power, Image*. Oxford: Oxford University Press, 2020.

Fung, Courtney J. *China and Intervention at the UN Security Council: Reconciling Status*. Oxford: Oxford University Press, 2019.

Hehir, Aidan. *Hollow Norms and the Responsibility to Protect*. New York: Palgrave, 2019.

Hopgood, Stephen. *The Endtimes of Human Rights*. Ithaca, NY: Cornell University Press, 2013.

Hunt, Charles T., and Phil Orchard, eds. *Constructing the Responsibility to Protect: Contestation and Consolidation*. London: Routledge, 2020.

Jacob, Cecilia, and Martin Mennecke, eds. *Implementing the Responsibility to Protect: A Future Agenda*. London: Routledge, 2020.

Menon, Rajan. *The Conceit of Humanitarian Intervention*. New York: Oxford University Press, 2016.

Staunton, Eglantine. *France, Humanitarian Intervention and the Responsibility to Protect*. Manchester: Manchester University Press, 2020.

Stuenkel, Oliver. *Post-Western World: How Emerging Powers are Remaking Global Order*. Cambridge: Polity, 2016.

Welsh, Jennifer M. "Norm Contestation and the Responsibility to Protect." *Global Responsibility to Protect* 5, no. 4 (2013): 365–96.

———. "Norm Robustness and the Responsibility to Protect." *Journal of Global Security Studies* 4, no. 1 (2019): 53–72.

INDEX

military intervention (*continued*)
(R2P), 4–5, 81–82; Somalia vs. Bosnia,
100; Syria and, 145–152, 196n25, 196n25;
theorists on, 10; United Nations (UN)
Security Council, 106, 127
Mill, John Stuart, 58
Miller, David, 90, 96–97, 103, 201n108
Milton, Patrick, 40
Mitchell, Jessie, 61
Mitterrand, François, 70–71, 136
moderns, international thought, 19, 24–29
Morefield, Jeanne, 82
Mornay, Philippe de, 168
Moyn, Samuel, 91
Münster, Treaty of (1648), 39

Nama, genocide against, 43, 62
Napoléon III (Emperor), 48
Napoleonic Wars (1799–1815), 42
national interest, 2, 88, 102–104, 142, 164
National Security Strategy, United States
(2017), 164
Native Americans, Spaniards and, 20–22
Nauru case, ICJ, 115, 126
Nazi Germany, 58, 66, 95
Nebenzia, Vasily, 159
Netherlands, 127, 178
New World, 19, 60
New Zealand, 61, 66, 69, 115
Nigeria, 68, 70
Nonconformist Union Association, 53
North Atlantic Treaty Organization
(NATO), 77, 83, 88, 137, 138, 143–145
North Korea, 163
nuclear weapons, 7
Nuclear Weapons advisory opinion, ICJ, 120
Nuremberg laws, 58
Nussbaum, Martha, 176

Obama, Barack: address to UN General
Assembly (2015), 88; arms sales to Saudi
Arabia, 156; Atrocities Prevention Board,
142, 164, 165, 171; human protection by
United States, 8, 96, 153–154, 158, 169–172;
international community and, 135; Libyan
intervention, 77, 81, 83, 89, 139–144, 171;
protection for Syrians, 7, 93, 150, 155; on
responsibility for human suffering, 170;
US intake of refugees, 163
O'Neill, Onora, 105
order of charity, 20
Organization of Islamic Cooperation, 178
Organization of the Islamic Conference, 81,
142

Orthodox Christianity, 44, 46, 57
Osnabrück, Treaty of (1648), 39–40
Ottoman Empire: Armenia (1894–96), 53–55;
Bulgaria (1876–78), 48–52; Christian
minorities in, 8, 37; Disraeli and, 48–52;
European great power interventions in,
95, 188n9; Germany and, 63; Greece
(1821–27), 44–46; persecuted Bulgarians
in, 7; protecting Christians in, 42–55; pro-
tection of Christian minorities, 64, 95, 108,
152; Syria (1860–61), 46–48; treaties, 42;
Treaty of Berlin, 52, 54; Treaty of Paris, 50,
51; Treaty of San Stefano, 52
Ouattara, Alassane, 154
Oxford University, 22
Özsu, Umut, 46

Pagden, Anthony, 18, 28
Pakistan, 68–69
Palatinate, 41
Paris, Treaty of (1856), 46–47, 49–51
Paris Peace Conference, 56, 63
Pattison, James, 95
Peace of Westphalia (1648), 2, 5, 10, 18, 37,
39–42, 136, 164
peacekeeping, 83–85, 104, 115–116, 153–154,
156, 160–163, 166, 173
Pedersen, Susan, 63
People's Republic of China, 161. *See also*
China
Pérez de Cuéllar, Javier, 138
perfectionists, international thought, 19,
29–32
Permanent Court of International Justice, 56
Permanent Mandates Commission, 63, 64
Peters, Anne, 117, 128, 131
Philippines, 62, 163
Pogge, Thomas, 101
Poland, 56, 57, 67, 95
Pol Pot, Cambodia, 68, 144
populist nationalism, 3; resurgence of, 163–165
Power, Samantha, 158
principle of self-preservation, 22–23, 25,
27–28
Pufendorf, Samuel, 7, 27–29; *De jure natu-
rae et gentium* (*The Law of Nature and
Nations*), 27–29; Grotius and, 28, 30, 33;
imperfect duties, 8–9, 11–12, 34–35, 38,
76, 88, 124, 129, 171; Leibniz and, 176;
natural law, 24, 27–29

R2P. *See* responsibility to protect (R2P)
racism, 11, 38
refugee protection, 36, 133, 163

Syria: atrocities and intervention in (1860–61), 46–48, 140, 152; chemical weapons attacks in, 165; civil war and crisis in (2011–), 100, 105; Druze and Maronite populations in, 46, 140; international politics of, 145–152; Obama and, 7, 93, 150, 155; refugees fleeing civil war, 87; Russia in, 164; violation example, 152

Tambadou, Abubacarr, 1, 178
Tamil population, Sri Lankan government against, 86
Tams, Christian, 131
Tan, Kok-Chor, 104
Temperley, Harold, 63
Teresa (Mother), 159
Thakur, Ramesh, 145
Thatcher, Margaret, 200n98
Thirty Years' War (1618–48), 39
Thomists, 18, 19–22, 24, 25, 29, 82, 102, 169
Thouvenel, Edouard-Antoine de, 47
Tiananmen Square massacre (1989), 76
Timor-Leste, 83
Treaty of Berlin (1878), 52–54, 56
Treaty of Küçük Kaynarca (1774), 44
Treaty of Lausanne (1923), 57
Treaty of London (1827), 45, 47
Treaty of Münster (1648), 39
Treaty of Osnabrück (1648), 39–40
Treaty of Paris (1856), 46–47, 49–51
Treaty of San Stefano (1878), 52, 54
Trump, Donald: "America First" by, 163–165, 172; arms sales to Saudi Arabia, 156; human protection by United States, 8, 96; populist nationalism and, 163–165; US ambassadors to UN, 159; US intake of refugees, 163
Tuck, Richard, 25
Türk, Volker, 123
Turkey, 50, 54, 56, 57, 60, 64, 96, 149
Tutsis in Rwanda, 68

Uganda, Idi Amin in, 83, 144
Uighurs, 162
United Kingdom: arms sales to Saudi Arabia, 156; authority of, 115; Bosnia, 117, 126–127; extraterritorial protection efforts, 129; human rights and, 66; international norms on human protection, 177; Libyan crisis, 140, 142; obligation requirements, 122; permanent Security Council member, 148; Rwanda genocide and, 127; Syrian conflict, 165; Yemen and, 164, 177

United Nations (UN): Charter, 37, 66–68, 69, 75, 106, 121, 123, 136, 138; Committee on Economic, Social, and Cultural Rights, 123; Global Compact on Refugees, 123, 163; peacekeeping, 83–85, 104, 115–116, 153–154, 156, 160–163, 166, 173; World Summit, 1, 3, 75, 80, 84, 109–111, 139, 148, 194–195n1
United Nations (UN) General Assembly, 69–70, 88, 104–105, 109–111, 121, 136–137, 150–151, 162, 178
United Nations (UN) Human Rights Council, 150, 163
United Nations (UN) Security Council, 1; activism of, 109; atrocities in 1990s, 153; authority of, 110; authorization, 5, 83, 104, 106, 116–118, 144, 155–156, 173–174; Côte d'Ivoire, 154; debate on Syria, 161; enforcement measures by, 67–69; failures of, 105; legal authority, 80; Libyan crisis and, 140–141; members of, 12, 103, 114, 116–118, 124, 130, 160–161; obligation of, 110–111, 131, 136, 138–139; peacekeepers, 166; preventing adoption of resolutions, 103; Resolution 713, 118; Resolution 1973, 77, 142, 143; Syrian crisis, 145, 148–151, 158–159; veto of resolution of, 127
United States, 68; airstrikes in Libya, 77; arms sales to Saudi Arabia, 156; Burundi and, 155; Bush Sr. administration, 100–102; Cambodia and Vietnam, 69; extraterritorial protection efforts, 129; human protection, 3, 8, 158; human rights and, 66; international protection responsibility, 110–111; intervention against Islamic State, 95–96; in Liberia, 84, 95; Libyan crisis, 89, 140–142, 146, 150–151; National Security Strategy (2017), 164; Obama on responsibility of, 170–172; obligation to prevent, 122–123; Ottoman Armenians and, 55; permanent Security Council member, 118, 148; responsibility to civilize, 62; Rwandan genocide and, 109, 127, 137, 152; slave trade and, 60; Syria and, 89, 165; UN peacekeeping, 160, 163; Yemen and, 164, 177
University of Alcalá, 19, 21
University of Salamanca, 19, 21

Vattel, Emer de, 7, 30–32; Grotius and, 31, 33; imperfect duties, 32, 34–35, 38, 76, 92, 124, 171; Kant and, 8–9, 12, 30, 34, 76, 93, 99, 102, 104; *Le Droit des Gens* (*The Law of Nations*), 30–32, 89; natural law,

A NOTE ON THE TYPE

This book has been composed in Adobe Text and Gotham. Adobe Text, designed by Robert Slimbach for Adobe, bridges the gap between fifteenth- and sixteenth-century calligraphic and eighteenth-century Modern styles. Gotham, inspired by New York street signs, was designed by Tobias Frere-Jones for Hoefler & Co.